THE ENGLISH LABOUR MOVEMENT
1700—1951

Also by Kenneth D. Brown
Labour and Unemployment 1900—14 (1971)
John Burns (1977)
(ed.) *Essays in Anti-Labour History* (1974)

KENNETH D. BROWN

THE ENGLISH
LABOUR MOVEMENT
1700-1951

GILL AND MACMILLAN

First published 1982 by
Gill and Macmillan Ltd
Goldenbridge
Dublin 8
with associated companies in
London, New York, Delhi, Hong Kong,
Johannesburg, Lagos, Melbourne,
Singapore, Tokyo

7171 0870 8

Origination by Lagamage Company Ltd., Dublin
Printed and bound in Great Britain by Biddles Ltd.,
Guildford and King's Lynn.

Contents

Introduction: Wage-labour, 1500-1800

The Growth of Wage-Labour

The history of wage-labour in Britain before the industrial revolution has never been satisfactorily written and perhaps never will be. Yet it occupies an important place in Marxist and non-Marxist historiography. Both see the sixteenth, seventeenth and eighteenth centuries as a period when capitalist modes of production – characterised by the concentration of large amounts of capital into the hands of a relatively small number of owners, production for distant markets, and the use of wage-labour – came into being. Considerable attention has been given to the first two features, but the third has been largely taken for granted. The reasons for this are not difficult to discover. First, the evidence is fragmentary. Our knowledge of wage-labourers comes from official pronouncements, such as statutes of the realm and judicial wage assessments; the comments of employers and economic observers; guild regulations; and only rarely from wage-earners themselves, who remain for the most part a submerged group in society. They are an obscure group, moreover, not merely because of evidential difficulties, but because the whole concept of wage-labour as a separate factor of production lacks precision before the late eighteenth century. All men laboured, except for a small minority who lived as gentlemen, but not all men laboured for wages by selling their labour on the market.

The difficulty of identifying wage-earners has occasionally led writers to minimise their importance in the economy. Thus Tawney wrote many years ago that in the sixteenth century the social problem of Europe was not the wage-earner, but the peasant.[1] If that were the case, it is difficult to

1

explain such legislation as the Statute of Artificers of 1563. More commonly, though, historians have exaggerated the number of wage-earners. W.G. Hoskins, for example, relying on the evidence of the lay subsidy returns of 1523-7, states that two-thirds of the population lived on wages during the reign of Henry VIII; while Everitt has calculated that between one-quarter and one-third of the rural population of Tudor England was 'peasant labourers'.[2] Studies of seventeenth-century towns, too, often imply that roughly two-thirds of the urban population was wage-earners. If these proportions are even approximately correct, they leave little room for an increase in the share of the population depending on wages during the two-and-a-half centuries before the industrial revolution. By the beginning of the nineteenth century, wages accounted for about forty-five per cent of the national income.[3] On the assumption that wage-labour received a disproportionately small share of the national income, that fraction also implies that around two-thirds of the population lived on wages in 1800.

In fact, it is probable that wage-earners were less numerous in the early sixteenth century than Professor Hoskins assumes, since the lay subsidy returns may be misleading on this point. The tax was charged on land, property or, in the case of those who had no property, wages. Since wages paid by far the lowest rate of tax, it was obviously tempting for taxpayers to pose as wage-earners. True, tax-gatherers had an interest in putting people into a higher tax bracket in order to maximise revenue, and the collection of the subsidy seems to have been well organised; even so, the suspicion remains that to claim to be a wage-earner carried fiscal if not social advantages. In a similar way, estimates of proportions of urban labourers in the late seventeenth century, based as they are on the evidence of the hearth money returns, may also be inflated. The proportions cited are of those in the population excused the tax on grounds of poverty, and it is perhaps too readily assumed that that group was composed of those living on wages.

In other ways, too, the size of the wage-earning population in Tudor and Stuart England has been made to appear greater than it probably was. Everitt's use of the phrase 'peasant labourer' is revealing. Many peasants occupied small plots of land, but they needed to supplement their incomes by working as wage-labourers for larger farmers. Other small-holders found work in domestic industry, making cloth, metal wares, leather goods or other articles. A few of these people were full-time employees, but many were like the stocking knitters in the north Yorkshire dales described by Willan: men and women who knitted the winter away making army socks for military contractors in London, and in the spring and summer returning to the fields to tend their livestock.[4] Sometimes it is difficult to determine whether a man working in putting-out industry was a wage-earner or not. For example, spinners and weavers in the west of England textile industry were generally the employees of the merchant clothiers who supplied them with wool and yarn; but the farmer-weavers of the West Riding were self-employed men who bought their raw materials from middlemen, although they sometimes became so indebted to their suppliers as to be indistinguishable from employees.

An even more obvious way of exaggerating the size of the wage-earning population is to treat women and children working on family farms or in family workshops as though they were employees working for wages. In underdeveloped countries today, the proportions of the population recorded as comprising the labour force very enormously according to whether or not family workers are defined as part of the economically active population. If a characteristic of wage-labour is the selling of labour in a labour market, then unpaid family workers cannot really be included as part of the wage-labour force. Much of the labour force in pre-industrial England was composed of women and children in occupations such as spinning, lacemaking, gloving and others, working for their husbands and fathers as part of a household unit.

Notwithstanding ambiguities in the evidence and difficulties with definitions, wage-earners were numerous in England at the beginning of the sixteenth century. Wage-labour therefore cannot be regarded simply as the product of an expansion of capitalism during the early modern period: it was inherited from the Middle Ages. The reasons for its development before 1500 can only be guessed at, but they may be connected with the fall in population at the time of the Black Death and the protracted demographic decline of the later fourteenth and fifteenth centuries. The consequential change in the balance between land and labour increased the rewards of the latter and made wage-earning relatively attractive. A long-term fall in food prices increased purchasing power and stimulated the demand for manufactured goods – and consequently for the labour that produced them – throughout western Europe, pushing up wage rates among urban craftsmen. The position in the countryside was more complicated. Movements in the relative price of grain and pastoral products encouraged the development of pastoral farming – which was less labour intensive – at the expense of arable, so reducing the demand for labour per unit of land. However, a reduction in the demand for rural labour could not go too far. Grain continued to be the main component of agricultural output and labour was needed to cultivate it. Furthermore, farms were on average becoming larger, sometimes getting too big to be managed by family labour alone. As a result there was a demand for farm servants working for wages.

Between the early sixteenth and the mid-eighteenth centuries the further development of wage-labour took two forms. First, the proportion of the population receiving *some* income from wages grew, although not perhaps by very much. Secondly, that part of the population depending *wholly* on wages increased. The social problem of the period increasingly became that of the wage-earner. For example, the state was intimately involved with determining the appropriate level of income for wage-earners even before Parliament passed the Statute of Artificers in 1563. That the statute was an attempt by employers to fix maximum wages at a time when labour was temporarily scarce is less significant than the fact that the House of Commons thought it necessary to legislate on the matter at all. Even more significantly, the wages of woollen workers assessed by the justices were soon accepted as minimum, not maximum, wages. The growth of wage-labour in this industry, in fact, had gone further than in any other branch of the economy, and no government sensitive to social welfare could ignore the conditions of textile workers. The widespread social distress caused by the depression in the textile trades in the 1620s is indicative of how important wages had become as a source of income. By the second half of the seventeenth century, wage-labour emerged as a major theme in the economic literature of the time.

Further evidence of the growing importance of wage-labour is provided by changes taking place in the structure of craft guilds, particularly in London. Guilds were organisations of master craftsmen, not wage-earners, but many contained within their ranks journeymen who failed to make the transition to master status but remained as employees. During the early seventeenth century, considerable friction developed between these journeymen and the master craftsmen, as the former became frustrated by their inability to advance. Sometimes conflict between masters and journeymen led to a split in the guild, such as occurred in 1638 when the glovers broke away from the London Company of Leathersellers to form their own organisation. In other guilds — including, for example, the curriers and cordwainers of London — journeymen remained within the guild but as subordinate members.[5] In the eighteenth century, disputes between journeymen and employers were frequent in many trades, taking the form of strikes by journeymen for better pay and conditions. These combinations provoked a reaction from masters, who instituted prosecutions and lobbied in Parliament for private combination acts to deal with insubordinate workers. The climax of such activity was the Combination Acts of 1799 and 1800.

How is the growing importance of wage-labour after 1500 to be explained? The answer to this question is less obvious than might at first appear. As the population increased and the potential stock of labour grew relative to the supply of land and capital, real wages fell. The index of the purchasing power of building labourers compiled by Phelps Brown and Hopkins shows that the real income of such labourers in the 1630s was only about forty per cent of the 1500 level.[6] Men and women were thus not attracted into wage-earning by the rewards it offered. Nor were they lured by the social privileges attached to the status of the wage-labourer, for there were none. During the late medieval and early modern period, there was a general increase in personal rights and freedom with the ending of serfdom, the clarification of property rights, and the development of a legal code protecting the wealth of individuals. Yet wage-labour – the selling of labour services – involved a curtailment of individual freedom: when in the pay of his employer, a worker was not his own master, could not determine his own hours of work, nor decide his own comings and goings. Although not a slave, he surrendered his liberty during the period that he was working for his master. Workers in putting-out industries retained more freedom than workers in centralised workshops, but even they gave up part of their personal freedom in return for wages.

The increase in population after 1500 did, of course, create conditions favourable to the development of wage-labour in certain circumstances, although much depended on the structure of land-ownership and the nature of agricultural tenures. If population grows within a mainly rural society and agricultural holdings are divided to accommodate an increasing number of people, then the inevitable outcome will be that farms become too small to support families by agriculture alone. By-employments of some sort will therefore be needed to supplement farm incomes. Such developments occurred in England in forest and upland regions where manorial structures were weak and the local communities imposed few barriers to sub-division of farms. In such regions, too, arable land was in short supply and farming tended to be pastoral, so absorbing comparatively little labour. Supplies of wool, wood, iron or skins were often available locally, providing the materials for industrial activity. Production at first was likely to be directed towards local markets and organised within self-employed family units; but as this sort of peasant manufacture eventually became commercialised, the rural labour became employed by entrepreneurs who supplied raw materials and sold the output in distant markets. Even before 1500, developments of this kind had taken place in woollen manufacturing districts such as East Anglia and the west of England, but they were greatly extended after 1500 and also spread into other industries such as metal-working and glove-making.

In many parts of England, farms were not divided as the population increased, but were kept intact by restricting the inheritance to a single person, usually the eldest son, leaving the younger children to find a living in some other way. Systems of primogeniture were widespread in those parts of lowland England which had been strongly manorialised in the Middle Ages and where manorial courts still supervised inheritance practices and tenures. The growth of population in these regions created a body of landless labourers, who had the choice of working for those farmers possessing farms sufficiently big to need wage-labour, or of moving to other areas where work was available. Rural industry did not generally develop in these regions, because the predominantly arable farming absorbed a good deal of wage-labour, and also because manorial courts, by controlling settlement patterns, made it difficult for a non-farming population to find somewhere to live. As manorial organisation collapsed, so the landless population could survive on odd patches of land – the squatters of the eighteenth century – and form a workforce that might attract the attention of entrepreneurs seeking cheap labour.

During the sixteenth and seventeenth centuries, midland counties such as Leicestershire and Northamptonshire displayed many of the features outlined above. They figured prominently among the counties affected by enclosure and depopulation in the early, mid- and late sixteenth centuries, although the bulk of land remained in open fields until the late eighteenth century. When sixteenth-century commentators condemned depopulation in these counties, they were, in fact, remarking on the difficulties experienced by a surplus population in finding employment in regions where industry was lacking. Some of the excess population moved to the local market towns in search of work, but some of them went further afield. The rapid growth of London during the sixteenth and seventeenth centuries, for example, was caused in large part by migrants coming from the Home Counties and the Midlands. Only when manorial control decayed did a large body of landless labour remain in the Midlands and find work outside agriculture; and at the turn of the seventeenth and eighteenth centuries London-based manufacturers moved into the area recruiting labour as framework-knitters or shoemakers to produce goods for London and overseas markets.

Wage-labour was not the only possible outlet for landless labourers. An alternative was begging. Town after town in sixteenth-century England complained of the rising tide of beggars and vagabonds flowing through their streets, and in 1547 the central government took the extreme, though short-lived, step of enacting legislation by which beggars could be made slaves. As a career, begging had its drawbacks, but it required little or no capital and entry was easy. Arguably, too, the rewards of the successful beggar were better than those of many wage-earners. Some other forms of self-employment were scarcely more difficult to take up than begging. It cost very little, for example, to set up as a cobbler or a peddlar: practically no fixed capital was necessary and stocks of materials could be bought on credit. Admittedly the credit standing of some men was better than others, and guilds made entry into urban crafts difficult.

Therefore, a man who had no land, could obtain no capital, was barred from entering a trade by a guild, and was not attracted to begging might become a wage-earner. Or he might be born the son of a wage-earner. But few men became wage-earners by choice.

So far, reasons accounting for an increase in the potential supply of wage-earners have been considered, but not why the demand should have risen. In general demand rose after 1500 because the demand for goods and services expanded, thus stimulating the demand for all factors of production including labour. But an increase in a demand for *labour* is not identical to an increase in a demand for *wage-labour*. A larger output of goods and services might be achieved by a multiplication in the number of self-employed producers. For example, as the population grew after 1500, there was generated a larger demand for boots and shoes, saddles and harnesses, and therefore for leather. This increasing demand for leather, footwear and saddlery was satisfied principally by a series of independent producers linked together by the market. Tanners brought raw hides and converted them into leather. They then sold the leather to dealers, who sorted it and cut it into sizes suitable for leather-using craftsmen. Leather dealers then sold the leather to shoemakers, saddlers and harness-makers, who manufactured leather goods which, in turn, they sold to the final consumers. No increase in the proportions of wage-labour employed was necessarily involved in the expansion of trade. Units of production did not become noticeably bigger, but the number of production units increased, as did the number of market transactions linking butchers, tanners, dealers, shoemakers, harness-makers, saddlers and final customers.

The alternative way of responding to increasing demand, which made use of wage-labour, was exemplified by the woollen textile industry. The whole process of production, from the purchase of the raw wool to the sale of the finished cloth, was organised by clothiers who employed combers, carders, spinners and weavers. As more cloth was demanded, more men and women were hired to spin and weave. Instead of a multiplication of market transactions linking the various production stages (as in the leather industry), there was instead a development of enterprises employing wage-labour.

The two models of production just described were not mutually exclusive. Tanners who bought raw hides to make into leather often employed labourers to move hides from pit to pit, just as shoemakers — the hero of Thomas Dekker's *Shoemaker's Holiday*, for example — employed journeymen and apprentices to cut and stitch footwear. In the textile industry, alongside spinners and weavers employed by capitalist clothiers were independent producers making yarn or cloth for sale in local markets and relying on dealers to sell them raw materials in small quantities. Much of the West Riding woollen industry was organised in this way. Nevertheless, the contrasts between the two systems of production are sufficiently clear and demonstrate that the employment of wage-labour was not an inevitable response to a rising demand for goods and services. This required the presence of special conditions. One of these was technical: some manufacturing processes needed expensive equipment far beyond the financial resources of ordinary labourers. Iron manufacture was such an industry. The cost of furnaces, forges, bellows and other equipment ran to several hundred pounds; and there were, in addition, the expenses of the ironstone, lime and charcoal to feed the furnaces. At the same time, the nature of the process demanded the use of labour on a fairly large scale. Much of this labour was unskilled and was provided by men without the money-capital to set themselves up as masters. However, technical requirements demanding large accumulations of capital operated only in a few industries in early-modern England. Most capital invested went not into fixed plant, but into stocks of raw materials which could often be bought for credit in small quantities. This was so in the woollen industry, where – more than in any other – wage-labour developed as a widespread form of production. Another explanation, therefore, beyond the need for capital is necessary to account for the employment of wage-labour.

The essential requirement was the nature of the market for the products. The capitalist clothiers of the woollen industry, the framework-knitters in the hosiery industry, and the entrepreneurs in the small metal industry all produced goods in large quantities for mass markets. Wage-labour had two attractions in these circumstances. First, it could be readily recruited, particularly outside the corporate towns away from guild control, from among agrarian populations that were otherwise chronically underemployed. The flexibility worked in both directions, for as demand slackened so labour could be laid off with little or no inconvenience to the employer. The other attraction was that the employer retained the ownership of his materials throughout the production process and was thus able to monitor the quality of the product.[7] This was particularly important for a commodity like woollen cloth, which was sold in highly competitive markets. Competition was on the basis of quality and price. There was little opportunity for a manufacturer to gain a competitive advantage through technological improvement. Therefore goods could be sold successfully only if they were a little bit cheaper or were superior in quality to the goods of competitors. A greater degree of control over costs and quality was easier to obtain if the entrepreneur owned raw materials throughout all stages of production than if goods passed from craftsman to craftsman through a series of market transactions.

Two further conditions of a general kind were necessary for the widespread use of wage-labour. One was the existence of an agricultural sector capable of producing surpluses of food that could be bought by landless labourers. Some wage-earners, such as Everitt's peasant labourers, occupied plots of land on which they grew food. Nevertheless, most wage-earners had to buy their food on the market. During the sixteenth and seventeenth centuries, English agriculture made important advances in methods of production. These took the form of increasing the amount of fodder and forage crops available; so increasing the supplies of meat and dairy produce and also, more importantly, of enlarging the supplies of animal manure applied in the cultivation of arable land. The long-term rise in food prices before the mid-seventeenth century suggests that agricultural production had difficulty in keeping pace with the expanding industrial and commercial sectors of the economy. Nevertheless, by the later seventeenth century there were ample agricultural surpluses to feed a large and growing wage-earning population.

The increase in agricultural output was accompanied by the second precondition: improvements in market mechanisms. There were more than eight hundred market towns in Tudor and Stuart England, which for many wage-earners were the normal source of supply. Public markets were supplemented by other forms of distribution, including middlemen, wholesale merchants, and retail shops. The activities of middlemen were strenuously resisted in the sixteenth century by central government and municipal authorities — as well as by clerics and preachers — who feared that they exploited the needs of consumers. Attempts to restrict the activities of food dealers were ineffective, and their failure simply demonstrated the need for an efficient food market to supply the growing towns and expanding non-agrarian sector.

The emergence of fully fledged wage-labour distinct from the twilight world of peasant labourers and family workers did not occur evenly over time, nor did it affect all sectors of the economy to the same extent. It was more of an industrial phenomenon than an agricultural one and was probably most widespread in the service sector, where the ranks of wage-earners were swollen by armies of domestic and personal servants and by casual labourers. These occupations required little skill and were ready havens for men, women and children without land, capital or training. On the demand side, although services such as cooking, barbering, portering or bedmaking could be bought on the market, there were obvious advantages to the consumer in having them instantly available on demand from an employee; just as today we choose to own cars and suffer the cost, rather than hire transport in the form of taxis or trains. The importance of tertiary employments persisted into the nineteenth century, although they changed in character with clerical and financial services becoming more important. Domestic service as a major source of employment survived into the twentieth century; and it is no accident that the term 'servant' was used in nineteenth and twentieth century Britain as a synonym for 'employee' in, for example, the titles of statutes (Master and Servant Act) and the names of trade unions (The Amalgamated Society of Railway Servants).

Wage-labour developed slowly in agriculture, where family workers persisted for centuries. As late as 1831, as Clapham has reminded us, there were only two-and-a-half farm-labouring families to every farm-occupying family.[8] When a farmer needed more labour than his household could supply, it was commonly provided by neighbours. Wage-earners were, nevertheless, well known in agriculture. The Statute of Artificers provided for the assessment of agricultural as well as industrial wages and even allowed for labourers to be directed into agricultural employment. Farm servants frequently lived in farmers' houses, although the practice seems to have been declining in the eighteenth century. At busy periods, such as harvest time, casual workers were employed. In the eighteenth century, these included short-term migrants from Ireland, who moved from region to region following the harvest. In July 1797, for example, Ann Hughes, a farmer's wife in Herefordshire, was 'verrie glad' that 'we shall not be bothered with the Irish folks this year . . . for the women was such great trollops and verie drabbie hussies, what the men did bring.'[9] Altogether different were the small number of specialist workers, such as shepherds or farm bailiffs, hired by the year on high wages. These were the peak of a hierarchy of agricultural employees, socially and economically distinct from common farm labourers.

In secondary industry, wage-labour became important in two types of occupation. One was the capital-intensive enterprises such as metal-smelting and mining, where expensive equipment needed a certain amount of labour to operate it. Such enterprises were eye-catching and have formed the basis of Nef's arguments for an industrial revolution in the sixteenth century, but they were unrepresentative of industry as a whole and employed only a tiny fraction of the workforce. In the late seventeenth century, for example, coal-mining throughout Britain employed, on Nef's own figures, no more than about 15,000 people.[10] The other important and much more numerous category of wage-earners was found in textiles, metal-working, leather-working, and similar occupations where wage-labour was combined with working capital to supply standardised goods of uniform quality and low price to national and international markets. The workers were not always fully employed the whole year round and were subject to bouts of idleness when trade was slack, but they formed a class of more or less permanent wage-earners with little prospect of graduating to better things. In this respect they were different from another group of wage-earners: the journeymen and apprentices of the urban crafts organised in their guilds, who had some expectation of graduating to the status of small masters. It is clear from the census of 1841 and 1851 that workers in craft occupations survived well into the period of industrialisation, although it remains difficult to distinguish between the self-employed and the wage-earners. It is also clear that such forms of employment were declining in importance relative to the numbers of wage-earners employed in capital-intensive enterprises producing for national and international markets.

The Operation of the Labour Market, 1500—1800

Wage labour is bought and sold on the market, the function of which is to equate demand and supply at a price — or wage — where those seeking labour will absorb those offering labour for sale. In practice, before 1800 there was not one but many labour markets dealing with many different kinds of labour. In practice, too, labour markets were very imperfect; for many institutions – guilds, municipal authorities, the state – impaired their smooth operation, while ignorance of market opportunities by both employers and employees restricted the free flow of labour. Even greater, possibly, were the difficulties caused by poor communications and by the forces of custom and tradition which contrived to make labour one of the most immobile factors of production. Furthermore, labour was highly heterogeneous in character. It was differentiated by skill and training, health and physique, attitudes and productivity, although the untrained and unskilled masses predominated.

A major difference between modern labour markets and those in earlier periods was created by the existence of under-employed agricultural labour in pre-industrial England. Such labour survived with the support of the more productive members of the community. On family farms, all members of the household shared the family income – even though the removal of one or two members would have had little adverse effect on the level of production. The contribution of marginal workers to output was zero, yet they received food, clothing and shelter from their families. Such labour, however, could be integrated into more productive employment by manufacturers who provided part-time industrial work on a putting-out basis. The conditions favouring the development of rural industry were the existence of 'peasant' skills among the rural community – such as the spinning or weaving of wool or linen – that could be commercialised; the growth of national or international markets to buy the products of such skills; and the presence of entrepreneurs able to harness peasant labour to satisfy the demands of the markets. In the woollen industry, entrepreneurial functions were performed by clothiers who organised all stages of production, from the purchase of raw wool to the sale of cloth to exporting merchants. Clothiers sometimes emerged from the ranks of manufacturers; others were merchants extending their operations back into manufacturing. In the case of framework-knitting and shoemaking, which extended through the east Midlands in the late seventeenth and early eighteenth centuries,

London-based producers came to the region searching for cheap labour to manufacture goods for the growing mass market of the metropolis. The expansion of the metal trades in the west Midlands, by contrast, seems to have been the work of local capitalists exploiting market opportunities in London and overseas.[11]

Putting-out was important in the long-term development of industry, since regions in which rural industry was located often became centres of machine-based industrialisation in the late eighteenth and nineteenth centures. Nevertheless, wage-earners in putting-out industries were probably out-numbered by the many thousands of wage-earners who worked as journeymen and apprentices in craft workshops found in every market town throughout pre-industrial England. In such occupations the normal method of recruitment was by apprenticeships regulated by the guilds, and the labour market was far from resembling the textbook perfection of a commodity market. Guilds controlled the conditions of apprenticeship, during which the workers were not paid wages. In addition to the regulations imposed by guilds, the Statute of Artificers (1563) established seven years as the normal length of apprenticeships in 'any art, mystery or manual occupation . . . now used or occupied within this realm of England or Wales'.[12] The statute also defined the ratio of journeymen to apprentices, as well as restricting the growth of industry outside corporate towns and limiting the recruitment of agricultural labour into secondary industry. Had it been rigourously enforced, the statute would have severely curtailed the geographical and occupational mobility of labour. Long apprenticeships were ostensibly a means of providing technical training, and to that extent they con-tributed to the stock of skilled labour; but in practice they limited the flow of new workers into overcrowded occupations. Apprenticeships for seven years were scarcely necessary in any of the crafts coming within the scope of the Statute of Artificers, but they protected established workers from competition and gave to masters the benefit of cheap, tied labour. It was this aspect of apprenticeship that survived into the late eighteenth and nineteenth centuries, after compulsory apprenticeships had ceased to be enforced in many occupations. Under the provisions of the poor law, pauper children could be put to work as apprentices; and in this way factory masters sometimes recruited cheap labour during the early stages of the industrial revolution.

Labour markets operated with fewest obstacles at the lowest levels of skill. By the end of the eighteenth century, even quite small towns possessed pools of unskilled labour that could be recruited into any manual occupation, while big cities such as London teemed with unskilled workers who were hired on a daily, even an hourly, basis whenever their services were needed.[13]

An important impediment to the operation of labour markets was the immobility of labour, although there was some movement from region to region and even more from occupation to occupation. Among the upper strata of society, for example, younger sons of land-owners travelled to London to be apprenticed to city merchants. At a less exalted level, the sons of yeoman farmers moved to London or to provincial towns to learn a craft. Their sisters, too, often migrated; for it was a common practice for adolescent girls to leave home and enter into domestic service. Girls from better-off homes sometimes went to the households of relatives and worked in conditions that bore little resemblance to wage-labour; but, for the daughters of poor farmers and farm labourers, domestic service was a widespread and menial form of employment. There was also migration of unskilled men and women from the countryside looking for work in the towns. The growth of population in the sixteenth and early seventeenth centuries coupled with a fixed supply of land created a pool of landless labourers, who drifted to the cities where they were often regarded as inseparable from the vagrants, vagabonds and petty criminals who posed severe social problems to local and central governments. The fact that many migrating workers were often treated as vagabonds suggests that a geographical movement of labour was not considered normal in pre-industrial England.[14]

The movement of workers from one occupation to another was regarded as undesirable by the government which passed the Statute of Artificers, as well as by the urban guilds. Yet it was common for unskilled and semi-skilled workers to shift from one occupation to another or to follow two or more jobs simultaneously. Sometimes the occupations were closely related. It was common in the eighteenth century, for example, to find cases of men described variously as carpenters, woodworkers or builders. The appellation 'labourer' was particularly vague, and a man thus described might work at various times in agriculture, secondary industry or trade. The whole system of employing men and women in putting-out industry depended on their following more than one occupation; such flexibility was part of the attraction. Of course, the shift of labour between one job and another could occur only within a narrow range of skills and was not possible where a high degree of training was required; but the great mass of occupations in pre-industrial England depended more on physical strength and manual dexterity than on arcane, technical skills – with the result that considerable movement of labour from one task to another was possible.

The imperfections in the labour markets were especially obvious in the fixing of wages. There were, broadly, three sets of influences at work: the interaction of demand and supply, the force of custom, and statutory regulations. It is doubtful whether the price of labour before 1800 – or afterwards? – was determined entirely or even largely by the intersection of demand and supply curves. Perfect competition in the labour market required both a large supply of labour and also a large number of employers, so that no individual could affect the supply price of labour. In practice, labour markets were composed of a large number of workers and a restricted number of employers willing to employ them. In the corporate towns, as we have already noted, craft guilds deliberately restricted employment opportunities by their apprenticeship regulations. Even in occupations not regulated by craft guilds, or falling outside the ambit of the Statute of Artificers, a weak effective demand for goods and services resulted in a limited demand for the labour that produced them.

In the countryside, the growth of population swelled the supply of underemployed farm labourers; and until the second half of the seventeenth century labour markets in England corresponded more to W.A. Lewis' model of an economy with unlimited supplies of labour than to perfect competition.[15] In these circumstances, wages offered by employers were below those that would have prevailed in competitive markets, although higher than the value of the marginal product of labour in agriculture would indicate. This was because industrial employers needed to offer a wage high enough to compensate a farming family for the costs of rearranging the farming tasks among those workers remaining within agriculture, when one or more of its members took up manufacturing. If a labourer shifted totally from agriculture, the wage offered had to be high enough to compensate him for the loss of the customary levels of subsistence supplied within farming communities. The importance of conventional views of subsistence was reflected in the widespread practice of paying wages partly in kind.

The forces of custom were very strong in determining wage rates over long periods of time and in establishing differential wages between different skills and occupations. Phelps Brown and Hopkins, for example, have shown that wage rates paid to building craftsmen remained unaltered for many years and that the relationship between the wage rates of craftsmen and of labourers was even more stable.[16] Possibly the sources used by Phelps Brown and Hopkins — wages paid to building workers employed on contracts by colleges in southern England — are biased towards a picture of stability, but their findings confirm Adam Smith's observation in 1776 that 'the money price of labour remains uniformly the same for half a century together.'[17] The builders' wages surveyed by Phelps Brown and Hopkins remained almost constant throughout the fifteenth and eary sixteenth centuries. They moved up in the 1540s, 50s, 60s and 70s, but then remained steady until the 1630s. A further long period of stability occurred from the 1660s — punctuated by modest upward movements in the 1690s and 1730s — until the 1770s. Throughout the centuries from the fifteenth to the eighteenth, craftsmen's wages were about fifty per cent higher than labourers' wages.[18]

Demand and supply, of course, exercised some influence in determining wages. In the long run the supply price of labour was fixed by the cost of subsistence, for if this was not covered the population — and hence the labour force —

would fall as a result of malnutrition and disease. Short-run fluctuations in the price of provisions, as Adam Smith noted, had little effect on wage rates. Variations in the intensity of demand, on the other hand, had a direct influence on wages. Earnings were generally higher in towns than in the country-side, because urban demand for labour was greater in relation to its supply. In the countryside, wages at hay-making and harvest times were higher than at other periods of the year. In the second half of the eighteenth century, there was a marked secular rise in money wages, reflecting a general growth in the demand for labour relative to its supply. It was during this time that Adam Smith wrote that 'the wages of labour have been continuously increasing' since the reign of Henry VIII. His explanation for the phenomenon was that the amount of capital employed in production had steadily increased; and 'people who have great stocks to employ frequently cannot get the number of workmen they want, and therefore bid against one another in order to get as many as they can, which raises the wages of labour.'[19]

Other influences on wages included the length of training involved, and 'the ease or hardship, the cleanliness or dirtiness, the honourableness or dishonourableness of the employ-ment'.[20] A more obvious influence was legislation, although its impact is very difficult to judge. The statutory control of wages dates back to the aftermath of the Black Death. During the fifteenth century, there were sporadic efforts to relate the level of wages to the price of food, and municipalities some-times tried to fix local wage rates. An act of 1514 introduced a national maximum wage; but by the mid-century inflation, combined with a temporary shortage of labour during the 1550s, produced a different approach. The Statute of Artificers (1563) had a number of objectives. One was to ensure an adequate supply of labour for agriculture and another was to restrict the movement of labour from occupation to occupa-tion. A third, as we have seen, was to establish a seven-year apprenticeship as the normal means of entry into a wide range of occupations. Finally the act empowered justices in the counties and mayors in the corporate towns to assess wages every Easter 'according to the plenty or scarcity of the time'. The rates so assessed were maximum rates; but those in the textile trades were usually accepted as minimum, a practice that was sanctioned by a further statute in 1603.[21]

It is doubtful whether the Statute of Artificers, despite remaining in existence until 1814, had a great deal of success. Wage assessments seem to have been made fairly regularly until the beginning of the eighteenth century but sporadically thereafter, although the number of assessments that have survived — under 1,500 — does not suggest that the whole country was ever adequately regulated. When justices did fix wages, the criteria they adopted are not clear, except that in many cases older rates were reissued unchanged. Unless the justices took account of the realities of the labour market in their assessments, it is unlikely that the official wages were heeded; and there is little evidence that either employers or employees were prosecuted for offering or demanding wages different from the assessments. Given the difficulties that modern governments have in regulating wages, it would be unwise to credit governments in pre-industrial England with other than sporadic and localised success in determining wages.

By the eighteeenth century, another institutional impediment to the free working of the labour market in determining wages had emerged: workers' combinations.[22] Combinations could, as Adam Smith observed, be of employers or employees, although it was the *ad hoc* formation of combinations by journeymen in pursuit of higher wages that attracted comment. Most of them were founded by workmen in crafts whose skills were acquired through apprenticeship, such as shoemaking, tailoring and currying. The combinations' influence on wages was limited. In a period of general labour shortage during the eighteenth century, combinations could perhaps have some temporary success — and the loud complaints about their activities indicate that employers were worried about them — but their power to bargain was not strong. Employers procured private acts of Parliament to crush them — and a general combination act in 1799 — or prosecuted them under the common law for breach of contract. If necessary, skills once thought obtainable only by long apprenticeship were suddenly diluted by employers recruiting untrained labour. The master curriers of London, for example, advertised for unskilled workmen in 1812–13 when in dispute with their journeymen over piece rates. They also opposed the renewal of the licences of those public-house keepers who had allowed journeymen curriers to meet and collect money on their premises. The master curriers also revealed a significant attitude when they accused their wayward workmen of 'haughtiness' and lack of deference by going on strike.[23] In a society where labour was fragmented, where the law was weighted towards the protection of property, and where lack of deference was a social sin, combinations of employees for higher wages had little chance of success.

Wage-Labour in Society

In 1610 Rowland Vaughan, describing a community of artisans that he claimed to be setting up in the west country, listed a large number of crafts and concluded by remarking, 'if I am mistaken in marshalling my Mechanicals, your Lordship must understand that I am no Herold: they be a disordered Company; the offence be not great to place one knave before another.'[24] The attitudes embodied in this remark were common throughout the three centuries before the industrial revolution and persisted into the nineteenth century. As Christopher Hill has shown, wage-labourers were despised, had no place in society, possessed no political rights, and were accorded no consideration except as producers of wealth.[25] Even in this role, common opinion was that they should remain as poor as possible in order to keep the costs of production low.

Attitudes towards wage-labour were composed of a web of paradoxes. The greatest was that a Christian society, whose God had been made man as the son of a carpenter, should so despise manual labour. More understandable, perhaps, was that most economic writers who articulated views about wage-labour saw no contradiction between arguing that the wealth of the country depended on having a large stock of labour fully employed and believing that wages should be kept as low as possible. It is true that by about 1700 a few writers were discussing the merits of high wages, but more believed that the nation could be prosperous only if the mass of its population was poor. This leads on to a further paradox: that, notwithstanding a general belief in the necessity for low wages, wage-earners in England were, by the beginning of the eighteenth century, among the best paid in Europe.

The contemptuous regard given to wage-earners in pre-industrial England was the obverse of the high regard in which the owners of land property were held. Land represented the largest stock of fixed capital in the economy. It was the source of agricultural wealth and, indirectly, of industrial and commercial wealth as well. The social value of land was even greater. The titled aristocracy was mainly, although not entirely, identical with the great landowners; and everywhere substantial landowners formed a body of county gentry, who exercised political and social power throughout the provinces. Men successful in industry and trade rapidly turned their profits into acres in a search for social acceptability. As Thomas Mun, East India merchant and author of *England's Treasure by Forraign Trade* (published in 1664 but written in the early 1620s), observed, a merchant's son 'scorneth the profession of his Father, conceiving more honor to be a Gentleman (although but in name) to consume his estate in dark ignorance and excess than to follow the steps of his Father as a Industrious Merchant'. The irony of the remark was that Mun's work was published posthumously by his son John, 'of Bearsted in the County of Kent, Esquire'.[26] If even successful merchants were despised, how much more the man who owned only his own labour? Merchants could at least buy land and thus purchase gentility, but of labourers 'no account is made of them but only to be ruled'.[27]

In the early sixteenth century, such attitudes were strengthened by the survival of a feudal theory that held that all men owed obedience to a superior lord. Wage-labourers were out of harmony with this concept of an ordered society, where the possession of property fixed a man's position in relation to his fellows. They were 'masterless men'. Even worse, they surrendered part of their freedom when they sold their labour to employers; they became servile and, as such, placed themselves beyond the pale of polite society.

Such attitudes were occasionally challenged. During the 1640s, for example, the Levellers and Diggers sometimes regarded wage-earners differently, even to the point of believing that they should have the vote. However the arguments of those radical groups were ambiguous and some strands of Leveller opinion seemed to exclude servants and wage-earners from the franchise.[28] Radical views surfaced again in the late eighteenth century, stimulated by the events of the French revolution. Rapid industrialisation was also reshaping relationships between employer and employee in some parts of the country, in the process probably widening the social gulf that existed between them. Gradually a working-class consciousness, challenging the rights of property and asserting the rights of men, became articulated. Until well into the nineteenth century, however, such radical views were held only by a minority of working men and the general opinion about the social position of wage-labour remained much as it had been in the pre-industrial period.

Attitudes concerning the economic position of wage-labour, as opposed to its social, are easier to explain. During the sixteenth and seventeenth centuries, they were shaped by two sets of assumptions. Most obvious among the first was the self-evident truth that in most industries labour costs were the largest component of total costs. Prices of goods, therefore, were directly related to the cost of labour: when wages rose, prices rose; if wages were kept low, prices would be kept down. Lying beneath this line of argument was a further assumption: that technologies were rigid and therefore little possibility existed of reducing the unit labour costs of production by the use of more efficient methods.

The second set of assumptions concerned the importance of overseas trade and the balance of payments to the economy. No economic writer in the sixteenth and seventeenth centuries disputed the importance of an adequate supply of bullion, for gold and silver were the basis of the money supply without which trade would cease. The only practical way for a country like England, lacking gold and silver mines of significance, to acquire bullion was to export goods of a greater value than were imported. Commercial regulations could help to secure a favourable balance of trade, but the only sure way was to produce goods at competitive prices that would sell well overseas. Thus theories about the balance of trade linked up with those dealing with the level of wages. They were complementary; and in periods of economic depression, such as the 1550s, the 1620s and the 1640s, both strands of opinion combined to produce powerful arguments in favour of low wages.

The inherent illogicality of arguing that wage-earners must be poor so that the nation could be rich was resolved, or at least glossed over, in two ways. In the first place, such a belief was entirely consistent with the argument that wage-earners had no social status. Secondly, it was widely assumed that labourers were naturally lazy: if they were paid more, they would work less; and the wealth of the country would be thereby diminished. As Petty wrote in the 1670s, 'It is observed by Clothiers and others ... that when corn is extremely plentiful, that the labour of the poor is proportionately dear: and scarce to be had at all (so licentious are they who labour only to eat, or rather to drink).'[29] The assumption of high leisure preferences seemed to have some basis in fact, for underemployment among labour was endemic in the sixteenth and seventeenth centuries. Underemployment, however, was more a result of the structure of the economy than of attitudes. Labour was concentrated in agriculture, where the vagaries of the weather and the seasonality of cultivation produced periods of inactivity. More generally, shortages of capital and inefficient forms of organisation both in agriculture and industry, combined with disruptions to trade caused by wars, epidemics or shortage of specie, often forced men into idleness. Demographic considerations also played a part. The proportion of children in the population was high, and although they laboured they did so intermittently and not very efficiently.[30]

In addition, many of the adults were weakened by disease and malnutrition. Also, the absence of economic opportunity created idleness. When the range of consumption goods is restricted, labourers become – in the modern jargon – 'target workers', working to satisfy only their conventional needs. In such circumstances higher wages lead to less work.

By the end of the seventeenth century, and more commonly in the eighteenth, such pessimistic views of labour were being challenged and gradually new arguments justifying high wages evolved. One reason for the change was purely pragmatic.

Wages were rising from the late seventeenth century, but England's competitive position in international markets was not impaired. On the contrary, overseas trade grew and became more diversified. Furthermore, the Dutch were well known in the seventeenth century both for their high wages and for the strength of their overseas trade. The explanation seemed to be that high wages would be matched by high productivity. As John Cary, a Bristol merchant, wrote in 1695, 'new projections are every day set on foot to render the making of our Manufactures easier which are made cheap by the heads of the Manufacturers, not by falling the Price of poor People's labour.'[31]

Two intellectual developments strengthened arguments in favour of high wages. One was a refution of the argument that labourers were lazy. 'The wages of labour', wrote Adam Smith, 'are the encouragement of industry, which, like every other human quality, improves in proportion to the encouragement it receives.' In direct contradiction of Petty a century earlier, Smith claimed that 'where wages are high . . . we shall always find the workman more active, diligent, and expeditious than when they are low . . . Some workmen, indeed, when they can earn in four days what will maintain them through the week, will be idle the other three. This, however, is by no means the case with the greater part. Workmen, on the contrary, when they are liberally paid by the piece, are very apt to overwork themselves, and to ruin their health and constitution in a few years.'[32] It is impossible to arbitrate with confidence between the opposing opinions of Petty and Smith, but studies of labour in underdeveloped countries show that attitudes change quickly as economic opportunities open up and, in particular, as new consumption goods become available. When there are things to buy, men will work to earn money to buy them. During the eighteenth century the range and quantity of goods available to English consumers increased, providing a strong incentive to work.

The other development was an appreciation that high wages were a reflection of a prosperous economy, even a cause of that prosperity by adding to effective demand. In 1677, the author of *England's Great Happiness* argued that high incomes 'put us all upon an industry, making every one strive to excell

his fellows'. In the early eighteenth century, Defoe argued of
labourers that '. . . if their wages were low and dispicable, so
would be their Living; if they got little, they would spend but
little, and Trade would presently feel it.'[33] In the *Wealth of
Nations*, the argument took a different form, with Adam
Smith stressing that rising wages caused workers to copy the
consumption patterns of their superiors. He welcomed the
development because wage-earners were the greater part of
society and 'it is but equity . . . that they who feed, clothe,
and lodge the whole body of the people, should have such a
share of the produce of their own labour as to be themselves
tolerably well fed, clothed, and lodged.'[34]

The growing acceptance of a doctrine of high wages in the
economic literature occurred at a time when English wage-
earners were among the most prosperous in Europe. Even in
the mid-sixteenth century, patriotic Englishmen claimed
themselves to be richer than Frenchmen or Germans. The
claim might not have been true; but Defoe was on more
certain ground in describing England as the most opulent
country in the world. Adam Smith diagnosed the cause of
high wages in England (and in Holland) as the application of
capital to production which increased the productivity of
labour and hence wages. Money wages in England had, in
fact, been rising since the late seventeenth century; at the
same time the price of basic foods had been falling. On the
eve of the industrial revolution, therefore, real wages in
England were higher than they had been for a hundred
years.[35]

The material conditions of the English labourer at the
end of the pre-industrial period, however, must not be
idealised. Although real wages were rising, this was in part
because they had been reduced so low during the sixteenth
and first half of the seventeenth centuries by the relentless
pressures of population growth and inflation. If the indices
of Phelps Brown and Hopkins are to be believed, the levels
of purchasing power enjoyed by wage-earners around 1510
were not again achieved until 1880.[36] For all the greater
prosperity evident to Adam Smith when he wrote the *Wealth
of Nations,* living and working conditions were by the standards of the late nineteenth century wretched. Men, women

and children toiled for long hours at manual labour, living on diets that were monotonous, precarious and often inadequate, and in houses whose squalor was concealed only by their rural settings. Mortality was high, especially among children, and life expectancies short. Attitudes towards wage-earners were still generally hostile or at best indifferent on the eve of the industrial revolution. The paternalism that conditioned relationships between masters and men was the paternalism that treated employees as servants who were expected to be docile and obedient, their interests subordinate to those of their masters. Fundamental changes in attitudes towards labour, along with fundamental improvements in their material conditions, occurred during the nineteenth century: the century of industrialisation.

1

Trade Unionism to c. 1840

In their great classic work on the subject, Sidney and Beatrice Webb defined a trade union as 'a continuous association of wage-earners established for the purpose of maintaining or improving the conditions of their working lives'.[1] They added that they had been able to find no evidence of trade-union existence prior to the late seventeenth century, a statement which was so extended by later writers that in 1948 R.F. Wearmouth could claim that 'the unions of the nineteenth century were not the offspring of the past, a heritage of history, they were born from the circumstances of the time.'[2]

The Webbs' treatment of early union history requires to be approached with some caution. For one thing, they were writing at a time of intense debate about the nature and future of trade unionism in Britain — a debate in which, moreover, they were themselves leading participants. It was only natural that they should wish to direct the movement's attention to its future rather than its past, and their cursory discussion of union origins was presented as a curtain-raiser to the far more important business of interpreting the character of contemporary unionism.

Secondly, their stress on the idea of continuous existence exposed them to the risk of being misled by the nature of the evidence which they found. Very often what is known about early trade-union activity is the product of sheer historical accident — a chance reference to some organisation which may well have had a continuous existence but of which there is no other record. For example, combinations among Liverpool tailors and shoemakers are first noted in a passing reference in *Williamson's Liverpool Advertiser*; but this

28

journal only began publication in 1756, and it is almost
certain that both unions were very much older.[3] Similarly,
history has left only a few traces of the Union of Small Ware
Weavers, but they indicate that it was continuously active over
a long period. In the 1760s it was prosecuting unapprenticed
weavers; in 1779 it received official thanks from the Manchester silk weavers for assistance rendered during a dispute;
then, after thirty years of silence, the union surfaced as one
of the affiliates of John Doherty's National Association for
the Protection of Labour.

Thirdly, the Webbs were able to sustain their interpretation
because their definition equated continuous existence with
formal organisation. However, it is clear that men regularly
brought together in the same workforce or area might well
have acknowledged leaders and developed their own customs
and practices without ever embodying them in regular
institutions. Thus it has been suggested that the pottery
workers of Staffordshire were linked by 'the natural union
which exists when men of one trade dwell and work together'.[4]
An eighteenth century visitor to the north of England made a
similar comment about local pitmen, saying that they were
'apparently cut off from their fellow men in their interest
and feelings. They all have the same vocation and stand out
as a sturdy band apart from the motley mixture of common
humanity.'[5] Formal organisation might only have emerged
in times of particular crisis, such as a strike. North-eastern
sailors struck work no less than twelve times between 1768
and 1825. It is certain that these strikes must have been
organised by committees — although no trace of their existence
survives — otherwise the implied degree of spontaneity in
some of the more serious stoppages 'passes belief'.[6] Certainly
one contemporary magistrate observed of the 1792 strike
that 'there has been through the whole of this affair a degree
of system of order unknown in former riots.'[7]

Many of the 386 industrial disputes listed by C.R. Dobson
for the period 1715—1800 do not seem to have involved
formal continuous organisations of the type described by the
Webbs, yet there is no doubt that 'trade-union' issues were
often at stake: matters such as wages, hours of work, and
control of the labour supply.[8] Some of these disputes would

fall into the category of what has been termed 'bargaining by riot', for workers could often secure their collective ends through violence.[9] In 1718 and 1724, clothiers complained to Parliament that west of England weavers were threatening to 'pull down their houses and burn their work unless they would agree with their terms'.[10] A major strike of northern miners in 1765 was accompanied by so much violence and systematic destruction of winding gear that arson in mines was specifically proscribed in an amended Malicious Injuries to Property Act in 1767. Perhaps it is unwise to generalise from the few incidents of this sort as are recorded, particularly as they are regionally very concentrated, yet the persistence of this form of activity well into the nineteenth century does suggest strongly that it did represent a long-standing tradition.[11] It *is* valid, therefore, to see in bargaining by riot an incipient trade unionism, though clearly not in the Webbs' sense that it depended on formal organisations with continuous existence. Certainly it had much to recommend it as a tactic in pre-industrial society. It was well adapted to meeting intermittent needs occasioned by sudden changes in wages and conditions, and was especially effective against small, local employers. It also had the advantage of encouraging communal solidarity and discouraging blacklegs.

Finally, in their effort to prove that trade unionism was a relatively modern development, the Webbs totally discounted such evidence as they found that the unions had any links with the guilds of an earlier period. Yet the evidence for such links is strong. Guilds existed to protect specific trades, controlling entry via apprenticeship; maintaining a rational balance between the numbers of apprentices, journeymen and masters; and defending standards against unqualified interlopers, whether journeymen or masters. The inner balance was maintained by the guild's own rules and agreements relating to apprentice numbers, wage rates, hours, etc. Protection against outsiders was conferred by the guild's right of search, guaranteed by municipal law and later by royal charter. From the middle of the seventeenth century, however, the guilds began to crumble. When the painters of Dublin announced in 1836 that they were forming a trade union 'in consequence of receiving no assistance from the guilds', they were responding to a situation which had been manifesting itself in Britain for well over 150 years.[12]

As economic opportunities expanded, many masters began to diversify their interests well beyond the business in which they had first started. Accordingly they became much less committed to their trade guild. In any case, many masters now found it convenient to let guild regulations lapse, especially those pertaining to apprenticeship. Rising markets and new technology offered the prospect of larger profits, but apprenticeship regulations prevented the spread and thus the cheapening of many industrial skills. One result of this was the spread of industry beyond the corporate towns where the guild mandate ran. Combined with rising population and in some cases the threat of mechanisation, the weakening of apprenticeship regulations posed an obvious threat to the status of skilled journeymen. Further, the growing scale of enterprise in the eighteenth century ended the hopes, cherished by most journeymen, of one day becoming masters in their own right. The net result of these developments was a growing divergence of interest between the masters and journeymen who had previously been linked through the guild. In tailoring, for example, new retailing methods — the response to rising demand brought about by population increase, growing purchasing power among the middle class, and the Napoleonic wars — produced a clear division between a small group of master tailors and a very much larger group of those who could merely sew. In a similar way, the main impetus to the development of combinations in the printing trade was the threatened influx of unskilled and unapprenticed workers occasioned by the vast expansion of the industry. Faced with masters no longer willing to abide by the rules of the Stationers' Company, journeymen printers formed their own organisations. In textiles, lacemakers and stockingers joined forces in 1802 and 1806 to put pressure on Parliament to get the apprenticeship rules of the Framework Knitters' Company enforced. They were unsuccessful but it is significant that the first officers of the Nottingham Framework Knitters' Union had all previously been journeymen members of the guild company.

It is adequate testimony to the disintegration of the guilds in the eighteenth century that so many groups of journeymen appealed to Parliament for the enforcement of company regulations and practices. Yet Parliament was unwilling to interfere. The Spitalfields silk weavers were almost the last group to appeal successfully for the legislature to regulate their wages in 1773. Thereafter, such requests generally fell on deaf ears, and several of the unions which came formally into existence in the late eighteenth and early nineteenth centuries first appeared in response to Parliament's refusal to uphold traditional forms of labour protection. Thus the 1799 manifesto of the Association of Weavers opened with the assertion that 'the present existing laws that should protect weavers etc. from imposition, being trampled under foot, for want of a union amongst them, they have come to a determination to support each other in their just and legal rights.'[13] Liverpool artisan pewterers announced in 1756 that they would not support any of their number who trained interlopers, i.e. men not formally apprenticed to the trade. At about the same time, small ware weavers were attempting to prosecute those who had not served a proper apprenticeship.

The tide of opinion was running strongly against all such efforts. In 1814, the general apprenticeship clauses of the Statute of Artificers were repealed, notwithstanding the eloquent plea of the London artisans who organised a vigorous national campaign to oppose the repeal.

> The apprenticed artisans have, collectively and individually, an unquestionable right to expect the most extended protection from the Legislature, in the quiet and exclusive use and enjoyment of their several respective arts and trades, which the law has already conferred upon them as a property . . . and it is clearly unjust to take away the whole of the ancient established property and rights of any one class.[14]

It would appear, then, that the early combinations were linked in purpose and often in personnel to the guilds, in that they represented attempts by journeymen to give themselves the protection formerly provided by the guild.

Further indications of the link are provided by the iconography of the unions — their signs, emblems and ceremonial were quite clearly derived from earlier guild practice. Would-be members of the masons' union, for instance, were blind-folded and taken before the officers. When the blindfold was removed a skeleton was unveiled and the chairman read a macabre poem about death and the brevity of life, doubtless to impress on the applicant the advisability of keeping union rules and secrecy — especially relevant in the period when the Combination Laws were in operation.

The tramping system also points to an early origin for the unions. Under this arrangement, journeymen in good standing with their local brethren could, on production of appropriate documentation, secure subsistence and some-times work by contacting fellow tradesmen in other places. Tramping was designed basically to relieve unemployment by encouraging mobility, and long journeys were reported. The records of the Scottish National Union of Cabinet and Chair Makers reveal that in 1834 they relieved men from as far away as Belfast and Manchester.[15] When Francis Place went to London, he discovered that many of the unions operated houses of call in the capital: among them hatters, smiths, carpenters, plumbers, bakers, painters, glaziers and book-binders. While the evidence thus suggests that the system was very widespread in the early nineteenth century, it is clear that its main principles had been established much earlier by the guilds. The masons appear to have originated it sometime in the sixteenth century with their provision for checking on strangers' credentials, giving them refreshment and, if it was available, securing work. The very fact that the tramping system did become so widespread after 1800 is in itself refutation of the Webbs' view that it was a novel departure, since it is difficult to imagine any system less well adapted to coping with the unemployment problems of an industrialising economy.[16]

All in all, then, there is ample evidence that, contrary to the Webbs, trade unionism did have a pre-industrial origin. It is also apparent that as the eighteenth century progressed more workers in manufacturing trades sought protection for themselves through organisation. At one level this can be seen in the rapid expansion of friendly societies during the last forty years of the century, an expansion which was heavily concentrated in precisely those areas undergoing the most dramatic economic and social change. It is reckoned that the number of such societies increased to about seven thousand between 1690 and 1800.[17] Even though the Friendly Societies Act of 1794 made a legal distinction between unions and friendly societies, it is often difficult for the historian to make that distinction. Nearly a quarter of the friendly societies failed to register, fearing that this would lead to official scrutiny of their funds. While many of them did operate exclusively as benefit societies, providing coverage on an insurance principle against sickness, funeral expenses and old age, it is clear that many of them functioned concurrently as trade unions, concerning themselves with conditions of labour, wages and so on. The demarcation line is particularly difficult to trace where, as happened quite frequently, the majority of members of a particular society were drawn from the same trade or industry.

This is partly why it is so difficult to get much idea of the scope of trade unionism at the turn of the century. Certainly it involved only a small minority of the labour force, almost exclusively male. It is known that there were women in the Manchester small ware weavers in 1747, and in 1788 as many as 18,500 females made up the Leicester Sisterhood of Female Handspinners. These were exceptions, because women were generally difficult to organise, and it was not until the 1850s that unionism made much headway among them. The numerical strength of male organisation was also very limited. Even after periods of quite extensive expansion in the second half of the nineteenth century, the first official count of membership, taken in 1892, revealed that only about 1,500,000 workers were unionised, about six per cent of the labour force. Before 1850, therefore, it is likely that the number of unionists was very much smaller, although firm figures are scarce. Prior to 1825, unions were illegal and had every incentive to keep membership details secret. Many only had a short life or were small, local bodies which later merged into larger organisations. Either way any records which may have existed have often been lost, and such figures as do survive have to be treated with considerable caution. John Doherty's Grand National Consolidated Trades Union of

1834 claimed a membership of 500,000 — but paying membership was in fact only around 16,000.[18] This accords with the
evidence relating to an earlier federal body, the National
Association for the Protection of Labour, which the Webbs
estimated had between 10,000 and 20,000 members.[19]

While it is certain that surviving figures represent only the
tip of the iceberg, certainly for the years before 1825, it is
difficult to get much further. It is not possible, for example,
to extrapolate any general figure on the basis of information
relating to individual branches or specific unions, as these
were so variable. It was rare for any branch of any union to
have more than five hundred members. The Edinburgh chairmakers fluctuated in the 1830s between sixty and one
hundred, although meetings of the London brushmakers
could be attended by up to 240. Individual unions also varied
in size. In 1833 the Operative Society of Masons had 4,000
members, the potters almost double that number, while the
ironfounders were considerably smaller with about 1,200 in
1832. The masons were organised into a hundred different
branches, although the ironfounders had only twenty-nine
branches in 1824. On the other hand, despite its impressive
sounding title, the United Friendly Society of Journeymen
Bookbinders issued its first rule book in 1794 to just four
branches — its entire membership.[20]

Several explanations for the limited spread of trade unionism
in the early nineteenth century have been offered. Some
writers have suggested that poor communications were partly
responsible, though it is a claim which will not stand close
investigation.[21] Of course, there were transport difficulties.
Despite a marked improvement in the postal service after
1784 and an increase in the number of accelerated stage-
coaches plying the main routes, Gravener Henson, leader of
the Nottingham framework knitters, told a select parliamentary committee in 1838 that he had often wanted to know
what was happening in other centres of the trade like Devon,
but 'we are as entirely ignorant of it as they were in the
centre of America.'[22] Nor did the advent of railways necessarily make things any better in this respect. As late as 1860,
one trade-union official in Lancashire had to carry money
personally to strikers in the Colne Valley on at least nine

occasions. Each time he rose at five in the morning to walk the twelve miles to the strikers' village along 'one of the worst roads I ever travelled in my life, over mountain and moor, over bog and mire, through byways and on highways'.[23]

Despite these deficiencies, however, it seems that few unions experienced much real difficulty in maintaining contact, often over quite substantial distances, with workers both within and outside their own trade. Each district union of weavers, for example, sent delegates to central committees in leading towns such as Bolton, Preston, Carlisle and Belfast. Between these centres, claimed a contemporary, 'a constant and active correspondence was kept up.'[24] Thomas Dunning tells how Nantwich shoemakers were quite easily able to send one union member off to Dublin in order to prevent him being called as a witness against the union in a forthcoming legal case.[25] One very obvious means by which such contacts were maintained was the tramping system. Its historian estimates that in 1800 there were substantial intertown contacts in at least seventeen trades, and in twenty-eight trades by the early 1820s.[26] It was also in this same period that several groups, including steam engine makers, mechanics, smiths, shipwrights and potters, adopted the system of the acting branch, whereby branches functioned in rotation as a general headquarters for the whole organisation. This could not have been very practical had communications presented a major obstacle. On the contrary, relative ease of communication probably helps to explain why so often in this period a wage claim in one part of the country was justified on the grounds of a similar increase granted elsewhere. Edinburgh compositors asked for an increase in 1803 because the London men had just had one. Manchester printers made a request in 1810, citing recent advances in London, Dublin, Liverpool and Bristol as precedents. Communication was also adequate enough to permit the London artisans to wage their campaign against the repeal of the apprenticeship clauses in the Statute of Artificers, the *Journals* of the House of Commons revealing that the legislature had been bombarded with protest from all over Britain. Nor did communication problems generally prevent mutual financial assistance during strikes. The London brushmakers aided

Dublin workers in this way in 1816 and others at Hull some years later. One contemporary estimated that during a strike of Lancashire spinners in 1810 their weekly strike fund contained between £1000 and £1500, made up of contributions from all over the north of England.[27] The steam engine makers were able to adopt a system of equalising the financial holdings of their various branches, a technique later extended by their more illustrious descendants, the Amalgamated Society of Engineers.

Finally, it should be noted that as early as the eighteenth century some workers, notably shearmen and wool-combers, were experimenting with national organisation, something which developed even more once the Combination Laws were finally modified in 1825. In the late 1820s and early 1830s miners, potters, building workers, and cotton spinners all tried to organise at district or national level, and there were also some attempts at general union. John Doherty founded the NAPL in 1830s, though it collapsed fairly quickly when its main supporters, the Lancashire spinners, were defeated in a strike and the secretary absconded with the funds. In 1834 an appeal issued on behalf of striking workers in Derby led to the calling of a general trade-union conference in London. The upshot was the establishment of the Grand National Consolidated Trades Union, mainly the creation of the London artisans. Although it did not survive very long once Robert Owen became involved and led it off in the direction of co-operation, its collapse had little to do with poor communications. Rather, the union dissipated its slender financial resources; and in any case many of its backers, who included farm labourers and a few women workers, were in no position to provide any sustained financial input.

It cannot be seriously maintained either that illiteracy or lack of education were major obstacles to union growth, though there is much disagreement about literacy levels at this time.[28] Thus while it is agreed that Lancashire experienced falling levels of literacy between 1780 and 1820, some take the view that this was a product of industrialisation, others that industrialisation reversed it.[29] Again, much controversy was sparked off by E.G. West's claims that 'the extra-ordinary literacy attainments in the towns' testify to the 'success of educational endeavour . . . during the period'.[30] If he is right then this was a situation from which the unions, essentially urban in their scope, must have benefited. It is true that the formal institutions of education left much to be desired, but it is possible that the deficiencies were made good by the Sunday schools. Not only did they teach basic reading and writing, but it has been argued that their influence was so pervasive that outside London virtually every working-class child must have attended one.[31]

Whatever one makes of this particular academic debate, it seems doubtful if rates of literacy as commonly measured (i.e. the ability to sign one's name) are of much relevance to trade-union development anyway. For one thing, well into the nineteenth century reading and writing were separately taught. Reading was learned first and writing introduced at the age of about seven, by which time many children had finished with school. The effect of this is seen in the results of one survey of 143 Scottish parishes, which revealed that while 250,000 people could not write, only 83,000 could not read.[32] It would seem, therefore, that the dissemination of news and ideas about trade unions could not have been seriously hampered by any lack of reading skill. If it was, it is difficult to explain away the thriving radical press of the early nineteenth century. Although most of the papers were local in influence, usually centred on Manchester or London, Cobbett's *Political Register*, Wooler's *Black Dwarf*, and Richard Carlile's *Republican* all achieved national circulations after 1815.[33] The existence of the stamp duty may well have placed some publications beyond the financial reach of individuals, but some papers refused to pay the duty, while organisations like trade unions purchased journals for the collective use of their members. Indeed, trade unionists in some cases produced their own papers. London workers published the *Trades Newspaper and Mechanics Weekly Journal* from 1825, but even before this the *Beacon* had appeared briefly as part of the campaign to preserve the apprentice clauses in the Statute of Artificers.[34] As far as writing is concerned, unions needed at most a couple of individuals capable of keeping such books and records as were required – perhaps not even this while the Combination

Laws were in force, since there was a premium on secrecy and the less that was committed to paper the better. That there was no lack of individuals with these skills is seen in the growth of friendly societies in exactly the same regions of trade-union strength.

In a different and more widely accepted tradition, trade-union development in this period has been seen as part of a working-class challenge to capitalist enterprise and its whole associated system of social, legal and political relationships. The movement's weakness can thus be represented as the result of class conflict in which all the aces were held by the rulers. It may be that at the height of the panic caused by the French revolution trade unions were viewed as a threat to stability, particularly as wartime inflation resulted in a growing number of industrial disputes. Yet there is not much hard evidence that the authorities suspected any link between the wage earners' trade societies and the corresponding societies. Jacobins were dealt with under the Corresponding Societies Act of 1799, not the Combination Laws. The trade societies frequently protested their fundamental loyalty and held very conservative views. Rule eighteen of the Seamen's Loyal Standard Association imposed a fine of five shillings on any member who spoke 'contemptuously of the present King and Constitution'.[35] A Falkirk building union excluded from membership anyone who was guilty of adultery or association with unclean women; while Manchester bricklayers laid down an alliterative trilogy of sins, denying benefit to any whose injuries were caused by fighting, football or fornication. While it is easy to dismiss such rules as products of the unions' need to *appear* respectable, they have to be seen in the context of a very long tradition of British working-class behaviour which has combined industrial militancy with political and social conservatism. In the same way, while there was naturally an element of calculation in employers' efforts to maintain good working relationships with employees by providing social amenities, these also represented in many cases a genuine effort to preserve old forms of traditional concern for those who were seen as social dependents. To interpret the limited development of unionism at this time as a product of class war is to accept a version of relationships between men and masters that is oversimplified and unhistorical.

For one thing, it is quite evident that trade unions often enjoyed a broad measure of public sympathy. The great northern seamen's strike of 1813 attracted considerable support throughout local society, although this might be explained by the sailors' crucial role in the war against Napoleon. No such explanation, however, can be behind the admission of magistrates that all sections of local society supported Manchester cotton spinners in 1838. Again, there must have been a great deal of tacit agreement between employers and trade unionists, for instance in the compilation of agreed price lists and wage rates. This was perhaps less marked in those sectors of the economy experiencing the most rapid change, but the evidence presented to the Select Committee on Artisans and Machinery in 1824 suggests that it was very prevalent in older skilled trades. Sometimes there was active co-operation between workers and masters, especially the smaller ones. In 1818, Bolton mill owners suggested to weavers that they should leave the employ of those who paid below the current agreed wage. When, as a result of so doing, the weavers' leaders were arrested and prosecuted for conspiracy, the mill owners gave evidence on their behalf. Similarly in Glasgow, at least half a dozen strikes in the first two decades of the century were started at the suggestion of small masters, while Doherty's Grand General Union of Cotton Spinners had the backing of many small-scale producers. In Coventry in the early 1840s most manufacturers encouraged the formation of the Ribbon Weavers' Association. Those who resisted found themselves pressurised not only by the weavers but also by the local magistrates, keen to see the implementation of an agreed price list. The select committee set up by the House of Commons to investigate the working of the Combination Laws was told that unions existed 'in more or less objectionable form' in almost every major manufacturing centre.[36] It is difficult to see how this could be so if there had not been a great deal of tacit acceptance of the sort mentioned above, and this is further confirmed by the appearance of many fully formed unions immediately after the Combination

Laws were lifted. It seems unlikely that the potters' union, which officially came into being in 1824, could have paid out as much as £3,000 in a strike in that year without a long, underground existence beforehand. Similarly, an investigation of 1818 into a wage agitation in the West India Docks revealed that the coopers' union was already so well entrenched that once a cooper had worked for the dock company (which paid below the current rates for the trade) he was not allowed to work for anyone else until he had paid 'heavy fines for working at less wages than this confederacy has been pleased to dictate to the trade'.[37]

This is not to deny, of course, that industrial bargaining in this early period was accompanied by a great deal of violence from one side or other. This was especially true of trades such as hand weaving, stocking making and wool cropping, which were transformed by technical innovation, producing large numbers of redundant workers. Mining was also notorious for bad industrial relations. Owners freely evicted strikers, employed blacklegs, and penalised union members. Even after the Combination Laws were repealed and unions as such were no longer illegal, blacklegs were widely utilised and many employers would only take on men who had signed the infamous Document, a renunciation of any intent to become involved in union activity. Coal mine owners on the Tyne and Wear had an agreement among themselves not to employ any miner unless he produced a certificate from a previous employer. Union leaders were frequently subject to harassment. Charles Shaw recalled that his potter father was threatened with ruination if he did not cease his union activity. 'It came true,' he added, 'and the family was driven into the workhouse. Such intimidation in those days could be easily carried out by employers . . . [a man] could be run down by their sleepless vengeance like a rat.'[38] It was largely the belief that trade unionism was synonymous with violence that explains its uniformly unflattering portrayal in contemporary literature. Whether in Mrs Gaskell's *Mary Barton* or Dickens' *Hard Times,* the impression is the same. Trade unionism was virtually equated with terrorism.[39]

Welcoming the more moderate stance announced by the Dublin painters in the 1840s, the *Freeman's Journal* observed that 'everyone condemned the violence of former periods', and here surely was the point.[40] Conflict and violence had been features of industrial bargaining long before the industrial revolution, witness the whole tradition of bargaining by riot. With rapid technical change and the growing scale of enterprise, it was inevitable that violence should persist, given the absence of any institutional means through which disagreement could be channelled. Yet industrial conflict is not necessarily the same as class conflict. Very often those workers responsible for violence were not themselves directly engaged in a particular dispute. Stoppages involving skilled men could easily result in the laying-off of considerable numbers of unskilled labourers, who — lacking any resources of their own — were often tempted to bring matters to a speedy conclusion by the use of violence. Rarely, however, is there any indication of industrial violence being turned against political targets. On the contrary, much of it was not even directed against employers but against blacklegs. The Glasgow cotton spinners arrested in 1837 were charged with arson and murder of blacklegs, not employers.

Thus it is an oversimplification to see industrial violence in this period as an expression of deep-seated class conflict. The same is true of the operation of the law, which in some of the cruder Marxist accounts appears as part and parcel of the process by which the employing class, allied in some mysterious way with the landed ruling class, exerted its will over employees. No one could deny that the unions did operate under considerable legal restraint, though some of the claims made for the Combination Laws in this respect — 'among the most blatant pieces of class legislation designed to injure the bargaining power of labour'[41] — have been exaggerated. In theory at least, the Combination Laws were directed equally against combinations of men and masters, and in practice they were not much used. Nottingham framework knitters got away untouched by the law when in the course of a dispute with the masters they smashed over three hundred frames in the village of Arnold. During the whole quarter century that the legislation was in force, only three prosecutions were brought against these framework knitters under its terms. The London brushmakers were able to ignore with equal impunity, as were several other unions, the clauses which barred the donation of money by one organisation to another. In any case, the laws only remained in effect until 1824 when, after a campaign largely instigated and orchestrated by Francis Place, they were repealed and unions granted exemption from prosecution for conspiracy under both common and statute law. This produced a rash of strikes and violence, leading to an amendment act in 1825 which protected the rights of combination and collective bargaining, but restored union liability for conspiracy. There still remained, however, a veritable battery of other statutes which could be deployed against the unions. These included the Master and Servant Act, the Statute of Artificers, acts against oath taking, and a whole range of laws relating to threatening behaviour and intimidation.

In some cases the operation of the law was more subtle. Before 1825, when they were illegal, unions could not bring court actions to further their ends. So when the bookbinders wished to take legal action to enforce apprenticeship, it had to be done in the name of an individual member, with the attendant risk that the individual would be victimised. Neither could illegal organisations hold money in a bank, which presented serious problems of security, as unions tended to accumulate considerable financial resources. Thus the founder of the Journeymen Steam Engine and Machine Makers' Friendly Society had to secrete as much as £6,000 in his chimney and cellar. The brushmakers adopted a different approach. Rule XI stated that 'when the stock of this society shall amount to £80 five members of this society shall be appointed to purchase £50 stock in the five per cents; and every succeeding £50 to have different stock holders.'[42] Even with the repeal of the Combination Laws, financial security remained a problem. Most simply an individual, usually an office holder, was permitted to hold the union's funds, but the large sums involved frequently provided a source of temptation which many failed to resist. The first secretary of the Bookbinders' Consolidated Relief Fund was dismissed for stealing the funds. The Edinburgh chairmakers were warned in 1835 by a London branch about the 'villinous [sic] conduct of their late treasurer who had purloined at different times to the amount of about £500'. They were further invited to 'treat him as he deserves should he come our way'.[43] Rather safer, perhaps, was the common practice of letting the publican of the house where the union met keep the funds, or at least one of the three keys usually required to open the cash box. This benefited the publican, too, in that the meeting of the union provided him with regular, guaranteed custom; indeed, many unions elected drink stewards and made a small liquor allowance to the officers at each meeting. Masons and carpenters in Newcastle went further, stipulating that members must each spend two pence on beer at each meeting. Despite all the difficulties involved in securing their finances, the early unions still raised some impressive sums. Journeymen bookbinders collected £2,000 in 1786 to help five of their members who had been arrested for petitioning for a reduction of hours. In 1824 the potters spent £3,000 in the course of a single strike.

Yet if the unions did labour under such legal obstacles, it does not necessarily follow that the law was an instrument of class oppression. The idea and practice of law is notoriously conservative, and its formulation tends to lag behind when society is undergoing very rapid social and economic change. This is particularly so when, as in the case of English common law, precedent is at its heart. Law and its interpretation need not necessarily reflect the prejudices of a ruling class but rather the values and practice of an older social system. In any case, local magistrates, who were largely responsible for law enforcement, were not as invariably sympathetic to employers as is often suggested. One of the reasons why there were so many prolonged disputes involving north-eastern seamen in the years round 1800 was that 'the shipowners knew that they could not rely on the local magistrates making common cause with them in resistance' to the sailors.[44] A similar picture emerges if we examine the working of the 1800 Arbitration Act for the weaving industry. Most of the cases were settled amicably enough, but ten of the eleven disputes referred to the magistrates were decided in favour of the employees. Even at a higher level, Lord Kenyon, who presided in the last decade of the eighteenth century over most of the King's Bench trials for conspiracy, considered

that labour disputes were best settled without the intervention of the courts.

Nor was much of the law actually enforced. In part this
was a reflection of the sort of sympathies noted above, in
part the result of an antiquated legal system which did not
possess adequate machinery for enforcement. The very fact
that it was necessary in the eighteenth century alone to pass
as many as forty statutes against combination is eloquent of
the law's ineffectiveness. The act of 1719, to give one example,
which made it illegal for publicans to permit working people
to use their premises for unlawful purposes such as combination or public debating, was widely flouted, and many
early unions were centred on public houses. The three original
branches of the London bookbinders met at the One Tun,
the Green Man, and the Jolly Butchers. Britain is still full of
pubs named after the unions which began their lives in them.
It was precisely because trade-union law was so ineffective
that when in 1834 six hapless Dorsetshire labourers, known
to history as the Tolpuddle Martyrs, were sentenced to trans-
portation for administering illegal oaths in the formation of a
union, they were charged under an act connected with the
naval mutinies of 1797.

If then the quality of early-nineteenth-century education
and communication did not present really major obstacles,
and if the bite of the law and public opinion which sanctioned
it were not always quite as bad as their bark, wherein lies the
explanation for the limited development of trade unionism
in the period? One obvious consideration is that the trade
union, like the guild, was essentially an urban phenomenon.
Its potential for expansion, therefore, was limited by the
fact that the bulk of the labour force remained in agriculture,
locked into an older social structure which, except in the south-
east, was not yet changing very significantly. In any case, few
rural workers received sufficient cash income to afford even a
modest trade-union subscription. The average agricultural
wage in 1800, for example, has been estimated at about ten
shillings.[45] Similarly the vast army of sweated workers was
also financially incapable of organisation, and the existence
within manufacturing industry of large numbers of semi-
skilled workers ensured that here, too, union development
was patchy.

While it is possible that the absence of organisation might well indicate strength, signifying the bargaining power of an individual whose skills were in high demand, it has been generally assumed that lack of organisation should be equated with weakness. Some historians have argued that development was bounded by the ebb and flow of the trade cycle. In periods of boom, it is argued, unions tended to be aggressive and expand, becoming more defensive in slumps. While there is a certain commonsense appeal in this approach, it is not always mirrored in historical fact. For example, the outburst of activity in the years 1829–32, which saw the formation of the cotton spinners' general union and of Doherty's National Association for the Protection of Labour, took place against a background of economic depression, not expansion. More useful perhaps is the idea that booms favoured the stronger groups such as old elite craftsmen and also the new elite of factory cotton spinners and engineers. In times of slump, the depressed and declining trades struggled, while the stronger groups were quietly defensive.[46]

Yet in a sense this only raises another, more fundamental question. What enabled some workers to establish and maintain strong unions in the first place? The key to this was the ability to control labour supply, an ability which in turn depended upon one or more of a number of variables – the secular trend in labour demand, the size of production units, the amount of skill involved, the existence of an apprenticeship system. The latter in particular was a very potent weapon. Increasingly the skill-learning element in apprenticeship diminished, especially in trades where technology was ousting old hand skills, and it survived mainly as a safety valve on entry. Labour demand was probably the most important single influence on trade-union development. If demand for a product was growing rapidly enough, it even enabled men to survive quite significant technological change. This was the case in the printing industry, where the iron press (patented in 1798) greatly reduced the amount of labour involved in printing. Yet such was the expansion in the demand for literature that the printers' unions were among the best organised and most highly paid of all.[47] The Tyneside keelmen, a powerful group in pre-industrial times, survived the immediate threat to their position posed by the advent of the spout — which loaded coal directly into the holds of barges — because the demand for coal and thus for their services continued to grow at a very fast rate.[48] On the other hand, organisation in industries such as coal and hand-loom weaving was hampered because of the ease with which people could move in and out of the trade. A major brake on trade unionism in the South Wales coal field, for instance, lay in the divisions caused by the frequent influxes of non-Welsh-speaking migrant labour.

In some industries, technological change was slow or even non-existent in the first half of the nineteenth century, and unionism flourished amongst workers in such trades. These included tailors and, perhaps more surprisingly, some engineers. Most of the engineering processes involved in machine tool manufacture remained for some time a matter of apprenticed craftsmen using hand tools. Demand for engineers was so high that in London their organisations were able to command wages of seven shillings a day. This group also included many of the rather quaintly named unions which did eventually disappear as technology overtook them — the Birmingham button burnishers, the brass-cock founders, the Sheffield hoop-hafters and scale pressers, various unions of cloggers in Lancashire and the vermin trap makers of Wednesfield.

Changes in the scale of production frequently supplemented workers' bargaining power. In the iron industry, Carron was employing a thousand people by 1773 and the Darbys a similar number by 1800. The paternalist attitudes of the early iron masters inhibited union growth for a while, but the Friendly Society of Ironfounders emerged in 1809. The early growth of the shipwrights can similarly be related both to their relative scarcity and also to the growing scale of shipbuilding. A national census of wrights in 1804 showed that there were only 5,100 in the whole of Britain, plus a further 3,284 in the royal shipyards.[49] Liverpool's experience was fairly typical of what was happening around the country. By the end of the eighteenth century, what had once been an industry composed of small, often part-time, family concerns building ships in small yards had become a large-scale industry concentrated in the hands of a few entrepeneurs, who in many cases had never themselves worked as shipwrights. Potters' unions also flourished as the industry grew in scale. The bargaining power conferred on the men by their skill was amplified by growing demand and the concentration of the industry which by the 1830s employed as many as six thousand workers, mainly in the north-west.

The coal industry affords some interesting contrasts. Although hewers had genuine skills, they could be replaced — at lower productivity and higher accident rates — by black-leg labour. In the north-east and Scotland especially, miners were often at the mercy of owners through their occupation of tied cottages. Nor was the miner's alleged social isolation always sufficient to confer bargaining strength upon him. In most coal districts in the first half of the century, miners were heavily outnumbered by other workers; and especially in the midlands mining communities were simply grafted onto existing villages.[50] Like many other workers such as black-smiths, most miners found it difficult to organise success-fully before the 1840s because the production units were small and scattered. The exceptions were in Northumberland and Durham, whose pits were among the first to benefit from rising demand for coal in the eighteenth century. By the 1840s there were already some fifty north-eastern pits employing two hundred men, at a time when the national average was around fifty men. Even this, however, was a double-edged weapon, since large-scale owners could more easily resist union pressure. Thus Tommy Hepburn's miners' union, founded in the north-east in 1831, collapsed quite quickly. Nevertheless, the insatiable demand for coal ensured the future of miners' unionism. By the end of the 1840s they were organised at county level in Durham, Northumberland, Staffordshire, Yorkshire and Lancashire. In 1842 these groups set up the Miners' Association of Great Britain, which soon claimed a membership of 70,000, a third of the industry's labour force.

Miners were not alone in finding organisation easier as their industry expanded and became more concentrated. Some textile workers were in a similar position. Even though their job was not particularly skilled, factory cotton spinners were able to form closed unions, i.e. ones which exercised strict control over entry; because they were initially concentrated in relatively few mills and localities. In Scotland the Operative Cotton Spinners formed the strongest union of all, benefiting from their concentration in 134 mills within a twenty-five mile radius of Glasgow. As early as 1810, they had been able to impose a closed shop. The median size of the unit labour force in spinning and weaving at this time seems to have been between two and three hundred, and so entrenched was union power that Roberts, Sharp and Co., manufacturers of the first working self-actor mule, listed as its prime advantage the fact that it would enable employers to dispense with spinners. In the other main branch of the industry, weaving, there was a tradition of association among the workers long before the advent of the factory. Contact between weavers had been provided by 'bearing home' day, when the week's work was brought in to some central point. Technical innovation almost eliminated the hand-loom weavers, as we shall see, but by the 1850s factory weavers had a network of organisation in Lancashire, their power resting mainly in their concentration because 'few weavers could undertake the more-skilled work, but most more-skilled operatives could weave if it came to the point.'[51]

There was one other crucial difference between spinners and weavers which suggests a more general explanation for the limited extent of early unionism. The weavers were almost unique in that they actively encouraged others to organise. The spinners, in common with other skilled workers, tried to restrict entry to their own trade and implicitly — sometimes explicitly — inhibited organisation among less skilled men. There was a similar division in many trades. The miners' unions were dominated by the hewers, who barred oncost workers in order to protect their own privileged status. Similarly in London, artisans in many trades frequently combined in supra-trade activities, but their motive was always to protect their own status against both employers who violated trade customs and dilution from below — a threat made particularly pressing by the existence of a labour surplus after the end of the French wars.[52] Although such attitudes are usually thought to have been more influential in shaping union development after 1840, there is no doubt that they did serve as a general constraint on the wider dissemination of organisation within those trades where unionisation had made some progress earlier. Sir Archibald Alison was even prepared to dismiss all trade unions as nothing more than a 'system of aristocracy of skilled labour against the mass of unskilled labour'.[53]

2

The Making of the Working Class?

The exclusive attitude adopted by many trade unionists is particularly revealing in view of the frequently made assertion that the early nineteenth century saw the creation of the English working class. The case has been most powerfully put by E.P. Thompson who has argued that 'in the years between 1780 and 1832 most English working people came to feel an identity of interests as between themselves, and as against their rulers and employers.'[1] By 1832, he adds, this single working-class presence was the most significant fact of British political life, a significance symbolised in a concurrent shift of terminology away from older words such as 'ranks' and 'orders' to the language of class. Thus in 1833 John Wade published his *History of the Middle and Working Classes,* in which he traced the emergence of 'an opulent commercial and a numerous, restless and intelligent operative class'.[2] The great radical orator, William Cobbett, spoke of workers' wage claims as likely to produce a situation in which 'one class of society united to oppose another class'.[3] A few years later another popular radical leader, Henry Hetherington, claimed in similar vein that 'the middling classes will never wish the poor and despised "mob", as even *they* call the working classes, to have equal power with themselves in any respect.'[4] Such usage is significant in that it reflects not only social change but also men's perception of that change.

Certainly the greatest social division of all in the early nineteenth century lay between workers and others. 'Between manual and non-manual occupations a great gulf was fixed . . . No matter how skilled he was, nor how high his earnings, his social status was determined by the kind of job he performed.'[5] Similarly, it has been observed of the new middle-

51

order social groups created by industrialisation that overriding
all their shadings of income, origin, education and culture was
'a common resistance to inclusion in, or confusion with, the
working classes'.[6] Whether men worked in field or factory,
for large or small employers, they were bound together in
Thompson's view by their 'common consciousness . . . as petty
consumers of the necessaries of life'.[7] Class was not a thing
but an experience, developing when 'some men as a result of
common experience (inherited or shared) feel and articulate
the identity of their interests as between themselves, and as
against other men whose interests are different from (and
usually opposed to) theirs.'[8] For Thompson, the common
experiences which bound men together and transcended their
differences in the early nineteenth century were those of
immiseration (impoverishment) and repression.

Of the groups generally reckoned to have suffered most
from industrialisation, the hand-loom weavers have been
most publicised. Even contemporaries who believed that the
general effects of the industrial revolution were beneficial
usually made an exception of this group, and later writers
have followed in the same tradition. The weavers therefore
appear in the works of John and Barbara Hammond as the
archetypal skilled hand workers ruined by the advent of
mechanisation; and it has been variously claimed that by
1815 they were 'already at starvation point', having been
'reduced to a level of misery and degradation probably never
before suffered by nominally free men'.[9] As a body, cotton
hand-loom weavers appear to have come into existence some
time in the 1770s, following the spread of the new spinning
machines and the rapidly growing demand for cotton goods.
Before their final disappearance in the 1840s their numbers
reached an estimated quarter of a million and earnings
fluctuated just as dramatically. After rising rapidly for several
years, the average piece rate for muslin weaving in Bolton,
for example, fell from 34s. in 1795 to 10s. by 1820.[10] In
calico weaving, the piece rate index dropped from 100 in
1815 to 40 by 1827.[11] The real cause of the hand-loom
weavers' problem was simply that entry to the trade could
not be controlled. The necessary skills could be picked up
very quickly and apprenticeship regulations proved very diffi-

cult to enforce, partly because the labour force was very widely scattered, partly as we have seen because Parliament showed no interest in their enforcement. The weavers' high leisure preference meant that output rose only slightly when demand boomed, so new entrants could flood in to meet the new demand. Conversely, when demand fell off, weavers could only get work by accepting much lower rates as there were so many of them competing for the work. Thus even before the advent of the power loom, the economic security of the hand weavers was weak, resting solely on the continuance of a rising market. Once costly machines had been installed, manufacturers naturally preferred to keep them running in times of depression rather than putting work out to hand weavers. As a result, wage rates in the trade were forced down. To the scattered weavers seeking a target on which to vent their wrath, the cause of their plight seemed to be the power loom itself. Edmund Cartwright had built his first power-loom shed at Doncaster in 1787, and although diffusion was slow — only gaining real momentum after the Napoleonic Wars — it was clear by the 1820s that 'weaving by machinery is destined, and at no distant period, entirely to supersede weaving by hand.'[12] Spasmodically in periods of depression violence was directed against the looms. Grimshaw's Manchester factory was burned down in 1792 by men who had 'sworn together to destroy your factory, if we dye for it, to have your lifes for ruining our trade'.[13] More looms were attacked in 1812 in the midst of another depression, but the worst outbreak of all occurred in 1826. It began at Accrington and, as soldiers marched out from Blackburn to deal with it, factories in that town were also attacked. The following day the wreckers turned on mills at Darwen, and — although the actual violence was short-lived — many manufacturers continued to receive threatening letters. Whiteheads of Rawtenstall, who had replaced their broken looms very quickly, were informed that their factory would be ruined 'by fire or otherwise' if they did not 'within three days decline weaving by power'.[14] Altogether Lancashire mill owners claimed some £16,000 worth of damages, and sixty-six men were tried in connection with the outbreak.

The earlier spate of loom breaking in 1812 was part of the

more general outbreak of machine breaking or Luddism then occurring, spreading out from its Nottinghamshire focal point. It represented a protest by some groups of workers against the way in which machines were being used to threaten their traditional way of earning a living. In Nottingham, protest was concentrated in the framework-knitting industry where wide frames were being used to make cheap and poor quality goods called cut-ups, thus giving the whole trade a bad name. These products also had the effect of depressing wages. The county had some 25,000 stocking frames in 1811 and of these about a thousand, all making the cut-ups, were destroyed. In Yorkshire, Luddism was led by the croppers whose control of cloth production was threatened by the development of the gig mill and shearing frame. Throughout 1811 and 1812 machine breaking of various types spread northwards, and troops were apparently powerless to stop it, the more so as many smaller manufacturers probably sympathised with the wreckers. At Middleton, five Luddites were killed during one attack. In April 1812 the owner of Rawfolds mill killed two men intent on attacking his property, but shortly afterwards the Luddites exacted their revenge, murdering William Horsfall, another prominent mill owner. Eventually machine breaking was made a capital offence, although the wave of violence had in any case already petered out.

The rural labourers of southern England, whose various protest movements culminated in the Swing riots of 1830, comprised the third main group of sufferers in this period. Under the impetus of wartime boom, the traditionally hierarchical and paternalistic rural social structure had begun to change. During the French wars, agriculture suffered from an acute labour shortage — there were traditions of petticoat harvests in some parts of the country at this time — and hiring agreements were frequently broken as labourers took advantage of relatively higher wages elsewhere. Although hiring fairs persisted in some parts of the country until the end of the nineteenth century, in the south they began to disappear as a means of labour recruitment during the Napoleonic Wars. The October Jack and Joan Fair at Canterbury, for instance, was defunct by 1799. The rising demand for agricultural produce encouraged farmers to utilise marginal land to an extent never since repeated, even during the later world wars. It also encouraged them to sell all they could on the open market, rather than using some of their product to pay workers in kind. They also took such opportunities as presented themselves to substitute mechanisation, mainly in the form of the threshing machine, for human labour.

The ending of the wars, however, transformed this situation. The demobilisation of the forces threw a quarter of a million men into the labour market at a time when corn prices were falling in response to improved domestic harvests.[15] Many farmers were thus caught with high costs in a falling market, and they responded by taking advantage of labour surpluses to impose severe wage reductions. In the south and east where hand threshing had traditionally continued until December or January, the widespread adoption of the threshing machine severely curtailed labour demand in the winter months when alternative farm work was at its most scarce. The effects of falling labour demand were exacerbated by the continued growth of rural population. Sometime in the eighteenth century, and for reasons which are still unclear, Europe's population had begun to increase. Although statistics are patchy and by no means comprehensive, it is reckoned that population in Britain as a whole doubled between 1780 and 1841. The rural counties of England and Wales grew by a million between 1801 and 1831, reaching 3.7 million.[16] The consequent rise in expenditure on poor relief led to a resurgence of the view that overgenerous relief was itself encouraging poverty, and several attempts were made to hold such expenditure in check.

Throughout the 1820s, therefore, rural poverty was endemic, and crime rose in what were to become the Swing counties. The labourers finally revolted in August 1830. Machine breaking began near Canterbury, and in the space of about eight weeks it spread rapidly along a belt from Lincolnshire to Dorset, accompanied by rick burning and anonymous threatening letters from the mysterious Captain Swing. 'This is to inform you,' ran a fairly typical example, 'what you have to undergo Gentelmen if providing you don't pull down your meshenes and rise the poor mens wages . . . we will burn down your barns and you in them this is the last notis.'[17] Before the movement was crushed by a specially appointed assize which heard charges against over two thousand individuals, the Swing rioters did a fair amount of damage. Machinery worth £13,000 and threshing machines to the value of £8,000 were destroyed, in addition to £100,000 damage caused by fire to property.[18]

These three groups – Luddites, rural labourers and hand-loom weavers – constituted the main victims of early-nineteenth-century economic change. Legal convictions do not offer a reliable guide to their actual numbers, because they only tell us of those who were caught and brought before the magistrates. Relatively few Luddites were arrested, but there must have been widespread communal support for their activities. This at least is suggested by the fact that very little ever emerged about the movement and many people, not necessarily directly involved themselves, must have been aware of the complicated arrangements inherent in the organisation of clandestine, night-time forays. The same must have been true of the Scotch Cattle and the rural labourers. When rick burning occurred on Lord Stafford's midland estates, his agent commented that 'there is something most seriously remarkable in the secrecy with which it has been acomplished,' a remark no doubt prompted by his own inability to apprehend the culprits.[19] Again, the historian of the hand-loom weavers has claimed that the outbreak of loom wrecking in 1826 represented nothing less than a 'massive display of resentment on the part of *an entire community*'.[20]

Against this must be set the arguments of those who have suggested on the basis of statistical evidence that industrialisation benefited most people. This of course was a question about which contemporaries disagreed and on which historical debate has continued ever since, largely because of the problems involved in finding accurate data. For example, the compilation of a cost of living index depends on knowledge of, or guesses about, the items on which consumers spent their money. Yet defining a typical basket of goods to cover the whole period of the industrial revolution is a hazardous task. Consumption patterns vary according to family size, occupation or regional custom. Beer consumption, for example, was notoriously high among heavy industrial workers. 'In the North of England, Scotland and Wales,' wrote Eden in a comment on regional variations in diet, 'the poorest labourers, however, regale themselves with a variety of dishes unknown in the South'.[21] Thus in the 1840s an East Anglian labourer, Robert Crick, spent ten shillings of his weekly wage of 13s. 9d. on bread and potatoes for his family of five children. At roughly the same period, an urban labourer with a similar income but a slightly smaller family could afford to buy items like meat and porter, both absent from Crick's budget.[22] The difficulties are further compounded by the fact that most surviving price data relate to wholesale rather than retail levels. Even if retail price figures were more readily available, it would not necessarily make cost of living indices more realistic, since many members of the working class probably bought most goods from small local outlets on weekly credit.

An alternative approach has been to examine the course of wages, but there are again considerable difficulties in making satisfactory generalisations about the industrial revolution period. Over and above the significant differences in earning power between that most basic of working-class divisions, skilled and unskilled, there were enormous variations according to trade. A London tailor in 1815 could earn as much as 36s. a week. A Manchester cotton spinner got 27s. a week in 1833, whereas a contemporary hand-loom weaver was down to 5s. 6d.[23] Even within the same trade rates could vary. Village framework knitters were much less well paid than their urban counterparts, while there were marked regional variations in many trades. In printing, for instance, a compositor earned 12s. to 19s. a week in Scotland, between 18s. and 22s. in the north of England, and as much as 25s. in London.[24] Nor can weekly wage rates make any allowance for payments and deductions of a sort that continued well into the industrial revolution. Some workers had to deduct from their wages certain expenses incurred in the course of their work. Yorkshire miners, to give one example, had to provide their own candles; and it is possible that they also had to pay a small sum to their 'hurriers', the individuals who hauled the filled corves to the pit shaft bottom. Conversely, but equally different to allow for, many workers were paid partly in kind and partly in money. In addition to their money wage, miners in Earl Fitzwilliam's Yorkshire pits all received free domestic coal; there must have been many similar arrangements in other industries. At the margin, such gifts could be quite significant. South Wales rural labourers in the early nineteenth century earned about nine shillings a week; but it has been estimated that allowances in the form of potato land, fuel and assistance with rent added the equivalent of two shillings (twenty-two per cent) a week.[25] In the midland nailmaking industry, the operation of the piece system and the use of several different kinds of iron, all of which were paid for at different rates, meant that it was impossible to speak of an average wage for the trade.[26]

The same writer goes on to assert that 'what mattered for Black Country life, however, was not the individual's earnings but the income of the family and this was far more difficult still to generalise upon.' In other words, even if we had satisfactory wage data, this would not help very much in the compilation of some index of living standards; because the income of most workers, certainly those with no particular skill, was supplemented by wives and children. This element is largely incalculable but must have been significant, because the industrial revolution did not – certainly in its early stages – change either the view that children were a legitimate source of income or the traditional practice of putting them out to work as soon as they could earn a few pence.[27] Thus when proposals were mooted to restrict child labour in the mines, a Sheffield paper was able to ask with some point:

> What would be the condition of a miner's family if deprived by the legislature of the weekly wages produced by the industry of the boys in addition to those earned by the females? The whole collier's family under thirteen will, if turned out of the pits, be entirely dependent on the scanty earnings of the parent for food, clothing and instruction.[28]

Finally, any computation of weekly wage rates cannot

allow for periods when the earner was unemployed or working irregularly. It has been argued that opportunities for female work at home declined in the eighteenth century, while industrial change deprived them of other work in some of the older industries. Before women were reabsorbed into the economy, therefore, it seems certain that this situation would have had an adverse effect on family income. Eden certainly took this view, writing in 1796 that 'the circumstance most to be regretted in the state of the labouring classes is the want of constant and suitable employment for women and children.'[29] Given the generally sparse attention paid to safety and health matters, it seems likely, too, that early industrialisation must have generated a fair degree of involuntary unemployment through a high accident rate.

Faced with these difficulties in calculating accurate retail prices and meaningful average weekly income rates in order to construct a satisfactory cost of living index, some writers have turned instead to consumption figures, on the grounds that changes in per capita consumption must reflect changes in living standards. The best generally available statistics are those contained in the customs and excise returns, which included four items of importance in working-class diets — beer, tea, coffee and sugar. Interpretation is, however, hazardous. The beer return ends in 1830, while trends in tea and coffee consumption frequently reflect not rising living standards, but rather the fact that they are substitutes for each other. Sugar consumption appears to have remained pretty well constant at around eighteen pounds a head until the 1840s, and it certainly did not 'break out of the circle of semi-luxuries'.[30] Supplies of bread, the main item of diet, were always dependent upon harvest yields, but generally seem to have been adequate once the French wars were over. Potato consumption increased, but it is difficult to know what to make of this, as in the south potatoes were widely regarded as inferior and an indicator of falling standards, whereas in the north they were apparently welcomed as providing a dietary variant. As far as meat is concerned, the main evidence relates to returns of sheep and cattle taken to Smithfield market. It suggests that the annual slaughtering of these animals did not keep pace with rising population, a conclusion verified by analysis of the excise duty paid on hides and skins. On the other hand, Smithfield was only one meat market, and it served the metropolitan area which may not have been very representative. The figures do not include pig meat either, which made up an important part of working-class diet. Nor does a simple head count of dead sheep and cattle take into account the possibility that breeding experiments had produced animals that were heavier and more meaty.

All in all then, the patchiness of the evidence and the difficulties inherent in its interpretation render statistical generalisation about the industrial revolution of dubious value and would not appear to offer a very sound basis on which to challenge Thompson's argument of immiseration. Yet despite all the problems, one fact stands out above all others. During the period of the industrial revolution, national income rose considerably. The immiserationists thus have to explain what happened to this extra wealth if it did not go to the working class in the form of higher incomes. One possibility is that output did not keep up with rapid population expansion, producing diminishing returns and a decline in wage rates towards subsistence level. Historically, however, this has no factual basis. Every production series which has survived indicates a growth rate faster than that of population. Food prices did not soar continuously during the industrial revolution, and most contemporary economists had concluded by the 1830s that wages were not being driven down to subsistence level. Alternatively, it might be that rising national income was swallowed up by rising investment at the expense of individual incomes. Again, however, this is not very plausible. With the exception of the building of the canals, the industrial revolution did not require much heavy capital investment. One important general study of this subject concludes that industrialisation took place 'without the massive investment which has been postulated', and it was not until the railway mania of the 1840s that investment absorbed anything like ten per cent of the national income.[31] Perhaps rising national income was accompanied by some redistribution which benefited the wealthy at the expense of the working class? Perhaps, as some have argued, income was shifted into the hands of landowners at the expense of wage-earners and capitalists alike? This may well have happened during the Napoleonic wars when agricultural prices and rents both rose dramatically, but it is difficult to see how any such redistribution could have been maintained in the less prosperous climate for agriculture after the war. Pessimists have more usually suggested that the shift of income was in favour of capitalists either through the medium of taxation or, more popularly, through sheer exploitation. It is quite feasible that debt retirement and interest payments on the enormous expenses involved in the wars against France had an appreciable effect on the distribution of income in Britain; so, too, did taxation. The wealthiest groups in society (defined as those with an income of over £130 a year in 1801 and over £200 a year in 1848) increased their share of the national income from twenty-five per cent in 1801 to thirty-five per cent in 1848.[32] Transfers of income from taxation to holders of the national debt absorbed about £30,000,000 a year long after 1815.[33] Always assuming that the figures on which such calculations are based are reliable, here is clearly one very plausible means by which to reconcile rising national income with little or no improvement in working-class living standards. It is certainly much more likely than explanations couched in terms of exploitation by capitalists, which assume that employers had the power to compel labour to work and also to collude about wage rates, in turn suggesting a very immobile labour force and a very tightly-knit employing community. Yet if wage rates were similar in particular areas, this was a reflection of the prevailing market forces, not employer collusion. On the contrary, employers frequently tried to poach skilled workers form each other. Thus Watt wrote to Boulton in 1786 that 'we must see if we can get some hands from another works which we are constantly in quest of but there is so much machinery going forward all over the nation that it is difficult to get any that are worth hiring.'[34] Of course employers did combine to break strikes or unions, but this was not indicative of any general collusion on the part of a cohesive employing class. McCord's study of the north-east lead him to suggest that individual rather than class interest was the main motive of employers' actions.[35] The favourite

exploitation model employed by the immiserationists, however, is that in which politically determined enclosures
drove workers from the land to become an industrial proletariat. Yet it is quite evident that the motive for enclosure
was purely and simply to increase the value and hence the
rental of agricultural land. Further, the immiserationists' view
of enclosure posits a degree of co-operation between rural
and urban employers for which there is absolutely no empirical evidence. In any case, it does not necessarily follow,
though pessimists assume it does, that enclosure drove people
from the land. Chambers' study of Nottinghamshire enclosures suggests that — far from destroying jobs — enclosure with
its higher demand for maintenance on hedges and ditches
created more work.[36] It seems likely, therefore, that the
industrial labour force came mainly from the continued
growth of population, not the compulsory displacement of
rural workers.

All in all then, a statistical approach to the question of
immiseration encounters many problems. The weight of
evidence would support the view that at least average living
standards did not deteriorate. For some workers the industrial revolution brought considerable prosperity. Those whose
products were in demand and whose skills had not been
replaced by technology did well; so, too, did those workers
whose jobs were at the heart of the industrialisation process
— puddlers, fine spinners, iron shipbuilders, various types of
engineer, building and factory operatives, and, later, railway
engine drivers. Women who moved into domestic service and
men who joined the growing number of white-collar workers
must also have experienced some improvement. Yet even for
such workers, it is argued, there was a price to be paid,
though not one which could be measured in statistical terms.
In J. L. Hammond's words, this price included 'the want of
beauty, the same want of pageants or festivals . . . the ugliness
of the new life, with its growing slums, its lack of beautiful
buildings, its destruction of nature'.[37] In similar vein more
recent writers have suggested that the costs included a
vulgarisation of tastes, enviromental deterioration, and
'cashbox aesthetics'.[38]

Much early industrialisation took place in rural areas, and

it was frequently necessary for manufacturers to provide housing and other social amenities for their new workforces. Conditions in such industrial villages were often quite good, but as industrialisation progressed it became increasingly synonymous with urbanisation. By 1801 Lancashire, the county at the heart of the industrial revolution, was the most densely populated region in England outside London, with about forty per cent of its inhabitants living in towns of more than ten thousand people. In the West Riding of Yorkshire, population density had risen to 212 per square mile by the end of the eighteenth century.[39] The population of Bradford increased by over fifty per cent in every decade between 1811 and 1851.[40] Such meteoric expansion, exacerbated by heavy influxes of Irish migrants, proved far too much for existing local government agencies to cope with. It was many years before urban evils such as overcrowding, jerry-building, street pollution, impure water supply and poor sanitation could be effectively tackled. In the meantime, conditions for the mass of urban dwellers remained appalling. In Liverpool, Frederick Engels reckoned that 'a full fifth of the population, more than 45,000 human beings, live in narrow, dark, damp, badly-ventilated cellar dwellings, of which there are 7862 in the city.'[41] Birmingham was no better. 'There are many bad districts, filthy and neglected, full of stagnant pools and heaps of refuse.'[42] The local Poor Law medical officer described Halifax in 1842 thus:

> Deplorable state of dwellings in certain quarters of the town. Irish lodging houses for vagrants and trampers of the lowest description and most abandoned habits. Want of attention in clearing away offensive matters in sewers, cesspools, privies, pigsties etc. surrounding the houses ... Compulsory draining and purifying of cottages much wanted.[43]

Of course none of this was qualititatively much worse than what prevailed in towns before the industrial revolution. Open sewers were not an invention of the nineteenth century, and as early as the sixteenth century the authorities in Northampton instructed local leather workers not to 'cast any dead horse, mare, or gelding, or any dog, hog, or other

such carrion, on the street, ways and ditches, or any ground
of the town.'[44] Further, we should be careful of comparing
nineteenth-century housing with some romanticised picture
of pre-industrial rural cottages. Indeed, Cobbett reckoned
that people went to the towns largely to find shelter 'when
the hovels in which they dwelt fall down about them'.[45] In
an age before transport had been revolutionised, houses tended to be built of local materials and their quality thus very
variable. For most people, houses seem to have been poor.
Walter Davies described cottages in South Wales at the beginning of the nineteenth century as 'huts of the most humble
plans and materials'. Even these, however, were preferable
to those in the north of the principality, which, he claimed,
'were habitations of wretchedness'.[46] At about the same
time, the steward to the Marquis of Bath claimed that labourers were obliged

> to live, or rather to exist, in a wretched, damp, gloomy
> room, of ten or twelve feet square, and that room without
> a floor; but common decency must revolt at considering
> that over this wretched apartment there is only *one*
> chamber, to hold all the miserable beds of the miserable
> family.[47]

Even so, this cannot offset the fact that many more people
were now exposed to the evils of urban living, because by
1851 slightly more than half the population dwelt in towns.
Fevers of various types prospered in the filth, particularly in
poorer districts, and death rates actually rose in the larger
cities during the 1830s. If the Black Death had finally
disappeared, the new scourge of cholera reached England
from India late in 1831. The first reported case was in
Sunderland, whence it spread rapidly throughout the north
east and reached London in February 1832. Eventually this
first major outbreak carried off about 31,000 of the 71,000
who caught it.[48] Somewhat paradoxically perhaps, some of
the larger cities escaped quite lightly because they had a
variety of water supplies. The people most at risk from this
water-borne killer were those dependent upon a single water
source. There were three later epidemics, in 1848-9, 1853-4,
and 1866. Of these the first was by far the most serious,

claiming at least 61,000 victims, though figures are not terribly reliable.[49]

By the same token, many more people than before were exposed to the hazards of adulterated food, since adulteration was essentially an urban phenomenon. Frederick Accum's scholarly account, published in 1820, revealed widespread abuse. In 1819 alone there were nearly one hundred convictions of brewers and brewers' druggists for using a variety of substitutes for beer and hops. Alum was freely used in order to whiten bread, while sulphuric acid was added to newly brewed beer to simulate the flavour of the hard, older beer which was more popular. Given that more than £67,000,000 were spent on drink in 1830 and that there were about 40,000 beerhouses in the 1830s, it is evident that a good deal of adulterated beer went down very many undiscerning throats; and this ignores the produce of the many illicit stills which were operated, often by Irish immigrants.[50] Those who eschewed alcohol in favour of milder stimulants were quite likely to be drinking preparations of tree, rather than tea, leaves. One official report estimated that some 4,000,000 pounds weight of tea made from ash, thorn, sloe, and elder were sold annually in Britain, compared with 6,000,000 pounds of genuine tea imported by the East India Company.[51]

Finally, in this consideration of the impact of industrialisation on the conditions of life, mention can be made of the effect on the family. Marx had no doubt that the quality of family life had been destroyed. The bourgeoisie, he claimed, 'has reduced the family relation to a mere money relation'.[52] He went on to argue that because of industrialisation 'all family ties among the proletarians are torn asunder, and their children transformed into simple articles of commerce and instruments of labour.'[53] Leaving aside the matter of what sort of family life could be enjoyed in a pre-industrial society where infant mortality was endemic, 'studied neglect' during nursing a common form of birth control, life expectancy low, and earnings generally irregular, Marx's claims can legitimately be questioned.[54] Although it is possible that greater economic opportunity in the eighteenth century encouraged young people to marry earlier and become economically independent of their parents, this did not necessarily disrupt family relationships. Each individual continued to meet what have been called critical life situations — unemployment, sickness, death, housing problems, old age. Neither neighbours nor organised relief agencies were adequate to cope fully with such problems, and it was more often to kith and kin that the individual looked. Despite increased mobility, the early industrial worker remained

> a member of a meaningful social network of kin and/or migrants from his own native village or town. While the services which this network could perform for him were severely limited by the poverty of its members, it was nevertheless his first recourse in the many crises which life inevitably posed for him . . . the impact of industriali-sation was not straightforwardly disruptive; the family continued to perform important economic functions . . .[55]

Studies of early-nineteenth-century family life have also turned up little evidence to support generalisations some-times made about the brutalising and neglect of children by drunken fathers or working mothers.

The fate of children has been central to a second conten-tious area in the quality of life debate — the conditions of factory work. Much stress has been placed on the working environment of parish apprentices who provided an important source of labour in the early years of the industrial revolution. As an illegitimate child, Robert Blincoe found himself apprenticed at textile mills in the east midlands. At Litton Mill he worked sixteen hours a day, was rarely washed, and had to scour local refuse tips for food. It appears, too, that he was subjected to a good deal of gratuitous cruelty. Despite the efforts that have been made to discredit his reliability, there is no good reason to dismiss his recollections as falla-cious.[56] What needs to be remembered, however, is that the conditions he describes were generally typical only of smaller, rural mills in the early days of the industrial revolution. Not all employers were uncaring, and many of their apprentices were in any case drawn from sectors of society where hunger, disease and poverty were already constant companions. More generally, it is by no means certain that the conditions to which factory children were exposed were any worse than those which had existed and which continued to exist in domestic industry. Thus the 1833 inquiry into the conditions of factory children claimed that of all the employments to which they were subjected 'those carried on in the factories are amongst the least unwholesome'.[57] Of course, it is possible to argue that all such inquiries were in the nature of white-washing exercises conducted in the interests of the employers, but even this cannot get round the truth of the claim that domestic working conditions were often themselves very unpleasant. One Yorkshire weaver was found in 1842 to have a room twelve feet square into which were packed mis-cellaneous items of lumber, three bedsteads, three chests, three looms, and no less than five children to work the looms. In those domestic industries such as nail and chain making where demand was intensified by the industrial revolution, working conditions certainly deteriorated and were not sub-jected to even the rudimentary official scrutiny provided by the early factory acts. Of nailers' workshops in the 1840s it was written that

> The effluvia of these little work-dens, from the filthiness of the ground, from the half-ragged half-washed persons at work, and from the hot smoke, ashes, water, and clouds of dust (besides the frequent smell of tobacco) are really dreadful.[58]

A similar, if fictional, description of a tailor's sweat shop is provided by Charles Kingsley in *Alton Locke*:

> A low lean-to room, stifling me with the combined odours of human breath and perspiration, stale beer, the sweet sickly smell of gin, and the sour and hardly less disgusting one of new cloth. On the floor, thick with dust and dirt, scraps of stuff and ends of thread, sat some dozen haggard, untidy, shoeless men ... The windows were tight closed to keep out the cold winter air; and the condensed breath ran in streams down the panes ... [59]

If factory working conditions were probably no worse than those of such domestic industries, the proponents of im-miseration assert that the transition to factory production or to more intensive techniques still involved a major, qualitative deterioration, in that men lost the freedom to be their own masters and determine their own work patterns. 'What was at issue was the "freedom" of the capitalist to destroy the customs of the trade, whether by new machinery, by the factory-system, or by unrestricted competition, beating-down wages, undercutting his rivals and undermining standards of craftsmanship.'[60] Pre-industrial work patterns, essentially dictated by the rhythm of nature, were increasingly shaped by the tyranny of the clock as entrepreneurs sought to instil into dilatory employees the notion that time was money. This effort to maximise the profitability of machines and other forms of capital investment necessitated a change in the habits of the average Englishman who, according to Defoe, would 'work until he has got his pockets full of money, and then go and be idle or perhaps drunk till 'tis all gone and perhaps himself in debt . . . he'll drink so long as it lasts, and then go to work for more.'[61] Breaking down this high leisure preference was by no means easy. Early managerial records are full of complaints about the difficulties of getting men to work regularly and consistently. 'Our men have been at play 4 days this week, it being Burslem Wakes,' complained Josiah Wedgwood in 1776. 'I have rough'd and smoothed them over . . . but I know it is all in vain.'[62] Some sixty years later a land steward was making a similar complaint that high wages were bound to produce 'drunkenness, idleness and loss of time'.[63] Employers might have been in a stronger position to impose restrictions on their workers had it not been for the surprisingly high degree of labour mobility and the scarcity, at least in the initial stages of industrialisation, of certain skills. Because of such difficulties, early factory masters frequently resorted to parish apprentices for their labour, and even when the scarcity was eased by growing population it was still necessary to exert heavy discipline. Wedgwood fined his workers as much as 2s. 6d. for throwing things or leaving fires burning overnight, while 5s. was the penalty exacted in one Stockport mill for swearing or drunkenness. Threats of dismissal were frequently used, though these were only effective against relatively unskilled men or in times of depression. Nor was this effort to inculcate new work habits confined to the factory; it spread to everyday life. Old leisure habits which undermined discipline or were incompatible with the values of the emerging industrial society were suppressed, blood sports (except those for the wealthy) coming under especial pressure.

At the same time, it is argued, the paternalism which had protected many workers against the vicissitudes of the free market was being rapidly abandoned both by individuals and by government. Pre-industrial paternalism, which characterised social relationships, was a two-way affair and one in which conflict and friction were always present, whether in strikes or bread riot.[64] Yet as labour became more mobile, old client relationships continued to decline as they had already done among clothing workers, urban artisans, colliers and some classes of general workers. As Archdeacon Wilberforce asked in 1840, 'Where . . . are the old bonds of mutual affection and respect — of natural care on the one side and generous trust upon the other, by which the peasantry and gentry were united?'[65] State paternalism also declined. As we have seen, state regulation of wages was no longer enforced; with the result that some groups of workers resorted to their own efforts, either by simple riot or through trade-union and friendly society activity. Yet it appeared that the state was intent on making this more difficult with the passage of the Combination Laws and other measures which limited working-class self-expression. This, it has been suggested, was tantamount to a demand by government 'to have their cake and eat it, to exact paternal discipline while denying paternal protection'.[66] This process, aptly termed by Carlyle the 'abdication of the governors', reached its climax in the attempt to abolish the poor law system.

The original act of 1601 had made it obligatory for all parishes to provide for the poor by levying a rate on all property occupiers in their bounds. By the late-eighteenth century, however, the view was increasingly expressed that the able-bodied poor (i.e. the unemployed) should be found work and subsidised from the poor rate if their earnings were too low, an idea embodied in Gilbert's act of 1782. Under the impact of industrialisation, a series of bad harvests in the 1790s, and the economic dislocation resulting from the war against France, many rural labourers found themselves in severe distress. Several expedients were adopted, the best known being named after the parish of Speenhamland in Berkshire, whereby scaled relief was given according to the size of the applicant's family, his income, and the price of bread. The result of these expedients was a sharp rise in the cost of poor relief, a rise which was acceptable to ratepayers as long as the wartime boom in agriculture continued. Once the war ended and farming began to contract, many agriculturalists found themselves overstretched financially. Pressure thus built up for reductions in poor law expenditure, which had reached over £8,000,000 by 1818. In 1817, the abolitionist case — originally associated with the name of Malthus — was accepted by a parliamentary select committee. Alarmed by the hostile reaction this decision provoked, the government established a fresh select committee which, while accepting the general condemnation of the current system, argued that in essence it should be maintained, as in fact it was with the passage of the Poor Law Amendment Act of 1834.

This, it is argued, is the economic background out of which the working class emerged in the early nineteenth century. Yet not all historians have been convinced. Some have suggested that the labouring population did not begin to 'show the characteristics which we associate with the designation of the concept of class' until around 1850.[67] Others have termed it a mistake to think of a homogeneous working class at any time before the late nineteenth century, while some have gone still further, arguing that it is misleading to talk even of 'the worker, so great is the impression of diversity'.[68]

The arguments used by Thompson's critics fall into two broad categories: firstly, that the case for the creation of the working class in the early part of the century is based on an oversimplification of very complex historical processes; secondly, that there is no tangible manifestation of the existence of a united working class. Taking the first, it is quite clear that in areas of rapid economic development social structures and relationships did change. A village like Bradford — which in the 1790s was described as 'only a small rural town surrounded by green fields and quiet country lanes ... a really pleasant and picturesque spot' — was transformed by 1845 into 'a most filthy town . . . with streets that would disgrace a Hottentot settlement'.[69] Residential segregation on class lines soon emerged in such towns, and old forms of government and social relationships collapsed. In Oldham, it has been argued, the new working class established control over most of the institutions of local government.[70] In older towns such as Bristol and Exeter, as yet less affected by industrialisation, large numbers of the working population remained 'in kindly and immediate dependence on the wealthy residents'.[71] Similar relationships also prevailed in towns like Birmingham and Nottingham where small-scale industries still tended to dominate. In some rural areas paternalism may have started to disappear, but it survived for much longer in Wales and the north of England where farms generally remained small and labour continued to live in. It is evident, too, that many of the rural gentry did try, in their capacity as magistrates, to preserve old paternal values.[72]

It is misleading to see state paternalism as being deliberately abandoned in the early nineteenth century. Economic hardship and change led many workers to appeal to Parliament for protection for either wages or apprenticeship qualifications; but Parliament was unwilling to grant such protection, since in practice much of it had long since fallen into disuse. This was certainly true of the apprenticeship clauses of the Statute of Artificers, which had depended for their enforcement in the first instance on the decaying guilds. In any case, the courts had ruled in the early seventeenth century that the clauses only applied to those occupations named in the statute, and an increasing range of jobs thus fell beyond its scope. In the same way, while it is true that magistrates were still meeting in the eighteenth century to fix wages, the existing assessments were usually reissued without change, and where revisions did occur the criterion was normally the state of the labour market, rather than the cost of living as the original statute had required. Thus government was not deliberately abandoning its paternalistic role. In some respects it had already fallen into abeyance. Nor was it long before new forms of protection, more appropriate to an industrialising society, began to appear in the form of the early factory legislation.

The changes in leisure habits also need to be put into a broader perspective than that allowed by the immiserationists. One possibility is that the high leisure preference of pre-industrial Englishmen was a myth. Irregular working habits might have been caused, it is argued, 'partly by a high prevalence of debilitating disease and by low and unpredictable supplies of food'.[73] In other words, men may have worked inconsistently because they lacked the physical energy to do otherwise. This is an interesting hypothesis, but one that requires more empirical support — particularly as it is contradicted by the evidence contained in surviving factory records. More serious, perhaps, is the objection that irregular work patterns were by no means universal in pre-industrial England. Well before the onset of industrialisation many trades already had a 'conception of a certain number of hours which made up a normal full working day'.[74] In most handicraft occupations, a ten-hour day was the norm by the middle of the eighteenth century, and weavers considered ten-and-a-half hours a hard day. What happened as the industrial revolution progressed was, at most, an increase in the numbers subjected to the growing regularity and intensity of work associated with industrialisation. There was also an increase in the number of those employed in sweated trades or on a putting-out basis. There is little evidence, however, (except in agriculture and the cotton industry) that working hours actually increased very much.

Nor was the demise of old leisure habits part of some deliberate capitalist plot against the working class. On the contrary, insofar as traditional pastimes did disappear this was as much the result of unpremeditated economic change, and particularly of urbanisation, as of legislation. In the countryside itself, enclosure reduced the amount of space available for events such as intervillage football in which the goals were sometimes as much as three miles apart. Many customs such as harvest feasts and Plough Monday were rooted in rural life and could not survive the transition to an urban situation — though some, like Saint Monday, did persist albeit in an attenuated form. More generally, however, far from diminishing leisure opportunities for the poor, industrialisation actually seems to have increased them.[75]

Some of the older customs survived far longer than is often imagined. In particular blood sports, boxing and wrestling — which were publicly disdained — all survived in back rooms, canal banks, and other remote places, as any reader of Mayhew will know. Popular drama and spectacle experienced a major boom in the early part of the nineteenth century; the end of the previous century saw the birth of both pantomime and circus. The net result was the emergence of a popular culture that can legitimately be described as new, even though some of its elements were old, or new versions of traditional habits. While it is true that evangelicals, police, magistrates and employers could all be found opposing it, they did not represent any united establishment alliance against working-class culture. For one thing, this new culture was not a working-class one in the sense that it held out long-term goals or visions of social improvement for the people. Rather it was immediate in its aspirations and hedonistic in its spirit. Secondly, there also existed a politically and socially very mixed group who championed this culture, asserting the rights of the poor and wishing to maintain aristocratic patronage of popular sports and pastimes. Thirdly, and probably most important, some of the most vociferous critics of popular culture were themselves working class. From widely differing perspectives, both secular radicals and Methodists regarded it as a distraction from other, more important considerations.

Great care must be taken lest the degree of freedom and independence enjoyed by pre-industrial labour is unduly exaggerated. The independent craft shop, the oldest of the pre-factory forms of production, had begun to disappear as early as the thirteenth century. As markets grew, so artisans became increasingly dependent upon middlemen both for raw materials and marketing. In fact, if not in principle, many apparently free artisans were already wage-labourers before the onset of industrialisation, selling their labour rather than their commodities. In this sense the coming of the factory entailed little loss of independence, and in any case the number actually involved in any such transition must have been relatively small. For one thing, the factory labour force was quite small in the early part of the century; for another, much of it was provided by the growing population. It was not, as is often asserted, driven from the land by expropriating landlords. Indeed, much early industry was based in the countryside, and population often flowed out of the towns to the rural areas. A similar flow often accompanied economic slumps as displaced persons returned to their original villages.

The loss of freedom argument perhaps best fits the domestic textile worker, yet even his independence was very limited. It is true that in parts of Yorkshire woollen weavers seem to have purchased their own raw material, but this was certainly not the case generally, as the majority depended on entrepreneurs for materials. The majority were free only in the sense that they owned their own looms (midland frameworkknitters generally rented theirs) and were able to determine the pattern of their own daily work routines. Since domestic weaving was mainly a rural occupation, the weaver's independence was further restricted in that there were often very few alternative employers available; and some weavers were bound to one entrepreneur by virtue of borrowing money or occupying a tied cottage. The much vaunted freedom of the weaver was limited still more by the fact that no restriction was placed on entry, and the skill involved was so minimal that plain weaving could be learned in three weeks.

The second broad objection to Thompson's thesis is that, although there was a vast social gulf between workers and the rest of society, the working population itself was internally divided between competing and often overlapping interest groups. Much of the trade-union evidence reflects occupational or sectional consciousness rather than any wider class sympathies, and there are indications that the early nineteenth century saw a consolidation of such collective behaviour within occupational groupings.[76] While this may have prompted some desire for contact with others in similar industrial circumstances, there still yawned an enormous gap between skilled and unskilled, one of the main causes of the collapse of the GNCTU. Most trade unions, as we have seen, catered exclusively for skilled men. Only the weavers tried to organise the unskilled, and in Oldham a recent study has shown that there was a high degree of residential intermingling and intermarriage between skilled and unskilled in the town.[77] Whether this was typical of other textile towns awaits further investigation. The skilled-unskilled dichotomy was most apparent in wage differentials, regularity and security of employment and status. The typical factory operative and most labourers were also marked out from the skilled elite in that for many of them the family remained as the basic earning unit. Politically, too, there were differences, noted by Henry Mayhew in his lengthy survey of London life. 'In passing from the skilled operative of the west-end to the unskilled workmen of the eastern quarter . . . the moral and intellectual change is so great, that it seems as if we were in a new land, and among another race.' The artisans, he reckoned, were intelligent and 'red-hot politicians . . . the unskilled labourers are a different class of people. As yet they are as unpolitical as footmen.'[78] This is confirmed by William Lovett's claim that the London Working Men's Association had a membership restricted to the 'intelligent and influential portion of the working classes'.[79] The existence of the division was also noted by a representative of the NAPL making a speech at Nottingham in 1830. If the audience joined the association, he claimed, it would give 'the death blow to all hurtful dissensions in their respective trades . . . *even* their respective labourers need not remain unprotected.'[80] Another significant division lay between urban and rural workers. Sometimes this even transcended the unity conferred by a common trade. Rural ribbon weavers, for instance, had little in common with their urban counterparts. Similarly, rural framework-knitters earned less than their brethren in the towns; since the industry was differently organised, being dominated by bagmen rather than by hosiers. Although farm workers were themselves differentiated by skill — those with specific trades such as hedging or thatching often working as independent craftsmen — the general level of rural wages (payments in kind notwithstanding) was much lower than that of the towns. On the whole, rural workers lived in smaller, more isolated communities and remained in deferential relationships with their employers and in more direct contact with them. In the eyes of some contemporaries this was a situation not without advantage. William Howitt claimed that

the state of morals and manners amongst the working
population of our great towns is terrible ... where the
rural population in its simplicity, comes into contact
with this spirit, it receives the contagion in its most
exaggerated form ... There spreads all the vice and
baseness of the lowest grade of the town, made hideous
by still greater vulgarity and ignorance, and unawed by
the higher authorities, unchecked by the better influences
which there prevail, in the example and exertions of a
higher caste of society.[81]

Regional variations were imposed over these differences to
make yet another internal division. It would appear that
regional wage variations grew more, rather than less, marked
during the course of industrialisation; with the result that by
1850 there were at least twelve distinct wage areas in Britain.[82]
Thus early-nineteenth-century compositors, to give but one
example, earned 12s. to 19s. a week in Scotland, 18s. to 22s.
in the north of England, 18s. to 24s. in the south-east, and
as much as 25s. in London.[83] Nor were these difference only
statistical. Beneath them there often lurked fierce regional
pride, well illustrated in popular song. William Oliver's *The
Newcastle Millers* (1824) taunted Londoners.

The fancy lads that thou can boast wad tyek an 'oor ti
tell
Let Cockneys tawk o' Moulsey Hurst, we'll crack iv
Barlow Fell.
Jim B------n hez up te Lunnin gyen, ti show them hoo to
hit an' parry;
But still we've bits iv blud at hyem, that for a croon wad
bax Aud Harry.[84]

Attachments of this sort operated at many different levels.
The *Spectator* claimed in 1712 that 'at the Seasons of Football and Cockfighting' many parishes would resume 'their
national Hatred to each other'.[85] At a different level most
Englishmen would unite in opposition to foreigners, particularly the Irish, who constituted another divisive element
within the working population. It is reckoned that there
were some 400,000 of them living in Britain by 1841, but in

some large northern cities they accounted for as much as a fifth or even a third of the population. Like all immigrants they tended to enter at the bottom of the social scale, becoming casual labourers or going into depressed trades like hand weaving. To that extent they were identified with English workers in similar occupations. Yet their segregation remained because of the Englishman's xenophobia, his suspicion of popery, and dislike of a group who were frequently utilised as blacklegs. In the agricultural depression following the end of the French wars, unemployed rural labourers in the midlands ganged up on Irish workers who had helped bring in the harvest. When the railways were being constructed, there was constant conflict between different national groups, especially in 1845 and 1846. Notices were put up near Dunfermline, for example, warning that 'all the Irish men on the line of railway in Fife Share must be off the grownd and owt of countey on Monday . . . or els we must by the strenth of our armes and a good pick shaft put them off.'[86] In this particular case the sheriff was able to warn off two hundred Scots intent on driving out the Irish, but elsewhere they were subject to much physical violence. The French observer, Gustave d'Eichthal, referring to the Irish in Bolton, commented that they had been treated very badly and while prejudice had somewhat lessened 'they are still spoken of with great contempt even by working men.'[87]

Given that there were these fundamental divisions within the working population, it is hardly surprising that many historians have opted instead for the term 'working classes', implicitly and often explicitly rejecting Thompson's thesis of a unified working class in existence by 1832. Thus 'it is extremely difficult . . . to see in what ways this alleged class consciousness resulted in working class solidarity or united action . . . especially if one looks at the multitude of small sectional trade societies in London and provincial towns.'[88] Again, it has been suggested that, while there were some indicators of class feeling among London workers at the time of the Reform Bill, these 'cannot be considered to imply any unified attitude'.[89] Criticisms like this are based on the assumption that it is legitimate to speak of a class only when a group is united in every conceivable way: socially, politically, economically, geographically, and also in terms of its response to given historical situations. Such an absolutist definition renders the very concept of class virtually meaningless, for it is unrealistic to equate it with a monolithic block of identical individuals. People have many different identities, for example as members of a particular sex, trade, workforce, race, religion, city or family. At any given time an individual may be acting primarily in his capacity as a man, a carpenter, an employee, an Englishman, a Protestant, a Londoner or a father; but none of these necessarily takes away from his general position as a member of the working class. What the question ultimately boils down to is whether working men in the first part of the nineteenth century were consciously acting as members of a class or in some other role. At one extreme, Professor McCord argues on the basis of his study of the north-east that 'any very comprehensive and continuous cooperation on the basis of a major social class has been abnormal and unusual rather than a typical situation.'[90] The whole history of the region, he concludes, shows that individual interest, among employers as well as workers, was much more powerful than any class loyalty. At the other end of the spectrum, John Foster has charted the development of working-class consciousness and activity in Oldham in the period up to 1850.[91] His interpretation has been challenged on the ground that what he sees as class activity was nothing more than trade-union interest.[92] Certainly it is difficult to see how, if class consciousness was as highly developed as he maintains, it degenerated so easily into the ten-hour movement, so obviously a trade-union concern.

It must remain a moot point as to how widely shared were the socialist analyses and class terminology which some working-class leaders and radicals were using, but it seems certain that class consciousness in Marx's sense (i.e. a self-perception by workers of their role as member of a universally redemptive class) hardly existed at all. It is also highly questionable as to how many people were directly involved in the revolutionary plotting which in Thompson's view is the ultimate proof of the working-class presence. Luddites, trade unionists, farm labourers, and corresponding societies are brilliantly woven together to produce a thread of revolutionary activity which, he maintains, was a constant theme of working-class activity before 1820. There are, of course, forms of social relationship other than conflict – deference, indifference, accommodation, co-operation – but leaving aside the question of the inevitability of social conflict, what evidence is there to support the case for the existence of a genuine revolutionary underground?

First of all, it is clear that there were plenty of instances of insurrectionary aspiration. In the period 1800 to 1803 and again during the Luddite disturbances, magistrates in various parts of the country, but particularly in Lancashire and Yorkshire, submitted reports to the Home Office of nocturnal drilling by armed men. In some places caches of arms were uncovered. The incidence of such drilling appears to have increased with the demobilisation which followed the ending of the war. 'Our drill masters,' recalled Samuel Bamford, 'were generally old soldiers of the line, or of militia, or of local militia regiments; they put the lads through their facings in quick time, and soon taught them to march with a steadiness and regularity which would not have disgraced a regiment on parade.'[93] Unemployed ex-soldiers are known to have participated in the numerous risings which occurred in this period and which are seen by Thompson as the visible tip of the revolutionary iceberg. In 1803 Colonel Edmund Despard and six others were executed for high treason, accused of planning to form a revolutionary army with which to launch a *coup d'état*. Despite his previous involvement in revolutionary scheming, Despard's connections with the enterprise appear to have been dubious. Recent research has revealed that the plot was the work of the United Britons, who took advantage of popular discontent following the passage of the Cotton Arbitration Act and the Combination Laws to regroup after their earlier disappointment in the Irish rising of 1798.[94] Designed to co-ordinate risings in Ireland and London with a French invasion, the plan was on a much more ambitious scale than contemporary authority realised; but the arrest of Despard, premature though it may have been in some senses, was enough to bring it to nothing. Some years later in 1816, another group of revolutionaries, followers of Thomas Spence, also faced charges of high treason arising out of their involvement in the Spa Field riot. The Spencean revolutionary strategy was simple if naive. The plan was to call a public meeting, inflame it, and then attack key public buildings. This, it was believed, would attract the support of London's lower classes, the army would join in, and revolution would then spread to northern industrial districts. The Spenceans had tried this several times before it finally succeeded – after a fashion – in 1816. Henry Hunt, the famous radical orator, stirred up the crowd; and Dr James Watson led a group away to sack gunsmiths' shops and then attack the Tower. They were arrested, although this time the charges did not stick. Among those released was Arthur Thistlewood. Four years later, tired of the futility of the Spenceans' efforts, he died on the scaffold, accused of being a party to the Cato Street conspiracy which had aimed to assassinate the cabinet. More overt still was the earlier Pentridge rising of 1817, a pathetic attack on Nottingham which its leader, Jeremiah Brandreth, claimed was part of a nationally co-ordinated uprising. It dissolved at the first sign of opposition and Brandreth was hanged.

Were these incidents part of a continuous revolutionary strand, and were they connected with broadly-based protest movements such as Luddism? There can be no doubt that the authorities were very concerned about the dangers of social unrest and particularly, as was in fact the case, that plotters would obtain assistance from the French with whom Britain was at war for much of the period. The background of almost constant war also meant that the government's military capability was severely stretched. Although nearly a quarter of a million men were in the army by 1812, they were so widely dispersed that the Guards had been withdrawn from London to be replaced by volunteer forces. Furthermore, there is evidence that the government was fearful for the loyalty of the army. One or two quite high-ranking officers were in fact dismissed on the grounds that they were politically suspect; and it was in the desire to segregate the army from subversive civilian influences that Pitt announced his barrack-building programme. As Windham put it in 1796, quoting a French comedy, 'if I cannot make him dumb, I will make you deaf.'[95] The regular army was supported by a county militia whose reliability was also in question. Since they were raised by ballot and substitution was permitted, they were generally drawn from the lowest social orders, and were usually posted away from their own counties for fear that they would sympathise with local cvilians.

This government concern, springing from its military weakness, was reinforced by the flow of information which reach the Home Office from the localities. Responsibility for local law enforcement rested on about five thousand magistrates of variable quality and energy. Since many of them were reluctant to spend money on raising local police forces, they tended to make excessive calls on the army to maintain order. This certainly added to government fears, but the incidence of such calls cannot be used by the historian to prove the existence of a major threat to law and order. Furthermore the magistrates were thinnest on the ground in the rapidly expanding urban areas, where the threat of lawlessness was deemed greatest and old social ties were weakest. Both Manchester and Birmingham had populations approaching 100,000; and it was claimed in 1817 that a 150-square-mile district around the Potteries containing 50,000 inhabitants had no active magistrate at all. In their absence, the government had to rely on its own agents to gain information about what was going on in these areas. Because such spies were paid by results and often recruited from unsavoury social elements, they had every reason to exaggerate the importance and magnitude of the movements on which they reported. It seems likely that in some cases, especially Pentridge and Spa Field, government agents — respectively Oliver the Spy and John Castle — had persuaded the participants to go further than they had themselves intended. The Cato Street conspiracy was also penetrated and betrayed by government spies. Clearly not everything can be dismissed as the fabrication of such *agents provocateurs;* as we then arrive at the logically implausible situation where, in the absence of any real revolutionary threat, government employed agents to create one so that it could be crushed. The point is, however, that government did not use agents to create a threat. It used them in the absence of any other method of obtaining hard information about revolutionary plotting at a time when the country was at war.

If government fears of social upheaval were wrongly root-ed in exaggerated information from spies and magistrates and in misplaced concern about the reliability of the army, there seems no doubt that there were dedicated revolutionary plotters at work. The Spenceans were such a group and one, moreover, with a well-thought-out alternative social and economic system. The Despard conspiracy had wide inter-national ramifications, and Brandreth believed he was acting as part of a national movement. The same shadowy figures link the different movements together. Thistlewood, for example, survived the Spa Field trial to participate in the Cato Street conspiracy. There is evidence of connections between the Despard plotters and revolutionary groups in Yorkshire, though it should be pointed out that the evidence for this rests mainly on statements made at their trial by former conspirators who had turned King's evidence. They had made much less of such contacts in their original deposi-tions, and there lingers a suspicion that the government deliberately highlighted such evidence in order to justify its own repressive policy.

There is little to suggest that the plotters had much consis-tent popular backing, even though it sometimes suited government purposes, for instance at Spa Field, to suggest otherwise. The bulk of the population could not be described as either loyal or disloyal. It was fickle and could be either loyal or disloyal in quick succession, depending mainly on changes of economic circumstances. Certainly plotters could capitalise on discontent, but they did not necessarily make converts to the revolutionary ideal. There are no records, for example, of Luddites turning against overt political targets such as town halls or magistrates' homes. A study of rural and urban discontent in the west midlands con-cludes that 'between the two outbreaks of social disturbance in the region – in the agricultural and industrial areas – there appears to have been no continuity and no connection.'[96] Again it seems possible that many apparently revolutionary acts were born out of personal pique rather than any deep-seated revolutionary aspiration. This, of course, is by its very nature difficult to prove; but an examination of rural unrest in East Anglia suggests that perhaps as many as a half or a

third of all cases of rick burning and farm fires in the first
half of the century, including this 'revolutionary period',
were caused by individuals with personal grievances against
their employers.[97] Again it has to be borne in mind that
riotous and violent methods of expressing discontent were
nothing new but were part of popular culture, witness the
bread riot and the tradition of bargaining by riot. Luddism
and the rural revolt of 1830 could both be fitted into this
tradition quite easily. In this context, it is worth pointing out
that modern sociological studies suggest that revolution is
more likely to occur when the social élite is disaffected. If
'intense discontent is found among ordinary people but not
the élite, and if that discontent extends only to a few conditions of life, the potential for riots and demonstrations is
high but the potential for conspiracy or internal war is low.'[98]
By no stretch of the imagination could the plotters who were
at work be described as a social élite.

Finally, if we concede for the sake of argument that there
was a genuine revolutionary threat, its failure to materialise
has to be explained. Over and above the sheer amateurism of
the plotters — in Sheffield in 1800 a meeting of local
'revolutionaries' to discuss the manufacture of pikes was
attended by a local Volunteer officer who, although recognised and challenged, was allowed to go free — two reasons
suggest themselves. One is that repressive legislation, the
Combination Acts, the infamous Six Acts, and the suspension
of *habeas-corpus* were part of a deliberately engineered
counter-revolution which crushed the revolutionary movement's prospects of success. There is little question that the
legislation was repressive and was born of a genuine fear of
social unrest. Yet it might be argued that such repression
helped to create the very situation it was designed to elimin-
ate. The Combination Acts had the effect of driving the trade
unions background. When the Hampden Clubs' parliamentary
reform petition was rejected in 1817, the government clamped
down severely on the March of the Blanketeers and *habeas-
corpus* was suspended. At least one member of the Pentridge
rising, William Stevens, said that there had been no thought
of physical resistance until this right had been suspended.[99]
Henry Cockburn was another contemporary who suggested

that, while economic distress was important in fomenting popular protest, 'the feeling was exasperated by the new and severe laws made for preventing popular meetings and punishing popular excesses.'[100]

The other explanation for the revolutionaries' failure has a longer pedigree — the diversionary effects of Methodism. In a much quoted metaphor, E. P. Thompson has likened Methodism to a 'ritualised form of psychic masturbation. Energies and emotions which were dangerous to social order, or which were merely unproductive . . . were released in the harmless form of sporadic love-feasts, watch-nights, band meetings, or revivalist campaigns.'[101] It was a view which some contemporaries also shared. George Herod said of the Luddite period in Nottingham that 'at this juncture and crisis the P[rimitive] M[ethodist] missionaries brought a counteractive influence to bear upon the masses and in multitudes of instances destroyed the baneful vines of infidelity and insubordination.'[102] A more recent writer recalled that in the power-loom breaking of the 1820s her grandparents remained uninvolved, their Methodism causing them to be 'resigned to their lot and accepting it as designed by Providence'.[103] Yet authority viewed Methodism itself with considerable suspicion. After Wesley's death in 1791, some of his followers tried to democratise the connexion's government, an ambition which it was feared might be taken to have more general application to society at large. Fear was increased by the tight, cell-like structure adopted by the Methodists — who, of course, were strongest in precisely those urban, industrial areas where government was weakest. The Anglican hierarchy was also suspicious, fearing the levelling tendency of the lay preaching system and dreading the fanaticism of the new converts. None of this necessarily invalidates claims about the real, as opposed to the imagined, effects of Methodism. Yet the movement's attitude to social questions was highly ambivalent, and it is an oversimplification to see it as a form of externally imposed social control. The New Connexion seems to have favoured radical movements, whereas the Wesleyan Conference did not approve. Thus Charles Shaw suggested that Methodist influence was responsible for the weakness of trade unionism in the Potteries area where he worked.

In any case Methodism was a two-edged weapon. Labouring people may have accepted it, but they shaped in accordance with their own needs and aspirations. Further it is doubtful whether Methodism was numerically strong enough to have had the impact Thompson suggests. While its most rapid gains were made in periods of high social tension, it still had only some 600,000 adherents by 1851 and by no means all of these could be described as members of the working class.[104] Finally, there is no inherent reason why frustrated revolutionaries should become Methodists. Disappointed Methodists were just as likely to turn to political radicalism. In this context, it has been argued that men became radicals or Methodists for much the same reasons and that there was no essential polarity between them.[105] It may be legitimate to conclude with one contemporary that the role of Methodism in preventing revolution was 'only fully known to God'.[106] It seems more likely, however, that its role was unimportant because, despite government fears and the undoubted existence of revolutionary cells, there was no real danger of revolution taking place, nor any united working class behind it.

If there is little tangible evidence of united working-class activity, there are plenty of indications of a sense of general bewilderment at the speed and magnitude of the social and economic changes then occurring. For much of the century, this bewilderment was perpetuated in the persistent myth of a lost rural paradise. Consider Edwin Waugh's poem for example (1817–1890):

My Gronfaither's house, wur a cozy owd shop
As sweet as a posy, fro' bottom to top.
Parlour, loom-house and dairy; bedrooms graght and smo'
An' a skin' owd kitchen, the best nook of o'.[107]

Samuel Laycock (1826–1893) took up a similar theme in writing of 'Mi Gronfeyther'.

He'd a farm ov his own, an' a noice little pond,
Wheer we used to go fishin' for treawt;
An' aw haven't forgotten when th' hay time coom
    reawned,
For us childer had mony a blow eawt . . .

An' then he'd a garden at th' backside o' th' heawse
Wheer eawr Bobby an' me used to ceawer,
Eat goosbris, an' currans, an' rubarb, an' crabs,
Or owt there wur else 'at wur seawer.[108]

Responses to rapid social change were many. Some, as we
have seen, tried to protect themselves through the medium
of trade unions or friendly societies. Others tried to opt out
of the new, less congenial world altogether and turned to one
or other of the millenarian sects which so abounded in the
period that Carlyle referred to 'the contemporary rage of
prophecy'.[109] D'Eichthal noticed this when he was in
Edinburgh in 1828: 'There is great interest in Mr Irving's
prophecies about the end of the world and similar things.'[110]
While there are obvious dangers in generalising about the
appeal of millenarianism, it can, in part at least, be seen as a
response to widespread anxieties and insecurities produced
by rapid change.[111] Certainly the Wroeites and the Southcottians had particular strength in areas of high economic
distress and protest. The commonest contemporary explanations of millenarianism were couched in terms of mental
derangement, which may well be true of spectacular exhibi-
tionists like Ebenezer Aldred, who sailed down the Thames
distributing tracts which predicted the imminent doom of
the capital, or of Joanna Southcott who claimed that at
sixty-five she would give birth to Shiloh, the man-child
foretold in *Revelation*, chapter 12. It is hardly likely that the
many followers of such leaders – one estimate reckons there
were some 100,000 Southcottians – were all mentally disturbed. Some were doubtless attracted by promises that the
millennium would be accompanied by a downward redistribution of material goods. For most, however, the appeal of
the sects has been aptly described as a 'sense of separateness
from the world . . . a congenial home, where the values and
goals were different from those of the wider society, and
where unbounded hopes of a future millennium could be
indulged'.[112] In a sense this was also offered by more orthodox creeds like Methodism although the millennium here was
very much a matter of a heavenly hereafter, since the Methodist work ethic ensured that adherents kept their feet firmly
in the secular world.

Many, however, were not content to await divine intervention and responded to industrialisation by trying to change
its direction away from private profiteering into some form
of non-competitive communalism. Although the Rochdale
pioneers finally shaped co-operation into the form of co-
operative trading within the existing economic structure in
1844, it is important to remember that the first co-operatives
were designed as a means of transforming capitalist society
into a socialist commonwealth.[113] The first society of this
type had been set up as early as 1821, and at the movement's
peak in the early 1830s it is reckoned that there were as
many as 500 different societies with 20,000 members.
William Lovett recalled that they were originally meant as the
first step 'towards the social independence of the labouring
classes . . . I was induced to believe that . . . they might ultimately have the trade, manufactures, and commerce of the
country in their own hands.'[114]

This was essentially the vision of Robert Owen in whose
ideas many workers, initially at least, found their response to
the industrial revolution. Despite his subsequent reputation
as a founder of the co-operative movement, Owen had little
time for retail trading stores.[115] Rather, his plans for social
reconstruction were based on the assumption that society
would be transformed if property was held communally and
the economy organised on a co-operative rather than competitive basis. To this end, he established seven communities
in Britain between 1825 and 1847. Although they ultimately
failed and the co-operative movement became little more
than a retail mechanism, Owen did have a considerable impact
on many working people. Many trade-union leaders active in
the ferment of the late 1820s and early 1830s acknowledged
their debt to his social analysis. Because he saw in the unions
the organised numbers through which he might build his new
world, Owen made a determined effort to capture them,
especially in 1833 when he engaged in a propaganda campaign in the north of England. At a meeting of the Grand
Lodge of Operative Builders' Union in September, he won
the union over to a scheme for a building guild that would
build directly for the public, thus eliminating the middleman.
He also persuaded the Staffordshire potters to embark on a

scheme of co-operative production. The following year his influence on working people reached its zenith when he was asked to participate in the GNCTU, although his involvement soon waned because his theories were too remote for ordinary workers concerned basically with more mundane matters of earning a living.[116] In a sense Owen's ideas combined those elements of reform, nostalgia and millenarianism which informed so much of the response to industrialisation. There was nostalgia in the backward-looking agrarianism and paternalism of his communities; reformism in his wish to deploy the new technology of industrialisation to destroy poverty and drudgery; millenarianism in the sense that his goal was a totally new form of social order based not on the family, which he regarded as the quintessence of private property, but on communalism. 'The Owenite who sang his social hymns in the Manchester Hall of Science was striving for much the same goal as his neighbour who sang Wesley's hymns in the Primitive Methodist chapel or listened to "the prophet" in the Southcottians' meeting place at Ashton-under-Lyme.'[117]

Early in his career, in 1815, Owen had launched a campaign to secure parliamentary restriction on the hours worked by factory children. The attempt to reform factory conditions represented yet another element in the popular response to industrialisation. It has frequently been asserted that the factory reform movement was founded, led and championed in Parliament, and generally dominated by Tories and churchmen.[118] This is seriously to underestimate the role of the workers themselves. The first short-time committee was established in Manchester as early as 1814 and had a continuous existence even after its founder, the cotton spinners' union, broke up after an unsuccessful strike in 1818.[119] In 1819 came the first success with the passage of Peel's bill limiting child labour to 10½ hours per day; it is significant that a Manchester paper printed a letter which referred in derogatory terms to 'the connection between Sir Robert Peel's Factory Bill and the present combination of spinners in Manchester'.[120] Yet the act, which had only passed in a somewhat truncated form banning the employment of all children under nine in cotton factories and restricting the hours of those under sixteen to a maximum of twelve, proved almost impossible to enforce. From the middle 1820s onwards, Manchester spinners were again prominent in trying to secure a ten-hour day for the whole industry, raising a number of parliamentary petitions to this end. In 1828, Doherty was instrumental in setting up a Society for the Protection of Children Employed in Cotton Factories in order to implement more fully Hobhouse's act of 1825 which had decreed a 69 hour week for children. Thereafter the initiative passed to Yorkshire when workers in several towns set up short-time committees and asked the Tory, Richard Oastler, to spearhead their campaign which culminated in the Ten Hour Bill presented by Sadler in 1832. After a major step was taken to restrict child labour with the passage of the famous act of 1833, the factory reform movement as such rather lost its way. Various elements of the working class continued to support it, even though increasingly distracted by agitation about the poor law. The Manchester factory reform committee was perhaps unique in the degree of support it had from the cotton unions; but spinners in Glasgow were prominent in that city's committee, and the Huddersfield committee was also dominated by radical workers.

One thing which the factory reform movement must have brought home forcibly to many workers was that the key to social change lay in political power, and thus the campaign for parliamentary reform formed a further element of working-class response. The belief in reform had been fostered in the years of the French Revolution by the activities of the corresponding societies and had survived the war to reappear in the Hampden clubs. For some, political reform was thought to be a goal capable of achievement only through violent means. To some extent this belief was institutionalised in 1830 with the formation of the National Union of the Working Classes. When in the following year the House of Lords rejected the Whig reform bill, there were scenes of violence in many places. The authorities lost control of Bristol for several days; large crowds appeared on the streets of London; Nottingham Castle was burned down. Yet this was also a period of economic depression and high unemployment. It is quite likely therefore that the violence was

prompted as much by hunger as by frustrated political aspirations. On the whole, the main tradition of working-class,
parliamentary reform activity after 1817 developed on peaceful lines, exploiting 'every means of agitation and protest
short of active insurrectionary preparation'.[121] This even
survived the tension created by the Peterloo massacre in
1819, when a reform meeting on the outskirts of Manchester
was forcibly and bloodily disrupted by the military. While
this incident has often been used as evidence of incipient
class conflict in the period, the very fact that it created such
a furore probably indicates that it was an exceptional, not
typical event. Most working-class political reformers — and
they were always, it should be stressed, a minority — supported the political unions which sprang up all over the country
after 1830. The majority accepted, wrongly as it turned out,
the 1832 reform bill as an instalment and foretaste of what
was to come.

Superficially perhaps, political reform, millenarianism,
trade unionism, co-operation, revolutionary plotting, and
factory reform did not have much in common. Indeed, the
different movements frequently vied with each other for
support, though they were by no means mutually exclusive.
Doherty, for example, was a trade unionist, was actively
involved in the agitation for parliamentary and factory
reform, and is sometimes thought to have had some sympathy
for the ideas of Robert Owen.[122] Yet these various movements did have an underlying unity in that they were all seen
as remedies for one common condition — the insecurity
produced by economic and social change of unprecedented
speed and magnitude. By the late 1830s, these many prescriptions for improvement were either fading in popularity or
had been re-mixed into a new, all-purpose panacea — Chartism.

3

Chartism

As a formal movement, Chartism can be said to have first appeared in the spring of 1838 with the publication of the People's Charter — a product of consultations between a number of leading radical MPs such as J.A. Roebuck and representatives of the London Working Men's Association (LWMA), established in 1836 to agitate for 'an equality of political rights'. The Charter thus took the form of a parliamentary bill incorporating the six reforms deemed necessary to secure this equality: annual Parliaments, payment of MPs, equal electoral districts, universal male suffrage, vote by ballot, and the abolition of property qualifications.[1] Yet the origins of Chartism can be traced well back into the 1830s, particularly to the disappointment felt by radical activists at the outcome of the 1832 Reform Act. Although they had campaigned vigorously under the aegis of bodies like the National Union of Working Classes (NUWC) to get the measure through a Parliament in which the upper chamber was especially hostile, little had been done in the bill to reduce the cost of electioneering which remained prohibitively expensive. In any case, despite the reforms the franchise remained very restricted, the Commons being elected by only fourteen per cent of adult males. Certainly the act came nowhere near meeting the demands of the NUWC for annual Parliaments, adult male suffrage and 'especially, NO PROPERTY QUALIFICATION for members of Parliament; this Union being convinced that until intelligent men from the productive and useful classes of society possess the right of sitting in the Commons House of Parliament, to represent the interest of the working people, justice in legislation will never be rendered unto them.'[2]

The LWMA was only one of several organisations created in the course of the 1830s to express this disappointment. Although more militant than the LWMA, the East London Democratic Association claimed in its prospectus of January 1837 to have similar objectives. Also in the capital, Feargus O'Connor and a group of Irish supporters had founded the Marylebone Radical Association. Elsewhere, Thomas Attwood's Birmingham Political Union, which had withered away after playing a leading role in the fight for the reform bill, was re-established in May 1837; and political unions also sprang up in other provincial cities like Manchester. The efforts of such groups to channel working-class discontent and to recruit support through both the printed word and the public lecture were greatly assisted by the activities of the Whig governments elected on the reformed franchise; for these served to confirm radical suspicions that they had somehow been duped. Thomas Cooper was writing of the 1835 Municipal Reform Act, but his words applied equally well to the parliamentary reform bill:

> How the scale has turned, since the greater share of boroughs where the poor and labouring classes threw up their hats at 'municipal reform' — and now mutter discontent at . . . the recreant middle classes whom municipal honours have drawn off from their hot-blooded radicalism, and converted into cold, unfeeling wielders of magisterial or other local power.[3]

The sources of this discontent were numerous, but four were particularly important. For one thing, the Whigs kept up a relentless war against the unstamped radical press. In the period between 1830 and 1836, some seven hundred sellers of radical journals were prosecuted. Typical of the victims was James Watson, summonsed at Bow Street for selling the *Poor Man's Guardian*. 'They considered me as bad as my friend Hetherington, and sentenced me to six months', he recalled.[4] Joshua Hobson of Huddersfield was also summonsed for a similar offence and his defence speech gives a good indication of why such publishers were pursued so resolutely by the government.

I was induced to publish the *Voice of the West Riding* because a paper was wanted to support the rights and interest of the order and class to which I belong . . . The object of the paper was to . . . drag the tyrant and hypocrite from their den of infamy, and to show up the hideous monsters to the gaze and virtuous indignation of every good man in the community — to teach the sanctified knaves that they could not with impunity practise those vices which they affect so loudly to condemn — to learn [sic] the oppressors of the poor that though they might for a time pass unnoticed, and be allowed to practise their unholy deeds unmolested, yet there was a point which they could not pass . . .[5]

The publicity afforded to many of the prosecutions left a residual antipathy towards the government even after 1836 when the duty was reduced from 4d to 1d. One of the leading organisations set up to co-ordinate the fight was the Association of Working Men to Procure a Cheap and Honest Press, a body which was disbanded in 1836. As one of its prominent figures, William Lovett, recalled, 'We had collected together a goodly number of active and influential working men . . . and the question arose among us, whether we could form and maintain a union formed exclusively of this class and of such men.'[6] The outcome was the creation of the LWMA, which was to play an important role in launching the Chartist movement itself.

The Whigs also followed a very repressive policy towards the trade unions, which were undergoing considerable expansion in the trade boom of the early 1830s with experiments in general unionism. Many prominent radicals, including O'Connell and Hume, who had found useful allies among the working class during the struggle for parliamentary reform, were bitterly opposed to the whole idea of unionism. The rift between middle- and working-class radicals which appeared in the disappointing aftermath of parliamentary reform widened still further over this issue. The prosecution of the Tolpuddle martyrs in 1834 was very significant in the process. Thomas Dunning, the radical publisher, commented that the martyrs 'were intelligent working men who had assisted in the agitation for the Reform Bill of 1832 which established the persecuting

Whigs in power. Save us from our friends!'[7] At least one of
the political unions created to press for the reform bill, that
in Bradford, collapsed because of internal disagreements among
middle- and working-class supporters about the Tolpuddle
case. Peter Bussey, one of its most active working-class members, quit to become a prominent, physical-force Chartist.

In Scotland the same pattern emerged. Many trade unionists
had joined in the celebrations organised to mark the passage
of the 1832 bill — the Edinburgh Trades Union Council
arranged a jubilee in the city — but the alliance between
working-class and middle-class radicals deteriorated when
members of the Glasgow cotton spinners' union were arrested
in July 1837 on suspicion of arson and murder. All over
Scotland and the north of England, unionists rallied to support a campaign on behalf of the accused men, who were
widely believed to be the victims of a government clamp-
down inspired by O'Connell. The militance expressed in
this campaign must have frightened off many middle-class
sympathisers. Augustus Beaumont told Glasgow workmen in
November 1837 that he was surprised not to find barricades
in the street, the time having come 'for a fight with the
aristocracy'.[8] Further south, Rev Rayner Stephens merely
suggested, somewhat more temperately, that they should
burn down the mills of 'the cotton tyrants'.[9] Not surprisingly,
therefore, there was a good deal of support for Chartism,
especially in its early stages, from trade unionists. Charles
Davies of Stockport, for example, was said by a government
official to have become involved because of 'the failure of
his attempts to increase the Wages of Working Men'.[10]
Lawrence Pitkeithly, who took the lead in organising assistance for the Glasgow spinners, later became a prominent
West Riding Chartist. Many of the men who drew up the
first Charter were also active in the campaign of protest
organised against the sentence passed on the Glasgow men.
According to the *Manchester Guardian*, the first major Chartist
rally in Lancashire was attended by over 3500 trade-union
members.

A further source of discontent was provided by the failure
of the reformed Parliament to produce anything substantial
in the improvement of working conditions, one of the main

aspirations of factory workers. Sadler's bill to restrict working hours to ten a day in factories had lapsed when Parliament dissolved after the passing of the Reform Bill. Although Ashley's act went through in 1833, it was deemed unsatisfactory because it only affected the working day of children, leaving adult hours unregulated. What benefit, demanded the Leeds radical, Robert Taylor, were operatives 'to reap from the Reform Bill, if they . . . were to work the exact number of hours which they were able to bear?'[11] Richard Oastler, the Tory radical who led the move for factory reform in the 1830s, claimed that the government's failure to tackle the problem was 'convincing proof that the ten pounders will do nothing for the people whom they promised should be liberated'.[12] The logical conclusion was that factory reform could only be secured if Parliament itself was further reformed, and in this way the frustrations of the factory reformers went to swell the rising Chartist tide. Many of the northern delegates to the Chartist Convention of 1839 had been trained in the ten-hour movement.

Many also had experience in another major campaign of the 1830s, that against the introduction of the new poor law, arguably the most unpopular of all the Whigs' legislative enactments. On paper, the act ended outdoor relief and created poor law unions. The commissioners responsible for implementing the legislation imposed a new, harsh test which restricted eligibility for aid. Then, ruthlessly segregating men, women and children, the commissioners packed them into workhouses which rapidly became symbols of Whig oppression. The veteran radical, Hetherington, already had damned it as 'a murderer's death blow to the operative classes'; but in the south its introduction passed off fairly smoothly.[13] When the commissioners began implementing it in the north, however, they ran into a stormy resistance. Once more it was Oastler who led the way, describing the measure as 'the Devil's own spawn, begotten by him when in a very bad humour . . . the Catechism of Hell! . . . the Devil's own book! It must be *burnt* out and out burnt . . .'[14] The factory reform committees rallied to Oastler's side; so too did O'Connor, Rayner Stephens, and metropolitan radicals like Hetherington and Bronterre O'Brien, the Irish editor of a number of important radical journals. Many of the poor law guardians themselves opposed the act; partly because they viewed it as interference from London; partly because in several instances they had already reformed their own local poor law methods and did not believe that the workhouse system could cope effectively with the results of widespread industrial depression. Indeed, it was the coincidence of the commissioners' arrival with a depression that made resistance in the north so strong. Manchester alone had an estimated 50,000 workers on short time or unemployed by 1837, and many of them faced a real threat of being assigned to one of the hated bastilles. Publications attacking the new system poured off the presses; massive public protest meetings were organised; every unsavoury aspect of the new act's workings was widely publicised; and in some areas attempts to operate it met with riot and forceful resistance. By 1838, however, the campaign was beginning to run out of steam. Oastler had been dismissed by his employer, and the loss of his leadership was a blow which could not easily be offset. The commissioners themselves bowed before the storm and modified some of the act's bleaker provisions. There seemed little prospect of getting the act nullified entirely, as the failure of John Fielden's parliamentary motion in March 1838 seemed to indicate. Gradually, therefore, the north turned to a wider based radicalism, convinced of the force of Fielden's own point that they 'should keep to this one single point . . . the suffrage and the suffrage only, should satisfy the working people of England'.[15]

Towards the end of the decade, then, the fear generated by the new poor law, the frustrations of the factory reformers, resentments over Whig attitudes towards trade unions and the radical press were all converging into a general demand for broadly-based political reform of a type which some had been demanding ever since 1832, on the grounds that this provided the only sure way of remedying their accumulated grievances. As Manchester Chartists put it: 'Repeal the poor law, the rural police, the game law, the money, or the corn law, or any one single law on the Statute Book, and leave the root of the evil untouched, and you will be only dabbling with the effects of class legislation!'[16] The crucial figure in producing the transmutation of these several grievances into a general demand for parliamentary reform was Feargus O'Connor. His electrifying oratory not only seized his listeners, it was capable of bridging the gap between the more sophisticated theoretical arguments of the artisans and the more basic concerns of those to whom Chartism was essentially a matter of 'plenty of roast beef, plum pudding and strong beer by working three hours a day'.[17] A contemporary has described one of his performances thus.

> The voice took on a fuller sound; the sentences became shorter, they were wrung in spasms from his seething breast, the fist drummed more wildly against the edge of the rostrum, the face of the orator became pale, his limbs trembled, the cataract of his rage had flooded over the last barrier, and onwards thundered the floodtide of his eloquence, throwing down all before it, breaking up and smashing everything in its way — and I do believe that the man would have talked himself to death if he had not been interrupted by an applause which shook the whole house and set it vibrating . . . O'Connor spoke for about three hours that evening. The impression he made on the meeting was indescribable. More than once did the women, surrounding the orator on the rostrum, dry their hot tears from their cheeks, more than once did they break out into interminable cheering. On the faces of the men one could read what went on in their hearts, the mood of the speaker was reflected in them.[18]

This ability, which O'Connor had used in a variety of radical causes up and down the country during 1830s, ensured that he was seen as a natural successor to Orator Hunt in the radical movement. He was able to assume Cobbett's mantle as well when towards the end of 1837 he began publishing the *Northern Star*, a paper which served to fill the gap left by the collapse of the unstamped press after 1836. Although the early editions concentrated on the anti-poor law campaign and the Glasgow cotton spinners, O'Connor always had in view a much wider radical programme, headed by the demand for universal suffrage. By 1839 the *Northern Star* had a circulation of 36,000. Coupled with his own personal charisma, this enabled O'Connor not only to establish his own organisation, the Great Northern Union, in 1838, but also to win a fair degree of support in the strongholds of the Birmingham Political Union and the LWMA.[19] Out of this convergence of the main streams of radical protest in the 1830s came the plan to hold a national convention of the industrious classes.

By the winter of 1838–9, therefore, British radicals were largely taken up with preparations for the forthcoming convention, whose task it was to present the Charter to Parliament backed by a grand petition. Its various elements were held together by a strong sense of resentment, engendered by the property qualifications of the 1832 franchise, a fear of strong centralised government, and by the example of 1832 in which demonstration and threat of violence had forced through major legislative changes. Yet we should be careful not to exaggerate the organic unity of the rising Chartist tide, for beneath and often on top of the surface lay all sorts of local variations in organisations, tactics and emphasis which gave the movement its kaleidoscopic appearance.

It is true that analysis of the occupations of Chartist supporters in different parts of the country reveals a remarkably consistent pattern. Rank and file support came in the main from domestic outworkers, whose whole way of life, and the nature and values of the communities in which they lived, helped push them into a radical stance.[20] The immediate cause of their involvement, however, appears to have been economic. Many came from trades depressed by the advance of technology. In other traditionally skilled artisan occupations such as tailoring and cutlery, employment was threatened not by machinery, but by great influxes of labour attracted by the growing demands for such products. It is thus significant that one of the characteristics of strong Chartist areas seems to have been rising population, which placed added pressure on jobs in easily learned and labour intensive industries.[21] In addition, the increasingly national scope of the market subjected many more artisans to the ebb and flow of the trade cycle. Every source, therefore, indicates substantial outworker participation. Of the 113 members of the Great Horton Chartist Association in the period 1840–42, three-quarters were hand-loom weavers and woolcombers; hardly surprising when it is remembered that Bradford woolcombers, who had commanded wages of 23s. a week in 1824, were only earning 6s. to 8s. by 1840.[22] W.E. Hickson concluded of Scottish hand-loom weavers that 'amongst the foremost remedies proposed by handloom weavers for their depressed condition is universal suffrage; not because they consider that giving every man a vote in itself will benefit his condition, but because they believe, very generally, that without it, as a means to an end, the grievances, real or imaginary, of which they complain, will never be redressed.'[23] Of the twenty-three local associations which bothered to reply to a questionnaire distributed by the convention when it met, only two stressed lack of parliamentary representation as a general grievance. The majority complained of economic hardship, scarcity of work, low wages, or dear provisions.

There was, secondly, a strong Chartist following among factory workers, particularly in the Lancashire textile region; their support was also mainly a matter of economics. It sprang partly from heavy unemployment associated with the depression of the later 1830s, and also from the easily-seen gap between worker and employer. Stephens sensed the mood correctly when he stressed that Lancashire Chartism was a knife and fork question, and there was much truth in Cooke Taylor's assertion of 1842 that 'in Lancashire the cry for the Charter means the list of wages for 1836.'[24] An arrested Stockport Chartist claimed that 'the great distress is the cause of our discontent — if the wages were what they ought to be, we should not hear a word about the Suffrage.'[25]

The factory workers tended to occupy an intermediate position between the rank and file outworkers and the artisans and small shopkeepers, who seem to have provided most of the leadership. In Suffolk, for example, tailors, shoemakers and building trade artisans looked to agricultural labourers for mass support. In Bath, artisans again provided the leadership, the declining cloth trades the rank and file. Most of the members of the Bradford Northern Union were woolcombers or weavers, but leadership was provided by artisans. In Aberdeen exactly the same picture emerges of a balance between numerically significant hand workers and a small but articulate artisan leadership. In the Tyne area, the leaders included fifteen pitmen, ten boot- and shoemakers, nine tailors, and six masons.[26] In London similar groups provided local leadership although they were not at all prominent in the LWMA. Of some 340 metropolitan Chartists about whom there is information in the period 1841–43, over a third were boot- and shoemakers, though such workers comprised less than ten per cent of the total LWMA membership.[27] Craftsmen of this type rose to prominence, partly because they had a long tradition of political radicalism, partly because (as one of the Welsh leaders put it) 'we are intelligent men', and partly because in several cases their occupations conferred upon them a welcome independence.[28] Peter Bussey, for example, ran the Roebuck Inn near Bradford.[29]

Like most early working-class movements, Chartism outside secularist London was imbued with religious language and metaphors; and some of its national leaders like Henry Vincent sought to give the movement a Christian rationale. It is perhaps worth noting, therefore, the important role played by non-conformist ministers in providing lectures and other facilities for the Chartists. It has been estimated that there were at least forty such clergymen, some of whom – like Rev Patrick Brewster in Scotland – were quite prominent nationally. Others were more important at the local level. In Bradford, for example, the radical movement was organised by Methodists, and a Methodist minister acted as the local Chartist missionary. In Loughborough a Primitive Methodist minister, John Skevington, edited the local Chartist paper. Ultimately, this form of Chartist influence became institutionalised in the Chartist churches of which about seventy or eighty have been traced.

The ability of the local leadership to attract and retain the support of the rank and file was affected by local circumstances which naturally varied from place to place. This goes far to explaining the bewildering complexity of the movement and also why it drew its main support from certain well-defined areas – south Lancashire, the West Riding of Yorkshire, the east midlands, parts of the Black Country, Scotland and Wales. In other areas, however, it never secured much support. Sometimes this was because of well-organised local opposition. In Ireland there were some stirrings in cities such as Belfast, Cork and Dublin; but the general suspicion by the Catholic church of O'Connell (on the grounds that Chartism would undermine society) and of the Young Ireland movement (because it was English) together ensured that Chartism had little impact. This is surprising in one way, because there was a considerable involvement of émigré Irish in the mainland Chartist movement, and the Chartists generally were vitally interested in the Irish question. In Cornwall, organised non-conformity opposed Chartism, competing with it for leadership and support, and generating an attitude of resignation to existing social conditions. Sometimes local opposition was quite overt. Shopkeepers in Bath and Merthyr were warned not to stock or sell Chartist papers, while in Devizes Vincent was knocked unconscious when he tried to address a rally. Ministers of many denominations disrupted Chartist meetings and warned congregations against signing petitions.

More generally, Chartism was weak in predominantly rural areas where habits of deference and traditional forms of political action remained strong. The rural labourers of East Anglia could not be convinced — at least for any length of time — by the urban radicals of Ipswich that the vote was the remedy for their economic difficulties. Threatened both by unemployment and the new workhouses, they reverted in 1844 to incendiarism. Even in rural Wales where the gap between urban and rural workers was to some extent bridged by their shared non-conformity and mutual hostility to the symbols of English dominance, Chartism was accompanied by more traditional protests in the form of the Rebecca riots of 1839 and 1842. In one way, the weakness of Chartism in rural areas was self-perpetuating, in that good lecturers would only reluctantly accept engagements in such places because they could not be guaranteed an audience and were likely to run into strong opposition from the combined forces of the church and the squirearchy. Peter McDouall recalled that during his tour of the Midlands in 1842 he lectured on one occasion 'in a barn where there were two pigs outside and two policemen inside'.[30] Thus the weakly organised areas tended to attract only those speakers least likely to have much impact, especially as they could not afford the fees commanded by the most popular lecturers.

In some areas Chartism was adversely affected by having to compete for working-class attention against other 'isms' or movements. Land societies, co-operatives or mutual improvement societies all vied with each other in presenting panaceas for social evils. More pragmatically, they also competed for lecture halls. Sometimes the solution to this sort of problem was to infiltrate existing institutions and turn them to Chartism. The literary society in Llanidloes for instance was converted into a Chartist literary society, and several of the local friendly societies turned into clubs for the purchase of arms. Elsewhere they had to provide their own social facilities to hold support. The Dumfries Chartists had to provide chess, draughts, dancing and ultimately cricket. Chartist co-operatives were very popular in some parts, but ironically perhaps it was the socialists who often provided the greatest distraction. Although there were significant points of agreement between Chartists and socialists – a belief in the labour theory of value, the predictable collapse of capitalism, the value of education – to permit some individuals to belong to both groups, such dual allegiance was difficult. Many socialists (which by the late 1830s meant Owenites) quit the Chartist movement because it was too militant and its objectives in their view too narrow. Rivalry and often open hostility was common, especially in areas where both sides had strong followings. In 1842 Owen even produced his own nine point Transition Charter in order to offset local complaints that Chartist agitators were turning people away from socialism.

Chartism grew weakly in other areas because the local social and industrial structure did not produce a very fertile soil for it. In Lancashire it was rooted very firmly in the self-evident social inequality between workers and employers in the dominant cotton industry. Although this feeling was not very often openly expressed, it 'underlay the whole story of Chartism in Lancashire'.[31] This seems generally to have been the case in large towns which depended almost entirely on one major industry. In Coventry it was the absence of this class dimension which kept Chartism ineffective. The major industry, ribbon weaving, was still organised on a sufficiently small scale to permit journeymen to become masters in their own right. In addition, city freemen enjoyed privileges which separated them from the rest of the working class and deprived it of a potential leadership. Finally, because ribbon weaving was so prosperous and because there was such an abundance of charitable provision in the town, very few workers had to resort to the hated poor law which did so much to fuel the Chartist fire in Lancashire.[32] The same was true of Cornwall, where the local tin-mining industry had no obviously bourgeois figure equivalent to the Lancashire cotton factory master or the Tyneside colliery owner. Landowners leased mineral veins to groups of shareholders who then paid the miners a proportion of the ore's overall selling price. In this way, therefore, miners and shareholders were engaged in a joint speculation, and there was little of the sense of class differences and exploitation which existed in the industry in other areas.[33]

The local variations in Chartist support and composition were compounded by political differences. There were in the movement 'Repealers and anti-Repealers, anti-Poor Law men and Malthusianism, O'Connorites, O'Brienites, Cobbettites, Churchmen, Dissenters, or no Church-at-all men and others . . . differing in their views of political economy, morals and religion, wide as the poles asunder'.[34] Depending on which group gained ascendancy, Chartists in different areas tended to stress different programmes alongside the Charter which was frequently the only unifying element. In Lancashire the stress was very much on factory and economic improvement, while in Nottingham and South Wales hostility to the new poor law remained paramount. There were differences, too, about how precisely the Charter should be put into effect, and this served to create local factionalism as well. The members of the Leeds Working Men's Association, for example, were split into three groups: one favoured O'Connor's dictum of 'peacefully if we can, forcibly if we must'; another leaned towards the moral force of Lovett and the LWMA; and a third was influenced by Owenite ideas. In Scotland Brewster led a moderate wing against a whole span of more violent Chartists. Julian Harney was later to observe that in parts of the country 'faction has cut the throat of Chartism'.[35] Such local divisions often tended to be reflections of those which existed at national level, particularly between O'Connor and Lovett's LWMA. For his part, O'Connor did not care for Lovett's stress on education and self-help, finding the LWMA altogether too tepid in its advocacy of Chartism, and fearing that its peculiar emphasis would blind people to the fact that democratic suffrage offered them more than education could. Lovett took the view that O'Connorites 'spurn, with Gothic ferocity, all knowledge, truth or justice; and, judging from their actions, they seemed to think that liberty can only be realised by violence and prescription'.[36]

The electioneering which preceded the meeting of the convention exposed these differences still more clearly as the various factions sought to consolidate their positions. Their manoeuvrings were undoubtedly aided by the fact that the elections for the convention were conducted with scant regard for those principles enshrined in the petition. The constituences were meaningless, and many delegates received multiple mandates. O'Brien, for example, represented six different areas. All through the summer of 1838 election rallies were organised. In August O'Connor was well received at a major rally in Birmingham. The following month the LWMA — alarmed both by the continued stress of the Birmingham leader, Attwood, on currency reform and the apparent acceptability of O'Connor's militance to Birmingham Chartists — organised a similar meeting in the capital. Even here, however, it was O'Connor who won the best reception while the more moderate counsels of the local MP were heckled and shouted down. Lovett was left to declare at a later meeting that 'if the people were to be called upon to arm . . . he would have nothing to do with them.'[37] In Lancashire, O'Connor's reception was equally favourable, except among some of the trade unionists who found him too extreme for their taste. 'I have commenced the battle of the suffrage,' he exclaimed, 'and you are the forces with which I will fight that battle, even to the death, if necessary.'[38] It was, however, as a delegate from Yorkshire's West Riding that O'Connor was returned to the convention, along with the equally vociferous Bussey. In Scotland, the Calton Hill resolutions disavowing the use of force were roundly condemned by O'Connor, Harney and Dr John Taylor. Attempts made by moderates to diminish O'Connorite influence were unsuccessful. In London the moderate LWMA, despite its unrepresentative nature and the welcome afforded to O'Connor, virtually managed to corner representation. As a result, some of the extremists led by Harney quit the LWMA and formed the pro-O'Connor London Democratic Association (LDA).

The struggles between the various Chartist factions were at once manifested and perpetuated in the movement's rapidly growing press, contrary to O'Connor's own assertion that a press was 'at once the cheapest, most expeditious, and the most certain means of keeping a party together'.[39] The LWMA sought to publicise its position by publishing the *Charter* from January 1839. The following month other London Chartists produced a rival in the *Chartist*. A few weeks later the LDA joined in with the *London Democrat*. In Scotland the moral force wing found support in the *Ayrshire Examiner*, which consistently opposed O'Connor's line. There can be no doubt that in the press battle O'Connor had the strongest weapon at his disposal. It would be wrong to suggest that the *Northern Star* was merely his own personal organ; for the editor, Hill, was not afraid to dissent from his proprietor's views nor to insert matter and letters critical of him. The *Star* was by far the most influential and widely read of the Chartist papers. Furthermore, many of its full-time reporters and agents also served as organisers for the movement, and they naturally tended to favour O'Connor.

In February 1839, the convention finally assembled in London. Twelve of the delegates, most of them sympathetic to the LWMA, represented the capital. There were eight from Scotland, two from Wales, and five returned by the Birmingham Political Union. The rest of the fifty-four who attended came mainly from the industrial areas of England, although not all of those who had been elected in fact turned up. Bailie Craig from Scotland was elected chairman and Lovett secretary, despite spirited opposition from O'Brien. Although Lovett's role ostensibly strengthened the position of the LWMA within the convention, he was given no clerical assistance, and the organisation was consequently plagued by administrative ineptitude. The minute books soon filled up with complaints from local associations about unacknowledged letters, lack of information about the availability of speakers, and failure to dispatch important documentation. This administrative weakness was all the more significant in that it hampered efforts to boost the disappointing number of signatures – slightly more than half a million – on the petition. Missionaries were sent out by the convention to those areas where support was weak, but they met with little success and considerable hostility. Acting on convention instructions, Lovett also sent round a questionnaire, to elicit information from provincial associations about local economic conditions, numbers of signatures procured for the petition, and so on. Only twenty-three associations bothered to reply, although this hardly mattered since it is evident that the convention members had given little thought as to what might be done with the information once it was available.

In one area, that of finance, this administrative inexperience was crucial. It had been intended to finance the convention's activities by the National Rent, collected by local associations and forwarded to the rent's administrators, the Birmingham Chartists, P.H. Muntz and R.K. Douglas. No clear instructions had been given about the overall allocation of financial responsibility, an oversight which produced several difficulties. When the convention decided in June 1839 to send Bussey on a lecture tour of Scotland, the West Riding delegate meeting refused to pay his travelling expenses on the grounds that they were properly the responsibility of the convention itself. Such difficulties meant that of the thousands of pounds raised from the National Rent only a small proportion ever reached the convention. There was only £967 available when the convention first met, well short of the £10,000 that Attwood had reckoned necessary. Lovett found it impossible to get an accurate account of income from either Douglas or Muntz, and for this reason he included in his circular to local associations questions about their contributions to the rent. Matters were not helped by the offstage activities of a hostile national press which busily purveyed stories of peculation. 'The Birmingham delegates have, we believe, all returned home,' said *The Times* in March, 'and one or two of them in new cloaks, and otherwise attired in spic-span suits of the most modern London cut, appear to have profited, at least as far as the outward man is concerned, by their trip to the metropolis.'[40] Such rumour-mongering merely added to the difficulties of the local collectors, with the result that some convention delegates did not receive any help at all from their local associations. The difficulties had another side effect, too. It is quite evident that in some areas the methods used to raise the rent were little short of criminal, and this did nothing to hold the support of the middle class. Shopkeepers were informed that if they failed to contribute their shops would be boycotted, while in some places Chartist retribution was more dramatic. In Loughborough, for instance, a farmer called Poynder had his haystacks fired after refusing to contribute, but blatant intimidation of this type was usually punished by due process of law. Leeds Chartists who tried to mount a boycott against unco-operative shopkeepers were convicted on charges of extortion.

The convention delegates spent their time in debate, sometimes on major matters, more often on rather trivial considerations. In the course of these discussions, as well as during the extra-mural meetings organised by some factions, the gaps among Chartists began to loom large. Indeed, they had been evident from the very first day when Dr Arthur Wade, representing Nottingham, opened the proceedings in prayer, beseeching 'thy blessing upon *all moral means* for obtaining our political and social improvement'.[41] Soon afterwards Wade quit the convention altogether when it rejected his motion to remove the phrase 'peaceably if you may, forcibly if you must' from the *Address to the Irish Nation*. He was followed by a trickle of other delegates as the weeks passed, a trickle which soon developed into a stream, frightened off by demands of the sort made by Harney that 'all acts of injustice and oppression should be met by resistance', or by the recommendations of another delegate that the best weapon to deploy against the new rural police was a loaded bludgeon.[42] By May most of the Birmingham and Scottish delegates had retired, one of the latter commenting that 'the people of Scotland were too calm, too prudent and too humane to imperil this cause upon bloodshed.'[43]

It was this issue of violence and the closely related one of co-operation with the middle class which did most to divide the convention delegates. In the eyes of some delegates, the convention was an anti-parliament, based on the belief that sovereignty lay ultimately with the people.[44] If, as seemed likely, the House of Commons rejected the Charter, what could the convention then do to further its campaign? Either it could continue with peaceful agitation in the hope of reversing Parliament's decision or it could resort to more forceful means to assert popular sovereignty. Over and above the qualms many delegates clearly had about the morality of such a course, there was the further consideration that it would certainly alienate middle-class radicals whose parliamentary support was vital. Against this, however, were ranged those whose experience convinced them that it was futile to expect anything from co-operation with the middle class. O'Connor expressed his reservations quite clearly. 'If the middle classes wished to join the people, they must not expect to lead, they must go into the shafts together: but the moment they got to Whig Cross, they flashed the dark lantern in your face, and said, "Good-night, Mr Chartist", leaving you to grope your way along as well as you could.'[45] Daniel O'Connell in particular was vilified by Chartists as an example of a middle-class radical who had betrayed his working-class allies. Some quite sophisticated economic arguments were also brought into play to justify the plea for separate class action. It was widely argued that labour was the source of all value and that its rights could therefore only be defended by labour alone; that workers were exploited because the existence of a reserve army of unemployed men enabled employers to keep wages down; that manufacturers in effect robbed labour and compelled it to work long hours. The manifesto issued in 1838 by the Barnsley Chartists used such arguments, explaining the existing system of government thus:

> Suppose twenty men produce wealth to the extent of twenty pounds a week, and suppose four other men had been imposed on them, or pursuaded, that they (the four men) had a right to make laws by which the twenty men should be governed. Well, the four men proceed to make

laws, and the first law that they make is that the twenty pounds' worth of wealth which the twenty men produce shall be divided; and the twenty men shall have one-half for producing the whole, and the other half must be given to the four for making laws . . . Well, things go on pretty smoothly under this law for a while, but by-and-by the extravagance of the four law-makers is so great that their income will not meet their expenditure; so they call their legislative abilities into exercise, and devise plans to increase their incomes; they know well where to begin, for they know that there is no wealth but what the working class create . . .[46]

It was a suspicion of middle-class motives that lay behind the opposition expressed by many Chartists to the activities of the Anti-Corn Law League set up in March 1839. Scottish Chartists, who tended anyway to be more favourably disposed towards the idea of co-operation with the middle class, welcomed the league's appearance; but in Lancashire, where radicalism was nurtured in the tradition of Tory protectionism by Oastler, Chartists were very suspicious. Why did the manufacturers favour repeal, demanded Manchester Chartists in 1841? 'Because with the reduced price of corn, they will be enabled to reduce the wages of the working man, in order that they may compete with foreigners who live upon potatoes.'[47]

In May 1830, thwarted in its intention to present the petition by the resignation of Melbourne's government, the convention decided to move to Birmingham where more militant counsels had begun to prevail after the early resignation of the city's convention delegates. Here the convention resumed its discussions of the ultimate sanctions which might be used in the event of Parliament rejecting the petition (which now had 1.28 million signatures.) Many ideas were mooted: abstinence from liquor and a refusal to subscribe to unfriendly journals appeared among the gentler suggestions, while others were disposed to more far-reaching methods such as encouraging supporters to withdraw all bank deposits, withhold rents, tithes and taxes, or take up arms. In the end because no agreement could be reached, the delegates decided to leave the matter of ultimate sanctions for local associations to consider. It was noticeable, however, that by now some of the hard-line militants, particularly O'Connor and O'Brien, were beginning to hedge when it came to the point of translating their fine-sounding rhetoric into concrete action. One reason was that authority had at last stepped up its activities against the movement. As Home Secretary, Russell had been content to follow a generally conciliatory policy, resisting pressure at the beginning of 1839 to bring in a disarming bill or to licence the arming of local, volunteer, loyalist groups. In the spring and summer of 1839, a harder policy developed. Drilling was forbidden, lord lieutenants were empowered to raise and arm special constables, and the size of the regular army was increased. Leading figures in the London and Lancashire movement were arrested; and the tempo of arrests increased after a riot in the Birmingham Bull Ring in July when two leading militants, Taylor and McDouall, were apprehended. Even the peaceful Lovett found himself in Warwick jail when he courageously led a public protest against the Birmingham arrests.

On 12 July, what was left of the convention, ravaged by resignation, default, dissension and now arrests, was forced finally to face up to the realities of ultimate sanctions, for the House of Commons threw out the petition by 235 votes to 46. It was difficult to know what the various local meetings had decided on, but on 17 July the convention voted 13–6 to hold a sacred month, which virtually amounted to calling a general strike. Doubts about the wisdom of such a step at a time of severe trade depression were soon being expressed. Of the twenty English and Welsh associations which contacted the convention, sixteen opposed the plan. Only five of the forty-three Scottish associations wrote in support of it. A few Lancashire Chartists who tried to put it into effect had to close down local factories by force, indicative of the lukewarm reception the idea received in the region. O'Connor, who had absented himself from the convention debate on the plan, now announced that he had always doubted its practicality and supported the successful efforts of another militant, O'Brien, to get it scrapped. Shortly afterwards the convention, shorn by this vacillation of any credibility which it may have had, was dissolved. Its dissolution took place against a background of continued arrests of prominent Chartists in many different parts of the country. Major trials were held in half a dozen cities, and those who had avoided arrest watched in dismay as their organisation collapsed along with many of their hopes and aspirations.

As the summer passed into autumn, there were a few outbreaks of violence. The most spectacular occurred at Newport in November and arose out of plans laid by local leaders to rescue Henry Vincent from his prison cell in Newport. Early in November parties of armed Chartists from three centres assembled at Risca and marched on Newport in pouring rain. The tardiness of their gathering ensured that any element of surprise was lost and, as they approached and fired on the Westgate Hotel, well-hidden soldiers from the 45th foot regiment returned their fire, killing fourteen and wounding about fifty. The rest fled in confusion, many of them, including leaders such as Charles Jones, John Frost and Zephaniah Williams, to be arrested in the succeeding few days. It was widely supposed at the time that the attack on Newport was to be the signal for a general Chartist uprising. It has never been possible to prove this one way or the other, as the evidence is difficult to interpret.

For one thing it is quite apparent that much depended on the attitudes adopted by local magistrates and police. Potentially explosive situations could be defused by sympathetic handling. Dunning recalled that in Nantwich local police officers regularly attended Chartist meetings. 'Had Mr Superintendent Laxton been a political policeman, he might have caused arrests to be made for the making use of seditious language. However, as he knew us all to be peaceable citizens, he allowed us to read speeches from the *Star*, sing, and talk as we pleased.'[48] Similarly, General Napier of the army's northern command met privately with Lancashire Chartist leaders and promised to keep troops and police away from a major rally at Kersal Moor as long as they met peacefully. This local reaction was particularly significant because violence might well have flared up and spread from some local flashpoint. This was why Napier was so indignant about magistrates who overreacted in potentially dangerous situations. 'Alarm! Trumpets! Magistrates in a fuss! Troops! Troops! Troops! . . . I screech at these applications like a gate, swinging on rusty hinges, and swear! Lord, how they make me swear.'[49] Certainly plenty of magistrates seem to have employed *agents provocateurs*, and many played on public fear of armed rebellion. During trials at Chester in 1839, for instance, the barrister's table was covered with pikes, guns and swords found in the defendants' possession. This, it was believed, 'was for the purpose of influencing the jury to convict . . . During the Assizes a quantity of gunpowder, etc., was brought through Chester . . . It was generally understood these explosives had been consigned to a Chartist agent . . . This report must have been circulated to influence both juries and the citizens generally, for it was proved the gunpowder, etc., was a purely commercial transaction.'[50] A typical magistrate's letter to the Home Office, written from Loughborough in 1839, claimed that in local smithies 'pikes are being fabricated'.[51]

Even if such reports were exaggerated, it is still quite evident that Chartists in many parts of the country had taken seriously the words of some of their leaders about arming. In Merthyr some of the local friendly societies had been converted into arms-buying clubs. Dunning was informed that a Birmingham gunmaker had supplied 'a considerable quantity of arms' to the Potteries. As early as February 1839, the authorities in Trowbridge had learned that local blacksmiths had received orders for pike heads and that muskets were being brought in from Bath.[52] Of course, it does not follow from this that there was any intention of using the weapons; nor does it necessarily follow that the Newport rising was the signal for any more widespread insurgency. There is little real evidence in Home Office records that the arming and drilling reported in the area prior to 3 November were anything other than sporadic, although this may be indicative of deficiencies in Home Office intelligence rather than the absence of a plot. Furthermore, it seems that much of the firmest support received by Frost and his colleagues came from districts where Scotch Cattle activity had traditionally been strong, suggesting that some of the participants at least were more interested in revenge against individual employers and magistrates. While it does not necessarily invalidate the belief that Newport was part of a general plot, much of the evidence at the ensuing trials was about intimidation rather than sedition.

On the positive side, Chartist memoirs give the idea some credence. Robert Lowery's account presents Newport as the culmination of plotting which had gone on since the late summer of 1839.[53] General Napier, who was a highly competent soldier, also believed in the existence of a broad plan. Lovett's autobiography claims that a Yorkshire rising was arranged to support the Welshmen; and it seems almost certain that Bussey, who held a conference at Heckmondwike, perhaps to co-ordinate the plot, was in touch with northeastern militants like Taylor and Devyr. There are also some hints of planning in Birmingham and Lancashire. Frost is known to have visited Lancashire in October, though the purpose of his visit remains a mystery. Whatever plans were in fact laid at these and other meetings, little support was forthcoming when the Newport men launched their effort. Having apparently agreed to support a rising, O'Connor was in Ireland when it actually occurred. It is tempting to wonder whether, when he returned on 6 November, he was equally prepared to assume leadership in the events of the rising's success or disown it in the event of its failure. In Yorkshire, Bussey, who had once urged his supporters to purchase 'a rifle . . . a musket . . . a brace of pistols . . . a pike', also proved unable to live with his own oratory.[54] He feigned illness, sent one of his lieutenants around the county, perhaps to cancel the rising, and then fled to America where he was to remain for the next fourteen years. Ironically, perhaps, the Home Office records indicate a marked increase in the amount of drilling and arming among Chartists in the months *after* the Newport rising. Early in 1840, plans were laid to avenge the Newport fiasco. Once more, however, O'Connor — having given his blessing — apparently backed down, much to the disgust of Taylor. He complained bitterly in a later letter to Lovett that 'so long as O'Connor possesses any influence, the people will never be allowed to fight with any chance of success . . . the man who according to his own account was to die in the last ditch in the defence of Freedom, would not stir across the gutter to obtain it if there was a chance of even wetting his feet.'[55] The rising quickly fizzled out after a couple of nights' disturbances in

Bradford and Dewsbury and some brief success in Sheffield. Taylor, however, could perhaps derive some satisfaction from the fact that, this time, O'Connor was among those arrested.

By the summer of 1840, therefore, the rank and file of the Chartist movement was in a state of some confusion. Many of the journals had collapsed, and most of the movement's energies were devoted to agitating for the release of imprisoned leaders. A petition for Frost's release (the original death sentence on him had been commuted) contained over two million signatures when it was submitted in May 1841. To a considerable extent Chartism in this period depended, perhaps as never before, on the ability and dedication of local leaders; and it is ample testimony to the hold which the movement had on ordinary people that it survived at all. However, many different emphases now began to appear more strongly within it, and in some cases means began to subsume ends. The Chartist church movement which had prospered in Scotland began to spread southwards, flourishing especially in the Birmingham area and in Vincent's west country. In London Lovett, who had passed his time in prison preparing *Chartism: a New Organisation of the People*, proposed to launch a new organisation called the National Association for Promoting the Improvement of the People. He stressed the need for workers to try to win the vote by showing that they were an acceptable and responsible part of society. To this end, his plan was to encourage education and self-help, 'to redeem by reason what had been lost by madness and folly'.[56] Lowery was another who came to believe that social reform could not be effective unless supplemented or even preceded by moral reform. Henry Vincent, released from prison early in 1841, toured the country on behalf of teetotal Chartism so successfully that local Teetotal Chartist societies sprang up in many places. Hetherington, Hill and Cleave also shared his enthusiasm on the grounds that 'the ignorance and the vices of the people are the chief impediments in the way of all political and social improvement ... We especially appeal to all leaders of the Chartists to adopt the teetotal pledge.'[57] In Leeds and other provincial cities, Chartists turned to municipal electioneering, and councillors were elected at various times during the 1840s in Merthyr, Newport, Penzance, Nottingham, and in parts of Lancashire, Yorkshire and Scotland. In some places, success verged on the spectacular. By November 1849 Sheffield had twenty-two Chartist councillors. In the decade after 1843, eighteen of the twenty-five Chartist candidates were returned in Leeds. Elsewhere Chartism showed signs of its hybrid origins as the various elements from which it had been forged began to reassert themselves. At Nottingham, for instance, local Chartists took up the poor law issue again, bringing false charges against the administrators of the Basford workhouse in the hope of discrediting the system and gaining publicity for themselves.[58]

Despite these tendencies, some semblance of unity and national organisation was still provided by the National Charter Association (NCA), formed in July 1840 at a meeting of twenty-three Chartists in Manchester. Many Chartists, including Lovett, feared that the new body's constitution might be deemed illegal under the Corresponding Societies Act of 1799 and refused to join. Others, particularly in Scotland and parts of the midlands, were suspicious of its determined policy of centralisation. Growth was therefore slow, and by the end of 1840 just under three hundred local associations had affiliated. They were heavily concentrated: sixty each in Yorkshire and Lancashire, twenty-five in the Nottinghamshire-Derby area and thirty in London. Many of these, however, were probably nothing more than gatherings of dedicated Chartists. Although O'Connor later claimed a membership of 40,000, few seem to have made any consistent financial contribution to the NCA executive. As Matthew Fletcher disparagingly said, the NCA consisted in large part of 'miserable knots of a dozen or two in each town, meeting generally in some beer-shop'.[59]

Nevertheless the NCA was the only one of the new Chartist departures which O'Connor regarded with any favour. As for the rest, he feared that they threatened the movement with fragmentation. They would, he felt, 'lead to sectional and party dispute, and, ultimately, to class distinction . . . Get your Charter,' he advised, 'and I will answer for the religion, sobriety, knowledge, and house . . .'[60] O'Connor's suspicions also sprang from his fear that the new trends smacked of middle-class interference, and his fears were not without foundation. Lovett's association, for example, had considerable middle-class backing and its monthly subscription of 8d was in marked contrast with the subscription required by the NCA – also 8d, but per year. The success of Chartist municipal candidates in Leeds owed something to the efforts made in the city to reforge a Chartist-Radical alliance. The winter of 1841–2, which witnessed quite widespread public burnings of Peel's effigy by hungry workers, also saw agreements reached in several cities between Chartists and corn law repealers. O'Connor took the view that the Anti-Corn Law League offered working people the minimum necessary to gain support for its own ends; and in Lancashire there were open clashes between O'Connorites and corn law repealers who supported O'Connell.

There were also signs that some Chartists were turning to the Complete Suffrage Union, launched formally in Birmingham by Joseph Sturge in 1842, shortly before the second petition on behalf of the Charter was rejected by 287 to 49 in the House of Commons. Sturge's programme was designed to reconcile the middle and working classes. It included the repeal of class-based legislation and a declaration that the exclusion of a majority of the population from the franchise was both unchristian and unconstitutional. This attracted a good deal of interest, not only from middle-class reformers but also from those Chartists who had been alienated by the violence of 1840–1. In Scotland Sturge found a ready supporter in Brewster, while Vincent encouraged the movement in the west country. Dr Wade, Lovett and Place also lent support. At the first rally organised by the Complete Suffrage Union in Birmingham, O'Connorites were systematically excluded; and other towns adopted similar tactics in organising their own suffrage unions. Expedient as ever, O'Connor performed a rapid about-turn and declared his support for a middle-class alliance, even going so far as to support Sturge's candidature in a Nottingham by-election.

Before the alliance could be formally cemented, however, Chartist leadership was once more decimated by a fresh wave of arrests which took place in the aftermath of the Plug Plot riots. Against a background of deepening industrial depression, miners on the North Staffs coal field struck work in July. This was followed by a rash of strikes in the Lancashire textile industry, when employers tried to meet the depression by reducing wages. Mobs of strikers travelled through the county enforcing an almost total stoppage by drawing out the plugs of the factory boilers. Within weeks the strike wave spread across the Pennines into Yorkshire and then up to Scotland, where miners struck against wage cuts. In several towns troops were called in to quell civil disturbances. Almost as swiftly as it had begun, however, the movement began to die away, as strikers were forced back to work. Most historians have rightly dismissed the idea that the strike wave was launched by the Chartists and have suggested that their role was essentially one of trying to exploit the situation for their own ends. Yet their involvement was perhaps rather deeper than this might indicate. It is clear that many of those who spoke at the Manchester meetings which started the strikes in the textile industry were Chartists who had no connection with the cotton trade at all. A second opportunity for organised Chartist intervention was presented by a series of regional trade conferences held in August. Chartists were once more prominent in getting these conferences to adopt the Charter as the strike's main aim; and in cities like Manchester, Glasgow and London there was some convergence of Chartist and trade-union activity.[61] On the whole, however, the Chartist leadership was too divided to be able to take full advantage of the strike movement. If McDouall was in favour of pledging the NCA to support the strikers, both Harney and Hill opposed him. The unions themselves had little central machinery capable of organising anything very substantial in the way of a co-ordinated effort.

The Plug Plot movement had two adverse effects on the Chartists. Firstly, the effort made by some of them to organise the strikes for their own ends led authority to blame them for the strikes, hence the wave of arrests in September, including O'Connor who later got off on a technicality. Secondly, though by no means a universal reaction, trade-union disillusionment with Chartism probably increased. Thus in Stockport, for example, there was a large group of workers who consistently insisted that the strike was a matter of wages and conditions. They set up their own strike committee and issued a statement affirming that 'neither Politics nor Religion' should be permitted 'to interfere with the subject of Labour and Wages'.[62]

It was against this background that the NCA and the Birmingham Complete Suffrage Union (CSU) met in December to discuss their joint programme. The whole project collapsed in confusion, however, when CSU supporters rejected even the name of Chartism and proposed a ninety-six point bill of rights as a substitute for the Charter. This sacrifice was too much, even for moderates like Lovett, and it was at his prompting that the meeting rejected the CSU proposals. Sturge and his supporters thereupon quit the conference hall to draw up their bill of rights which subsequently was heavily defeated in the Commons. Lovett had no intention of remaining to work with O'Connor, and gradually he and others of like mind withdrew to pursue their own various forms of peaceful agitation. After a few disagreements with some of remaining national figures, O'Connor emerged firmly in control of the formal Chartist movement — which he promptly led off in entirely new directions.

One of his advances led into a dead end. The trade unions had provided many rank and file Chartists, particularly in London where the lower trades provided the bulk of the local leadership as well. After McDouall's unsuccessful recruiting efforts during the Plug Plot, the *Star* had given more coverage to industrial matters; and in 1845 it became the official organ of the National Association of United Trades for the Protection of Labour. Formed in March 1845, this association was composed mainly of the same type of craftsmen who backed metropolitan Chartism. Despite the association's high-sounding title, the *Star* was forced to confess of its inaugural meeting that 'Wales is absent; Scotland is absent; Ireland is absent; many parts of England are absent', adequate testimony to O'Connor's lack of success in tapping union support, probably because his own militance had alarmed them.[63]

If this was unsuccessful, O'Connor's land plan, which was accepted by a reshaped convention of fourteen delegates in

1845, proved to be a highly attractive proposition. It had been maturing in his mind for some time, although some of the credit should probably have been given to his friend, W.M. Wheeler, who helped him to write *A Practical Work on the Management of Small Farms* (1843).[64] Certainly as presented to the convention, it seemed to present not only an appealing programme, but also one which could prevent Chartism from fragmenting completely into the various elements of which it was composed. Basically the idea was to raise capital for a land company by permitting the purchase of shares at 3d or more a week. With the cash, land would be purchased and made into smallholdings complete with the necessary buildings. These holdings would then be rented to shareholders chosen by ballot. The idea was not novel, as there were already several similar schemes in existence. Initial progress was slowed by technical difficulties in securing legal recognition for the Chartist Land Company (partly because of the balloting procedure). Momentum gathered way once O'Connor purchased the first site near Watford. On May Day 1847, O'Connorville took its first tenants. Subscriptions soared. The plan had a general appeal in that it was rooted in land programmes derived from a line of radical thinkers including Spence, Paine and Cobbett.[65] It also struck chords in the hearts of those who believed that economic progress in the form of the machine had somehow dehumanised the individuality which had characterised the pre-industrial age. It seemed to represent an attempt to put the clock back and reverse the process of industrialisation. This mood was well caught by Ernest Jones, probably the most significant of the many Chartist poets.

> UP! Labourers in the vineyard!
> Prepare ye for your toil!
> For the sun shines on the furrows,
> And the seed is in the soil.[66]

O'Connor also benefited from the fact that he launched his scheme at a very auspicious time, when rising unemployment had generated increased interest in emigration and home colonisation as possible outlets for surplus labour. Many trade unions had started emigration funds, while other groups were running allotment societies. Accordingly, most of his initial support came from the industrial midlands and the north, although enthusiasm for it soon spread southwards.

By 1847 he had gathered sufficient cash to purchase for the re-named National Cooperative Land Company further estates at Lowbands, Snigs End, Minster Lovell, and Great Dodford. Some 250 people were already in occupancy, and in that one year of 1847 over £76,000 was subscribed by shareholders. O'Connor's personal position was further strengthened by his election as MP for Nottingham. He had high hopes that the third petition, now nearing completion, would be backed by five million signatories. Although this revival of Chartist fortunes was perhaps a modest one – Scotland had twenty active branches as against 169 in the peak year of 1839, for example – it still represented a substantial improvement in the movement's national reputation and standing. Nemesis, however, was very near.

Authority generally was uneasy at the Chartists' plans to present the third petition. For one thing, there were fears that Britain would be infected by the revolutionary spirit then sweeping across Europe, especially since Harney's Fraternal Democrats, organised in 1845, had been in contact with European radicals. Then there were fears lest the measures being proposed by the convention, which had assembled in April 1848, would tie down the army at a time when Irish militants were threatening rebellion. Certainly the numerous Irish connections of Chartism, not least O'Connor's own, gave added credibility to the claim made by *The Times* that 'the true character of the present movement is a ramification of the Irish conspiracy.'[67] Strong precautionary measures were therefore taken for 10 April when the third petition was due to be presented. Thousands of provincial Chartists arriving to accompany the petition to the Commons found London more akin to a fortress than a thriving commercial city. Eight thousand troops and 1500 Chelsea Pensioners had been drafted in to complement the thousands of hastily-sworn-in special constables. As before, these signs of government resolution were enough to frighten O'Connor into asking his supporters not to hold the procession which, he suggested, would merely give authority a chance to attack them. When he was summoned to meet the police commissioners after the petition had been ceremonially escorted to the mass meeting on Kennington Common, he agreed to call of the proposed procession to the Houses of Parliament altogether. In a characteristic speech, full of veiled threats and testimonials to his own record, he persuaded the vast crowd (estimated variously at half a million by O'Connor, 20,000 by *The Times*, and almost everything in between by the rest of the press) to disperse peacefully. Apart from a few minor scuffles with dissenters, therefore, the actual presentation of the petition had little of the dramatic impact for which the convention members had hoped.

Worse was to follow. Two days later it was announced that O'Connor's five million signatures included those of the Queen, the Duke of Wellington, and other equally unlikely individuals such as Pugnose, Nocheese and Snooks. O'Connor's bluster in the House of Commons fell even flatter when his five ton petition was officially weighed at a little over a quarter of a ton. For a few more weeks the convention, various local delegate meetings, and finally a national assembly considered various lines of action. They were paralysed however by internal disagreements and long-windedness to which was now added a great deal of mutual suspicion and recrimination. In London a second mass meeting was held on Bishop Bonner's Fields on 12 June and the authorities again responded with a heavy display of force. Once it was peacefully disbanded, a small committee appeared to begin planning a national rising with Irish support and the connivance of the NCA. After some hesitation, however, the government responded by arresting the ringleaders, and the plot was broken.

The final blow was not long delayed. In May Parliament had appointed a select committee to investigate the land company, which had come under scrutiny when O'Connor had tried to give it legal protection by amending the Friendly Societies Act. At the end of July, the committee reported that the company could not be registered as it was illegal. It further made the point that while there was no evidence to substantiate the rumours of fraud, the records and accounts were confused and inaccurate. Already having difficulty in getting rents from some of his tenants, O'Connor now found that the flow of share capital was drying up as well. After exploring several possible avenues to save the scheme, he finally took the route recommended by the select committee and wound the company up in 1851.

The following year Engels observed to Karl Marx that the Chartists were 'so completely disorganised and scattered, and at the same time so short of useful people, that they must either fall completely to pieces and degenerate into cliques . . . or they must be reconstituted'.[68] Within three years O'Connor was dead, dying demented in an asylum; and Gammage, one of Chartism's first historians, was lecturing on reasons for the movement's failure. In a technical sense he was perhaps a little premature, for Chartism did not immediately follow O'Connor into the grave. Its journals still flourished, though increasingly as the mouth-pieces of their individual owners or editors. Throughout the 1850s Chartist conferences continued to meet; although according to one hostile source the final assembly, attended by a mere forty-one delegates, only represented about five hundred people. Ernest Jones and his charter socialism achieved some following, especially in London among lower grades of craftsmen resentful of growing trade-union influence. Chartists also continued to be active in local politics, though this probably had less to do with their Chartism than with the fact that the sort of men who emerged as Chartist leaders tended to be the natural leaders in working-class communities anyway.[69] By 1860, however, organised Chartism was most certainly moribund. The last conference gathered in 1858, and two years later the NCA was formally wound up.

The disappearance of the movement and the failure to secure the Charter sprang from the fundamental organisational weaknesses. The whole process by which the convention was organised and financed exposed a crucial lack of administrative experience and imagination, while the rejection of the Charter showed how little parliamentary support the Chartists enjoyed. The parliamentary reformers of 1832 and the Anti-Corn Law League both used similar tactics to those of the

Chartists in order to whip up outside pressure, but in the end they were successful because they could rely on support within Parliament itself. The Chartists could not. Many middle-class radicals could go along quite happily with the Chartist political platform. Where they parted company was over the social component of their programme – hence the doubts expressed by many Chartists about the wisdom of working with the radicals at all.

Without much parliamentary backing or solid, middle-class support, the movement had either to give up altogether, repeat (as it did) the whole exercise of raising public support through petitions, or opt for less peaceful methods. The question of ultimate sanctions thus became a further divisive issue within Chartist ranks. In practice, the gap between physical and moral force was never as wide as it appeared. Many of the moral force men used very strong language, while many of the militants (O'Connor included) apparently shrank from putting their words into action. In fact, it has been suggested that there were not two but three Chartist strategies: moral force involving the use of economic pressure; intimidation by using the language of menace; and physical force, supported by Bussey, Harney and Taylor who tried to exploit all possible opportunities to stir up violence.[70] O'Connor's own actions certainly appear much more consistent in the light of such analysis and are aptly described as intimidation by strong language.

Just as the issue of tactics divided Chartists, so too did the precise aims and purposes of the movement. All were agreed on the injustices and imperfections of the prevailing social system, and it was this agreement which gave Chartism its underlying ideological unity. For a while, it also transcended the many different remedies and emphases to be found among Charter supporters; but there is no doubt that Chartism meant different things to different people. To Lancashire textile workers, it held out the prospect of economic improvement and factory reform. To the London artisan, it pointed the way to political equality. In Wales it was tinged with nationalism, in Scotland with the ethics of self improvement. East Anglia and Wales saw the mingling of Chartism with older forms of protest and traditional targets. Similarly, the various national leaders had different ends in view. Lovett saw the franchise as one element in a general programme of social improvement: indeed, he was accused by one critic of wishing to 'reform men in a middle class image'.[71] For Ernest Jones, Chartism was equated with socialism, which is probably why he contemptuously dismissed Gammage's *History* as 'disgusting trash'.[72] Frost and Stephens saw the movement primarily as a means to oppose the new poor law. To O'Brien, the success of the Charter would bring with it the opportunity to secure currency reform and land nationalisation. O'Connor viewed a democratic franchise as the political counterpart of his plan to re-establish a revitalised peasantry on its own land. If all these differences were symptomatic of a general resentment against the existing order, ideological unity did not extend to organisation. The only tangible symbols of unity were provided by the Chartist press, particularly the *Northern Star*, the convention, and the Charter itself. Once the convention lost credibility, once the papers collapsed or became outlets for individuals, and once the petition was rejected, the various interest groups with varying degrees of alacrity began to seek alternative ways of realising their ends.

Failure, however, is not to be equated with insignificance. The Chartist movement was important in that it embodied the shift from older forms of pre-industrial protest to new ones, or at least consideration of new ones, such as the general strike and attempts to exert pressure through mass organisation — both more relevant to the newly emerging industrial urban society.[73] It also encompassed the transition from the old radical critique of traditional landed society to more appropriate anti-capitalist criticisms. Thus Jones was to be found putting forward the Marxian theory of value. Harney's views included the claim that non-workers had 'no right to exist'.[74] O'Brien did much to popularise the concept of wage slavery. Even O'Connor, for all that he was no socialist, based his land plan on the premise that industrial society required a permanent reserve army of unemployed in order to keep wages down. It was no coincidence that in the socialist revival of the 1880s Chartist literature was much in evidence. It has even been claimed that, with their intense interest in European affairs, Harney's Fraternal Democrats were 'the first organised international group to raise the banner of proletarian solidarity, before even the First International'.[75] This is misleading, however. Chartist internationalism, like that of the later socialists, was heavily tinged with xenophobia.[76] The influence of the Fraternal Democrats was pretty much confined to London, which tended to attract European exiles anyway. Provincial Chartists were much more concerned with bread-and-butter questions, and the delegate at the 1846 Convention who raised the matter of Polish independence was very promptly ruled out of order.

Chartism has been seen as the first, organised, mass working-class movement in British history: a valid description if one considers both the geographical and occupational breadth of its support and also the unprecedented involvement of women. At least eighty political unions and Chartist associations for women have been traced for the period 1837–44; there may well have been others. Even allowing for the large number of bogus signatories, the five million names on the third petition were a significant achievement. 'Movement' is perhaps misleading, however. Chartism did not draw in the trade unions in any formal way; the Plug Plot being nothing more than an industrial dispute which local Chartists, against the advice of national leaders, tried to exploit. Little was done to bridge the gap between rural and urban workers. The Webbs (and others) with their Whiggish view of history may have seen Chartism as a vital stage in the inevitable onward progress of organised labour. It was nothing of the kind. There may well have been those who shared the ideologies of Harney, O'Brien and Ernest Jones, but Robert Lowery was probably nearer the mark when he commented upon the overwhelming ignorance and apathy of the masses.[77] For most of its supporters Chartism was a matter of economics. This primary concern with knife-and-fork issues explains why the peaks of agitation coincided with the depths of slumps in the later 1830s and again in the late forties. The impact of such slumps was much more severe in the urban-industrial environment, since there was often little alternative work and traditional relief agencies either did not exist or were (like the poor law) in the process of being modified. To many therefore, the heady rhetoric of the Chartist leaders had a natural appeal. In particular, the land plan appeared to hold out hopes of security and independence which industrialisation was felt to have undermined. It was here that O'Connor's influence in particular was so crucial.

While many historians have explained the Chartist failure in terms of organisational weakness, internal division, and a reluctance to use violence, others have argued that it was murdered by O'Connor. In part such verdicts are a product of sources which are very heavily biased against him. Much of our knowledge of Chartism is gained from evidence prejudiced in favour of LWMA's standpoint – that organisation's own minutes, the papers of Francis Place, and the autobiography of Lovett who damned O'Connor explicitly. Lovett replied to O'Connor's attack on his proposals for the establishment of a national association by stating that he had been anxious 'to redeem by reason what had been lost by madness and folly'.[78] O'Brien left a similarly jaundiced portrait in his work, *De Brassier: a Democratic Romance.* Although he denied it strongly, there is little doubt that this story of a wealthy aristocrat entering politics to escape his debts and satisfy his own ambition was based on the author's opinion of O'Connor. It must be conceded that O'Connor's carelessness with figures and accounts contributed to the final collapse of the land plan, that his oratory alienated as many as it attracted, and that he deliberately drove out of the organisation many able leaders. Yet it can be said in his defence that in driving out his rivals O'Connor probably helped to preserve the movement's basic unity longer than might otherwise have been the case, because he insisted on keeping the Charter as the primary objective. Further, his oratory, his newspaper and general charisma did more than anything else to create and then sustain the agitation. It says much for his hold on the popular imagination that his supporters endured with apparent equanimity his several changes of tack. Indeed, George Weerth suggested that O'Connor had this place 'precisely because of his less desirable qualities . . . his frequent imbecility . . . his blind enthusiasm . . . his homely and only too frequent childish humour'.[79] Perhaps this was because he not only successfully conjured up for ordinary people the exciting vision of an alternative society, but in the land plan came closer than anyone else in the nineteenth century to realising that vision. O'Connor tapped not some inherent working-class instinct for unity, but rather that sense of bewilderment and insecurity which characterised so much early-nineteenth-century labouring life.

4

The Years of Adjustment, 1850-75

In March 1863, Richard Cobden observed somewhat dispiritedly to his friend, William Hargreaves, 'I suppose it is the reaction from the follies of Chartism which keeps the present generation so quiet.'[1] In much the same vein John Snowden wrote to Ernest Jones about the Halifax area. 'Many of those that were once active Chartists have emigrated. And others, though residing here as usual, have become so thoroughly disgusted at the indifference and utter inattention of the multitude to their best interests that they too are resolved to make no more sacrifices in a public cause.'[2] For its part, government seemed much less afraid of popular aspirations in this period. By the 1860s, only twenty years after rumours of armed Chartists had caused such alarm, Parliament was confident enough to sanction financial assistance for the Volunteers: an armed, mainly working-class militia whose members kept their weapons at home. In the preface to *Alton Locke*, Charles Kingsley commented that the existence of the Volunteers was an 'absolute proof of the changed relation between the upper and lower classes . . . these volunteer corps are becoming centres of cordiality between class and class.'[3] Similarly, fears expressed in the early nineteenth century that the rising crime rate was part of a general social threat had moderated by mid-century to 'a view of crime as a normal problem inherent in industrial society, to be dealt with on a normal day to day basis by preventive, detective and penal measures'.[4] Historians, too, have been struck by the swift transition from the turmoil of the Chartist forties to the relative social harmony of the next quarter-century. Several explanations have been offered, though these are by no means mutually exclusive.

One is that the key to social harmony in the period lay in the non-militant nature of the intellectual influences to which the working class was exposed.[5] The briefly-important Christian socialists advanced a theory of co-operation which had a social as well as an economic purpose. It was designed, said F.D. Maurice, to show 'how a human relationship may be substituted for the mere animal connection between Driver and Slave'.[6] The Christian socialists were succeeded as the labour movement's intellectual mentors by positivists such as Frederic Harrison, E.S. Beesley, and Henry Crompton: all of whom played an important role in the campaign to reform trade-union law. They, too, had an essentially humanitarian appeal and were opposed to violence. They had only come together in the first place to seek ways of minimising social conflict of the type which occurred during the London building strike of 1859. Since such influences were brought to bear only upon labour movement leaders, it is difficult to see how they can account for a *general* shift in attitudes, unless the untenable assumption is made that the labour movement and the working class were the same thing. Secondly, it seems highly unlikely that individuals would be swayed by theoretical arguments about social harmony which may well have contradicted their own experience of social and economic reality. Finally and most damning, the explanation assumes that working people were incapable of generating any radical militant ideas of their own. One has to look no further than the contemporary activities and beliefs of the Soho O'Brienites, never mind those of earlier radicals, to see the fallacy of this.[7]

Another school of historians has taken the view that the changed social climate can be explained with reference to civic incorporation theory: that once the working class was incorporated into the nation's political structure by means of universal suffrage, its threatening stance gave way to an acceptance of the status quo.[8] Certainly popular interest in franchise reform did not die away with the demise of the Chartists. Individuals such as O'Brien continued to preach the message, and others contested elections. Jones stood at Nottingham in 1859 and F.R. Lees at Ripon the following year. Many important working-class leaders voiced their belief in the inherent right of their class to have a say in political affairs. Thus Robert Applegarth of the Amalgamated Society of Carpenters and Joiners could assert that 'we must not forget that we are citizens, and as such should have citizen's rights.'[9] When in 1862 the two Georges of the labour movement, Howell and Odger, launched the Trades Unionist Manhood Suffrage and Vote By Ballot Association, it was on the basis of a belief in 'the natural and God-given rights of every man to equal political rights'.[10] The formation in 1864 of the International Working Men's Association gave a further focus to working-class interest in franchise extension. At the beginning of 1865, these various elements merged in the Reform League. Quite soon this body had a hundred branches in London and three times that number in England and Wales.

In its national campaigning for a reform bill, the Reform League worked quite closely with the middle-class Reform Union. This was partly because middle- and working-class radicals had been drawn together in the early 1860s by their response to the American civil war, enthusiasm for Garibaldi's visit to London, and their mutual sympathy for the cause of Polish independence. At a more mundane level, however, the league was heavily dependent on the union for finance; and this weakened its ability to hold firm to the Chartist principle of one man, one vote against the union's willingness to accept the compromise of household suffrage. The defeat of Gladstone's reform bill in 1866, however, prompted Bright and other middle-class reform leaders into fuller and more generous co-operation with the league. It also ushered in a more militant phase of agitation. In July the authorities tried to ban a reform rally in Hyde Park, but the police were unable to restrain the vast crowds. For three days the park was occupied by demonstrators. All through the autumn of 1866 the campaign was intensified through public meetings and lobbying of influential figures. The Conservative government of Disraeli and Derby, however, seemed unconcerned and apparently had no intention of bringing in a bill in 1867. Although pressure from within the Conservative party itself and also from the Liberals forced Disraeli to change his mind, the household suffrage measure which was produced satisfied none of the reformers. Weekly demonstrations were organised in Trafalgar Square and plans made for a large-scale public meeting in Hyde Park. The Home Secretary, Spencer Walpole, mindful of recent events in the park, tried to prevent the meeting from taking place. Although police were massed and backed by troops summoned from Aldershot, by 4 May it is clear that the government had privately decided to ignore its own prohibition. The meeting went ahead as planned on 6 May, watched but not stopped by the forces of law and order. Shortly afterwards the reform bill of 1867 was passed, shorn now of most of the restrictions which had previously made it unacceptable to the reformers. Some of the larger industrial towns were given greater parliamentary representation, while the vote was extended in the boroughs to house-holders who had been in residence for a year and to lodgers paying more than £10 per year in rent. In the counties, the vote was granted to occupiers of houses rated at more than £12 a year and to leaseholders in premises worth at least £4 per annum.

It is difficult, however, to fit these events and their outcome into any theory of civic incorporation. For one thing, the act of 1867 merely extended the franchise. It did not introduce universal male suffrage: this was not achieved until 1918. Even the assumption that the measure enfranchised all industrial workers who were householders is ill-founded. Because of the way the act was implemented, some qualified industrial workers were excluded, as were all those living outside borough boundaries. This had the effect, for instance, of omitting significant numbers of miners, especially those in the north-east.[11] Secondly, the theory begs entirely the question of why and how a moderate labour movement was able to secure from a relatively strong government a measure of political incorporation in the 1860s which a more aggressive and militant movement had been unable to wrest from a much weaker executive in the 1840s. Clearly, one cannot discount entirely the effect of pressure from below in securing the 1867 bill. The fact that Disraeli conceded amendments very shortly after the Hyde Park meeting seems to nullify his assertion that he was not bowing to popular pressure. It is doubtful, too, if Parliament would have accepted the inevitability of reform without popular pressure. On the other hand, there is no doubt that Disraeli's main concern was to dish the Whigs; and it is also apparent that much of the middle-class support for an extension of the franchise sprang from a conviction that some sections of the working class were now worthy of voting, because they had *already* appeared to be willing to abide by the rules of middle-class society. Finally, it is perhaps legitimate to question the notion of incorporation when those workers who did receive the vote still had no option but to cast it for the nominees of the two main parties. It is true that the election of 1874 did see the return, under Liberal auspices, of the first two working-class MPs, Alexander Macdonald and Thomas Burt, both miners. On the whole, however, the Labour Representation League, which emerged when the Reform League was wound up in 1869, did not prove very successful in its stated objective of getting working-class candidatures for parliamentary vacancies. Liberal opposition was far too strong.

There can be little doubt that what made the crucial difference to the campaign for political reform was the more positive attitude taken by the trade unions once Gladstone's 1866 bill was defeated. While individual members had been actively involved in the reform movement, the unions themselves had tended to be lukewarm, just as they had been in the Chartist era. One counter-tendency to this, however, was the emergence in most major cities of local trades councils in the 1850s and early sixties. Sheffield Trades Council was launched in 1858, Edinburgh's a year later. In Dublin thirty unions set up a United Trades Association in 1863, and the Birmingham Trades Council came into being in 1866. London traced its continuous history from 1860. The initial purpose of most of these bodies had been to organise action and policy on local industrial matters, and many grew out of *ad hoc* committees set up to monitor particular local strikes or lock-outs. In both Birmingham and Sheffield, for instance, it was the hated Document which provided the initial stimulus for the founding of trades councils. Gradually these organisations had been drawn into local political affairs. In Edinburgh the reform movement was organised by the trades council, which brought forward independent working-class candidates in municipal elections. As early as 1861 the Glasgow Trades Council had given a general lead by issuing an address which urged trade unionists to make themselves the basis of the movement for political reform. It was a plea given added weight by the economic crisis of the middle 1860s, which prompted one labour correspondent to claim that it was political power 'which gives the capitalist the social means and the social influence which enable him to throw out of employment and reduce to starvation a thousand workmen if they do not obey his orders'. What, he went on, 'but the want of political power dooms the workmen to that socially degraded state in which their dignity perishes and their independence with it?'[12] The *Bee-Hive* was observing a general trend when it reported in 1867 that the typical northern worker was 'finding out that the franchise has something to do with wages and the work, and even the very right to make a free bargain with his employer'.[13]

This comment undoubtedly provides the clue to growing trade-union interest in political affairs, for events in the 1860s had brought their whole legal status into question once more. The successful outcome of the union campaign against this threat is sometimes implicitly interpreted as an extension of civic incorporation theory. In this view, the dying-down of working-class agitation came about because the unions themselves were incorporated into bourgeois society. Increasingly they were accepted as the legitimate representatives of working-class aspirations and accorded due legal recognition and bargaining rights.

Trade-union law was still unclear in a number of respects by the middle of the nineteenth century. It was uncertain whether a union could legally own property, and the very right to strike was called into question by the application of the law of conspiracy to the London tailors' strike of 1867. The precise meaning of the Combination Laws Repeal Amendment Act of 1825 was not agreed either; since the measure had penalised violence, threats and intimidation, and referred to matters such as obstruction and molestation without offering any definitions of these terms, except violence. Thus there was scope for considerable judicial disagreement. Some judges held that the law should apply only to physical acts, while others maintained that the essence of the offence was the intent that lay behind an action. Two decisions of

1851 (Regina v Duffield and Regina v Rowlands) produced a situation in which the existence of unions whose purpose was to raise wages was deemed lawful, but the means by which wage claims could be pursued were heavily proscribed. Equally invidious was the operation of the Master and Servant Law. It left employers who broke contracts with their employees to be dealt with under the civil law, while employees who broke contracts were liable to criminal proceedings. The *Bee-Hive* reported in November 1866, for example, on the case of three miners who each received fourteen days' hard labour for refusing to enter a pit made unsafe by fire-damp.[14] Since employees were rarely given written contracts anyway, it was almost impossible to bring a case against an employer. By the 1860s, however, prosecutions against workers were running at 10,000 a year.[15]

Nor were union finances any safer under law than they had been earlier in the century. It is quite apparent that most trade unionists believed that their funds were protected against fraudulent conversion by the Friendly Societies Act of 1859, a belief based on a statement made by Gladstone when the act was passed. As one witness to the Royal Commission on Trade Unions said in 1867, 'I was under the impression that as long as the rules were deposited, if the rules were perfectly legal we should have the protection of the Act.'[16] Prior to 1867 legal opinion would seem to have shared this view; and it was thus both unexpected and unwelcome when an attempt by Bradford boilermakers to recover £24 from their absconding treasurer (Hornby v Close) was ruled out on the ground that unions operated in restraint of trade, were therefore illegal, and could not claim the protection of the Friendly Societies Act. William Allan of the engineers immediately affirmed that 'we are placed in a very different position from what we expected we occupied', while the *Bee-Hive* lamented about 'one of the heaviest blows that has yet fallen on trades' unions . . . the decision places all societies at the mercy of any of their officers or members who may rob them of their funds'.[17]

The Hornby v Close case followed hard upon the heels of another blow which the union movement had sustained in the form of the 1866 Sheffield outrages, when sawgrinders had attempted to murder a strike breaker by exploding gunpowder in the cellar of his house. Public reaction was well caught in an anonymous *Quarterly Review* article which condemned out of hand the 'system of terrorism that lurks behind these Trade Unions'.[18] Nor was this quite the over-reaction it might first appear, because there had been other similar incidents during the same period. Northamptonshire shoemakers demonstrated violently in the 1850s against the introduction of the sole-sewing machine which could produce some 300 stitches a minute as against the ten to twenty a handworker could manage. They held up its diffusion for some years, although ultimately they were defeated. In brick-making, the mid-Victorian boom had witnessed the development of automatic brickmaking machines, threatening the privileged position of the temperers who mixed the clay by hand and also of the moulders who shaped it. There was a sustained and often violent resistance as employers tried to work the machines with non-union labour.[19] Generally this type of activity was dying out among trade unionists and was largely confined to those trades undergoing rapid technological change, usually for the first time. In the public mind, however, there was little to chose between the Sheffield sawgrinders and the Glasgow vitriol throwers of thirty years ago. Both seemed equally representative of the same trade-union movement. Reporting a stay he made in Bristol at this time, Isaac Ironside noted the observation of a fellow guest that 'if there were a commission appointed to examine into all trade secrets, perhaps Sheffield would not look so bad.'[20]

In fact, establishing a royal commission was exactly what the government decided to do, spurred on no doubt by the fact that leading trade unionists had petitioned for some form of public inquiry in the belief that it could only improve their image. In particular this demand had come from George Potter of the London builders and also from his main rivals, the leaders of the London-based amalgamated societies, collectively christened by the Webbs as the Junta. The commission's mandate was a wide one, ranging from inquiring into union rules, industrial relations, and intimidation to making recommendations about legal changes. Its composition was scarcely calculated to inspire much confidence among

unionists, however, since it included the anti-union director
of the Great Western Railway and also the notorious anti-
union MP, J.A. Roebuck. Only Frederic Harrison and Thomas
Hughes were known to be at all sympathetic to the union
position. There was thus a good deal of truth in Potter's
claim that it was 'the old, old story, the wolves sitting on a
commission inquiring into the benefits and promotion of the
sheep interests'.[21] Yet the results of the inquiry were far
more favourable to the unions than they had dared hope, all
the more surprising because shortly before the commission
began hearing evidence the full extent of the Sheffield outrages was revealed, prompting *The Times* to comment that
'not only the Ten Commandments, but every law, human and
Divine, is suspended, and an arbitrary code of Trade rules
substituted in their stead.'[22]

The commission produced a majority report and three
minority ones, the most significant being the work of Harrison
and Hughes to which Lord Lichfield also subscribed. It was
this report that formed the basis of the government legislation
of 1871. The original intention was to leave the unions open
to prosecution under the 1825 act, but to confer legal recognition on them by permitting them to register under the
Friendly Societies Act. Intensive parliamentary lobbying
ensured that these proposals were in fact kept in two separate
bills. Thus the Trade Union Act of 1871 afforded legal status,
while the Criminal Law Amendment Act left them exposed
to prosecution and was so amended in the House of Lords
that it virtually prohibited even the mildest forms of picketing.
More intensive lobbying secured a further measure from the
Conservative government in 1875: the Conspiracy and Protection of Property Act. This legalised picketing and forbade
the application of the law of conspiracy to strikes, unless of
course acts which were in themselves illegal were perpetrated.
The Employers and Workmen Act followed, specifying equal
treatment under civil law for broken contracts by both
workmen and employers.

Almost certainly the highly favourable outcome of the
commission owed something to the appearance in 1869 of
Thornton's work, *On Labour*, which repudiated the concept
of the wage fund as developed along Ricardian-Malthusian

lines by Nassau Senior. The theory stated that the level of wages was determined by the means available for their payment. Since these means, or wage fund, were dependent upon profits, it followed that any attack on profits would reduce the source from which wages came. In the long run, therefore, it was argued that union efforts to increase wages (unless profits were also rising) were self-defeating, or could only be successful at the expense of other workers. In demolishing the logic of this, Thornton pulled away one of the main intellectual props for what had often been nothing more than sheer prejudice. More important, however, was the skilful way in which the union leaders organised and presented their case. Applegarth attended all the commission's sittings, carefully schooled his witnesses, and provided valuable assistance to Harrison and Hughes. Harrison subsequently recalled that while the employers had been 'well supplied with facts and figures by the masters' agents', they were 'not nearly so well supplied as we were by Applegarth, Howell and Allan, the Union Secretaries'.[23] Although they could not totally exonerate the unions from charges of restrictive practices, the union witnesses did manage to focus attention on their more acceptable activities, particularly their benefit functions. In the process they had to withstand some very probing questions from two actuaries brought in to prove that the financial basis of these operations was fundamentally unsound.[24]

Once the commission had presented its findings, there was a marked shift in public attitudes towards unions. *The Times*, so critical of the Sheffield outrages, now moderated its tone considerably. 'True statesmanship,' it declared, 'will seek neither to augment nor to reduce their influence, but accepting it as a fact will give it free scope for legitimate development.'[25] John Stuart Mill noted the new attitude as well. 'I have been happy to observe that the indiscriminate prejudice against trade unions which had been so much stimulated by the obnoxious crimes brought home to the officers of a few of them by the inquiries of the Royal Commission, has been greatly corrected by the general results of those inquiries . . .'[26]

One other important by-product was the emergence of the Trades Union Congress as a genuine focus of trade-union activity. Originally the creation of northern unions, the TUC was designed to provide a forum for the discussion of opinion. Once the legislative intentions of the Liberal government became clear in 1870, the Junta leaders — who had effectively dominated the union case before the Royal Commission — decided that they required wider backing than that provided by their own Conference of Amalgamated Trades. So although they had not bothered to attend the first meetings of the TUC, they were represented at the third conference, held in London in 1870. Immediately they made their presence felt by securing the election of their nominee, George Howell, as secretary. Howell's earlier links with middle-class reformers made him the ideal go-between for the extensive lobbying that the unions conducted in order to get the various trade-union bills amended. Furthermore, the importance of union legislation at this time caused the TUC to become something more than a talking shop. It developed interests in policy formation, and the Nottingham conference (1872) authorised the parliamentary committee to formulate standing orders to make congress procedure more efficient. It also authorised the officers to raise funds by levies and voluntary subscriptions. This guaranteed the future of the parliamentary committee as the *de facto* executive of the first effective, national trade-union body in Britain's history.

There can be no doubt that the appearance of the TUC, the election of the first working-class MPs, the securing of a much greater degree of legal protection for trade unions, and the granting of a much broader recognition of their place by employers and general public alike all mark out the third quarter of the nineteenth century as one of considerable progress for organised industrial workers. But to return to our original question, can this be seen as part of a process by which working-class discontent was nullified via incorporation? It seems unlikely. For one thing most of the developments so far discussed came far too late to account for a change which is commonly located in the 1850s. More important was the fact that the unions by no means represented the working class as a whole. 'Between the artisan and the unskilled labourer,' wrote Thomas Wright in 1873, 'a gulf is fixed ... The artisan creed with regard to the labourer is, that they are an inferior class, and that they should be made to know and kept in their place.'[27] Total trade-union member-ship remained small, fluctuating with changes in the level of employment and the incidence of strikes. Harrison estimated membership at about 500,000 in 1865; a decade later Howell claimed three times that number. This seems much too high, for it will be remembered that this was also the figure given in the first official count, taken in 1892 after a well-attested period of expansion. Men were still dominant, as women were difficult to organise and did not usually receive much encouragement from males who tended to regard them as a likely source of unfair (i.e. cheap) labour. Nevertheless, in some industries in which women made up a significant proportion of the labour force, attempts at organisation did occur. About half the members of the North East Lancashire Amalgamated Weavers Association (1858) were women. Female organisation received a further boost in 1874, when Emma Patterson established the Women's Protective and Provident League. Though not a trade union itself, this league was instrumental in encouraging the organisation of women. By 1875 women had made sufficient headway to gain official representation at the annual TUC conferences.

Not only was the union movement unrepresentative of the working class as a whole, it was itself very much a hotchpotch of different structures and its importance varied considerably from region to region. Outside of Dublin and Belfast, trade unionism remained generally weak in Ireland. Glasgow, the regional centre of shipbuilding and engineering, was the focal point in west Scotland. There were several important and well-established groups in London, mainly craftsmen, but the presence in the capital of a relatively high proportion of unskilled and casual workers had a generally debilitating effect. Unionism was strong in the north-east where mining, shipbuilding and iron working were well-organised, staple industries. Lancashire, dominated by miners, engineers and textile operatives, was probably the most highly unionised county of all. If it is clear that in the nation as a whole builders, textile workers, shipbuilders and miners were among the most highly organised groups by the third quarter of the nineteenth century, figures for union density are difficult to find and often contradictory. Alfred Mault, secretary of the General Builders Association, suggested in 1867 that only about seventeen per cent of masons and ten per cent of carpenters were members of trade unions. He was a notorious anti-union figure, however, and his figures differ markedly from those of George Howell — though Howell's own estimates of sixty-six and fifty per cent respectively may well reflect that same optimism noted above. What is certain is that trade unionism was still generally restricted to miners, factory workers, and craftsmen; though the 1870s saw the first stirrings of organisation among both relatively unskilled groups, like dockers and farm labourers, and some white-collar workers, like school teachers.

It is still more difficult to see the unions as the vehicle of working-class incorporation when it is remembered that the movement was itself divided. It is here, perhaps, that the dead hand of the Webbs lies heaviest, for they all but succeeded in obscuring important tactical and structural differences. While they were certainly correct to emphasise the role played by the leaders of the amalgamated societies in orchestrating the campaign for trade-union law reform, they greatly exaggerated the overall significance of these societies. For instance, they placed great weight on the general influence exerted by the so-called new model unions on trade-union structures in this period. These unions, best exemplified in the Amalgamated Society of Engineers (ASE) which was established in 1851, had highly centralised systems of policy and financial control and provided quite comprehensive, insurance-based relief for those members who were on strike, unemployed or sick. In order to facilitate these operations, the union (according to the Webbs) followed a very pacific policy of industrial relations, wherever possible encouraging branches to resort to arbitration rather than strike action. The ASE's stress on benefit functions was not new: it was an adaptation of practices adopted earlier by several unions, including the steam engine makers out of which the ASE itself had grown. Nor did the engineers provide an organisational model in any meaningful sense for other workers. Other unions may have adopted the term 'amalgamated' as part of their title, but only the carpenters and joiners consciously modelled themselves on the ASE. Insofar as there was any general tendency towards centralised control of the type favoured by the engineers, it owed more to the bureaucratising tendencies inherent in the accumulation of large funds and to the increasingly national scope of the labour market. In any case, many unions did not adopt centralised organisation. Lancashire's cotton unions remained only loosely federated; and the miners still functioned primarily at county level, though the first national organisations – the National Miners Association and the Amalgamated Association of Miners – had been established in 1863 and 1869 respectively.

Nor were the Webbs correct in asserting that the amalgamated societies provided a general leadership for the union movement. In London itself they were opposed by Potter of the builders, who had re-established the LWMA in the 1860s and who also enjoyed considerable influence through his control of the *Bee-Hive* newspaper. Although of limited appeal, the *Bee-Hive* was a well-produced paper and enjoyed a much wider readership than its peak circulation of about 8000 would suggest.[28] There were also powerful unions, mainly in the north of England, who looked upon the amalgamated societies with suspicion. In 1866 these unions had established the United Kingdom Alliance of Organised Trades to provide mutual assistance in strikes against wage reductions. This body had also asked the London Trades Council (LTC) to organise a conference to discuss industrial unrest, which was sweeping the country in the late 1860s. The LTC, however, was under the domination of the amalgamated societies who ignored the request. Potter promptly stepped in and convened the meeting under the auspices of the LWMA. It was attended by delegates representing some 178,000 members. Although there was some double counting, it certainly warranted the later verdict that it was 'a pretty representative assembly'.[29] The conference produced a pamphlet highly critical of the Junta unions, and Potter kept up a ceaseless barrage in the *Bee-Hive*. 'The conduct of Messrs Odger, Allan, Applegarth and Coulson,' he stormed, 'has been characterised by a degree of selfishness, spleen, petty jealousy and untruthfulness that . . . must disentitle them to any further confidence as leading men in the union movement.'[30]

On the whole, therefore, it is difficult to see how either

the extension of the franchise or the relaxation of legal restraints against the unions could account for any general lessening of social tension, simply because neither development affected more than a minority of the population. This has not deterred historians of the left from suggesting that working-class quiescence was due to the anodyne leadership provided by this privileged minority of trade unionists or labour aristocracy. Anxious to explain why British workers failed to revolt against a system which (according to Marx) should have progressively impoverished them, they have argued that capitalism was able to contain this revolutionary potential by buying off the skilled workers who were the natural leaders of the working class. This group thereby acquired a vested interest in preserving existing social arrangements and the values which buttressed them. Thus the moderate nature of the labour movement at this time, it has been asserted, 'derived from a decision by the ruling class to use the profits of empire to create a privileged social stratum, a Labour Aristocracy'.[31] This was the phenomenon to which Engels referred when he complained that 'the British working class is becoming more and more bourgeois.'[32] As one more recent writer has put it, this labour aristocracy 'did not wish to destroy the Capitalist fortress, but merely knocked humbly at its gates in the hope that they would be let in'.[33]

There is no doubt that some workers did do rather better for themselves than others in this period, establishing better working conditions, higher wages, and greater prospects of security and advance. There is also some evidence from local studies that such workers tended to isolate themselves socially from the masses. Marriage registers for Kentish London indicate a considerable amount of intermarrying among the labour aristocrats' families and also some reaching out towards the non-manual strata.[34] In Edinburgh, higher paid workers moved to the more attractive parts of the city; the same was true of Stourbridge glassmakers, who began to move in the 1850s to the more select area of Ambelcote, north of the town.[35] There were still marked regional variations in wage rates and, less commonly, in hours of work; but the most authoritative account reckons that generally the differentials between skilled and unskilled were very marked in the 1850s and changed only very slowly over the next sixty years.[36] Yet it remains difficult to identify with any precision exactly who the aristocrats were, a problem compounded by the fact that the term was not widely used in working-class circles until the 1880s.[37] While wages did mark off the skilled from the unskilled, there still existed other divisions which cut across even this line. Industrial development had progressed very unevenly in the nineteenth century, and skilled machine operatives were still in the minority. The presence of a substantial proportion of Irish workers in the labour force was still a divisive element. Within the rural workforce certain jobs could be classified as aristocratic which could not be so designated in the context of the labour force as a whole. Where too are the growing numbers of white-colour workers with their generally lower wages but higher social status to be placed in relation to the labour aristocrats?

Engels himself seems to have thought of the aristocrats in terms of those who had served an apprenticeship, but even this definition is not without its difficulties. Formal apprenticeship in which skills were learned survived in trades such as boilermaking and printing, but more generally it was declining in the nineteenth century under the impact of continuous technological change and migration from rural areas. Howell reckoned in the 1860s that only about a tenth of trade unionists had been properly apprenticed. Even if apprenticeship was losing its connotations as a skill-learning process, other forms of controlling labour supply could be developed: particular groups of workers had special scarcity value, held strategic positions in production, or were strongly organised. In mining, for example, workers progressed through a succession of tasks more or less quickly according to local conditions and their own aptitude, until they reached the prestigious and most highly paid job of all — hewing. The highest grades of workers in the iron industry served no formal apprenticeship but depended on qualities such as strength and stamina. Engineers and joiners had a system whereby any man who had served five years at the trade was deemed to have completed his apprenticeship, and the number of such trainees was strictly limited in order to control the supply of time-served men. In textiles, the well-organised spinners were able to insist that machine minders should be recruited by seniority at individual mills from the piecers, who were restricted to two per machine.

From these systems has developed a more refined definition of the aristocrats as those who were employed in industry as pace-setters and technical supervisors.[38] By now mechanisation had rendered many traditional engineering skills unnecessary, but it is argued that their practitioners remained in the industry in positions of authority over less skilled machine workers. In the same way, spinners emerged as pace-setters in cotton textiles, becoming managerial tools in the enforcement of work discipline. Thus, it is argued, it will not do to dismiss the theory of the labour aristocracy on the grounds that such aristocratic workers had existed before.[39] This aristocracy was a new one that owed its existence to, and was a product of, modern technological development. It had, so it is argued, no history unconnected with that of capitalism and no history beyond the industrial revolution. There is perhaps some substance in this approach when it is applied to engineering, but it is difficult to see how it can apply to the cotton industry. Here the pace-setters and the workers whom they were supposed to dupe in the interests of managerial profit were frequently members of the same family. How, one wonders, could the former betray the latter? Further research into other industries is needed before the general validity of this approach can be verified.

What we seem to have in this period, as indeed in earlier ones, are indications that the working class was divided into many different and sometimes conflicting interest groups according to population, income, residence and so on. Effectively the labour aristocrats seem to be almost synonymous with the trade unions. It does not follow from this that the aristocrats meekly accepted contemporary bourgeois values as the price to be paid for their privileged position; certainly this was not the case as far as industrial relations was concerned. Contemporary political economy was based on the assumption that there was a harmony of interest between employer and employed. Yet Allan told the Royal Commission on Trade Unions that the two were diametrically opposed, while G.D. Pownall proclaimed that by their every action unions asserted that 'capital and labour have pitched in opposite camps.'[40] Trade unionists showed little interest in schemes of profit sharing or co-operation of the sort pioneered by Henry Briggs or Fox, Head and Co., and designed to give tangible form to this assumed identity of interest.[41] On the contrary, the middle years of the 1860s were marked by a severe wave of industrial unrest. Yorkshire and Staffordshire miners struck in 1864, as did Staffordshire ironworkers. Woollen workers in Dewsbury were locked out in 1865, and the following year masons and ironworkers in the north-east struck, as did Clydeside shipbuilders. It may be true that union witnesses before the Royal Commission generally stressed their role in encouraging peaceful industrial negotiation. Thus Applegarth referred to the practice of the Amalgamated Society of Carpenters and Joiners (ASCJ) of circularising all branches contemplating strike action with requests for details about the prospects of success. This acted as a dampener on ill-thought-out, hasty action; and Applegarth added that in this way about a third of all strike initiatives had been stifled over the previous five years. But, as we have seen, while the amalgamated societies may have dominated the union case before the Royal Commission, they did not call the tune for the whole movement. Further, they had a vested interest in presenting themselves in as favourable a light as possible to the commissioners. Nor can it be assumed that a reluctance to sanction strike action which had little prospect of success indicates any rejection of the principle of industrial conflict. It suggests simply a natural preference for husbanding financial resources.

A similar pragmatic explanation lay behind the unions' growing involvement in the arbitration and conciliation which were such a feature of this period. Government had attempted to intervene in industrial negotiation as early as the 1820s, although the 1824 Arbitration Act and later amendments in 1837 and 1845 had never been much applied. The National Association for the Promotion of Social Science had provided a forum for advocates of conciliation from its foundation in 1857. The first successful scheme was established in the Nottingham hosiery industry in 1860, mainly under the guidance of A.J. Mundella. Many others followed and by

the mid-seventies there was hardly a unionised industry
which did not have either a standing committee of workers
and employers or experience of settling disputes through
arbitration. By 1875, when the National Conciliation League
was formed, there also existed a recognised group of arbit-
rators, prominent among them being Mundella, Thomas
Hughes, Henry Crompton, and Judge Rupert Kettle. Most of
the schemes had written constitutions which provided rules
for the composition of committees, functions of chairmen,
and formal procedures for the resolution of deadlocks.[42]
The growth of interest in such bargaining machinery was
partly the product of a less abrasive attitude on the part of
major employers like Mundella, Titus Salt, Brassey (the railway contractor), Samuel Morley, and the Bass brothers. Such
men, it is suggested, had been alarmed by the signs of social
polarisation which had loomed so large in the 1840s and were
also aware of the opportunities they had as employers to
minimise the danger.[43] From the unions' point of view, it
clearly made sense to devise ways of settling grievances peacefully, since it was cheaper in both monetary and human
terms. There thus developed in this period a number of very
close relationships between employers and union leaders,
frequently thrown together in the course of industrial negotiation. Mundella was very friendly with Applegarth; Lord
Elcho, for all his warning that the convergence of political
reform and strong trade unions would result in the trampling
underfoot of British liberty, still enjoyed the confidence of
Macdonald, the miners' leader.[44] Other pairs included Morley
and George Howell, and the ironmaster Crawshay and John
Kane, leader of the ironworkers' union.[45] General and specific
studies make it quite evident, however, that the conciliation
movement grew out of a particular conjunction of economic
circumstances, in particular the combination of rising demand
for both labour and the product in industries where labour
was well organised and prices tended to fluctuate.[46] The
general enthusiasm waned once the economic climate changed
in the 1870s. In other cases it seems apparent that union
leaders accepted sliding wage scale agreements, for example,
not because they accepted the contemporary economic maxim
that wages had to be determined by profits, but because they

preferred automatic wage adjustment through conciliation boards to direct industrial conflict of a sort which broke so many unions, especially in coal and iron.[47]

Trade unionists and labour aristocrats, insofar as they were synonymous, do not appear to have acted, in the contemptuous phrase of one writer, as 'adjuncts of the ruling class'.[48] A similar, though much better argued, case for a slightly later period has been presented for the building industry.[49] Here, it is claimed, trade-union officials were agents of capitalist discipline, a position which increasingly divorced them from their own rank and file. Yet it is difficult to see how such situations could have occurred if workers and employers were as implacably opposed as is usually asserted. It is much more likely that in working closely with employers trade-union leaders were reflecting their members' views much more accurately than is often allowed. They were, after all, elected by and accountable to their men. On the industrial front, both groups acted consistently and rationally in their own self-interest. That their actions often cut across the interests of other workers is undeniable, but this primacy of group over class interest was nothing new in this period. Certainly they showed no sign of wishing to make fundamental social change in society; but to suggest that this represented a betrayal of broad working-class interests rests on two assumptions, neither of which is a self-evident truth, Marx and his followers notwithstanding: that workers will always and inevitably be desirous of controlling the society in which they live and that there is an objective, perceived, working-class interest which can be betrayed. Further, the argument of a quisling aristocracy still begs the question of how a minority of labour aristocrats was able to influence and shape the mass of workers with which it naturally had very little to do.

Another approach to the question of social quiescence in the third quarter of the nineteenth century has been to look at it in terms of social control. Social control theory was first fully developed by E.A. Ross in *Social Control* (1901) and has since been much used to explain how societies are held together. Simply put, it suggests that the ruling groups will use social institutions in order to propagate their own values, representing them as being in the common interest. In this tradition it is suggested that the mid-Victorian working class was subjected to a ceaseless barrage of propaganda from both public and private agencies on behalf of a value system supportive of capitalism and embracing ideas of self-help, competitiveness, punctuality, laisser faire, submission to authority, sobriety, respectability, and the mutual interests of labour and capital. According to this line of argument, the problem facing the rulers of Victorian Britain was two-fold. They had to destroy those characteristics thought to be incompatible with industrial capitalism and to replace them with the desired virtues. The thrust of this effort developed along four lines.

First of all, there was the attempt to shape leisure pursuits. Direct controls had swept away most blood sports in the earlier part of the century and this was reinforced by the activities of the Royal Society for the Prevention of Cruelty to Animals (RSPCA), founded in 1824. It is clear from Mayhew's accounts of London life in the 1840s that many traditional forms of animal sports persisted well into the century, but the society did its best to inculcate a more humane attitude towards animal welfare. Gradually it established a nationwide inspectorate; and the number of prosecutions rose dramatically from some 1300 in the 1830s, to 9000 in the 1860s, and almost 24,000 in the following decade.[50] Inevitably the bulk of such cases were brought against ordinary working people, if only because they had responsibility for the care of animals used by their employers. Other popular pastimes were hounded by the new police forces, which have been aptly described as 'domestic missionaries'.[51] Great resentment was engendered, especially among street traders, by police determination to prevent crowds gathering. Usually in response to local pressures, direct action was taken to stamp out gambling, sport, illicit drinking, and overt prostitution. Constant surveillance was usually sufficient to drive socially undesirable pastimes off the streets and into remote rural areas or behind closed doors. What this police activity meant for one local community, Batley, was well expressed in 1880.

The first policeman came into our midst, to plant the thin edge of the wedge, which was . . . to revolutionise our manners and customs. Since he came . . . we have lost all trace of mumming; all trace of Lee Fair . . . most of our mischief night; as nearly all peace eggers. I put a deal of this severance from ourselves of old customs down to the advent of the policeman in uniform.[52]

Heavy drinking was another activity which came under attack from the social controllers, since it not only interfered with the reliability of the workforce but was also associated with many of these brutalising pursuits which the refiners were seeking to eradicate. In practically all major industrial towns, one contemporary noted in 1828, all the workers' 'spare cash goes in strong drink, and this leads on to heated discussions, quarrels and fights'.[53] The heavy consumption of alcohol in the early part of the century was not simply because it provided, in the words of the contemporary quip, the quickest way out of Manchester. It was a safer and cheaper thirst quencher than most of the alternatives, though the price of coffee was probably comparable by 1830. In towns, drinking water was scarce or drawn from dangerously polluted sources. Milk was expensive and invariably adulterated. Beer functioned as a pain killer and was also believed to impart physical strength to those engaged in heavy manual work. In addition, alcohol was intimately involved in many popular rituals. Gloomy funerals and joyful weddings alike were enlivened by its presence. The tiding or drink gift symbolised a man's honourable intentions in the marriage market, while completion of the various stages of apprenticeship was often accompanied by some form of beery celebration. Attempts to foster sobriety were not new in the nineteenth century, but the 1820s saw the emergence of an anti-spirits movement which was 'only one of several contemporary attempts to propagate the middle-class style of life'.[54] What became the British and Foreign Temperance Society held its first meeting in June 1831; and the Band of Hope was launched in Leeds in 1847, based on the premise that the younger converts to abstention were made, the likelier they were to remain constant. By the end of the century, the movement claimed to have had contacts with some three million children, all of whom had been exposed to 'a new cultural identity'.[55]

Wresting working men from their traditional recreational

habits was not merely a negative process. On the positive side, alternative outlets had to be provided. When Rev Henry Solly founded the Club and Institute Union (CIU) in 1862, his letter of appeal for funds made the point that 'it would be as reasonable to expect the heathen world to convert itself to Christianity as to expect the great bulk of the working men to give up the public-house and establish private Clubs, without some impulse and guidance from those above them.'[56] There was substantial middle-class involvement in Solly's movement. By 1867 some three hundred clubs had been established, all of them temperance, and the CIU has been described as 'the largest and most successful of all the efforts through which Victorian England set out to ensure an assimilated and acquiescent proletariat'.[57]

The club movement was not all that dissimilar to the earlier mechanics institutes, though the latter placed much more stress on the acquisition of useful knowledge. The first of the institutes had been established as early as 1823 by working men in Glasgow, and others had followed in Bradford (1825) and Manchester (1829). The middle class had not been slow to realise their potential, summed up by Lord Brougham as providing a bulwark against irreligion, cultivating 'a taste for rational enjoyments' and engendering 'habits of order, punctuality and politeness'.[58] Thus many of the 1200 or so institutes which existed by 1860 began under the aegis of middle-class patronage. In Newcastle the initiative may have come from a radical publisher, but his appeal for financial support was directed to 'public-spirited gentlemen'; and the institute's president and eight vice presidents were all drawn from the middle class.[59] Apart from educational and recreational facilities, the institutes also provided useful platforms for the propagation of middle-class values. Thus at the annual Christmas party of the Manchester Institute in 1849, speakers from several different social groups complained about the tendency of Londoners to believe that Manchester was perpetually on the verge of revolution and to listen to 'any tale of Manchester life which seems to paint vividly the crimes and violence of one class or the selfishness and hard-heartedness of the other'.[60] James Hole prefaced his *Essay on the History and Management of the Literary, Scientific and Mechanics' Institutions* (1853) with a quotation from Southey.

Train up thy children, England,
In the ways of righteousness, and feed them
With the bread of wholesome doctrine.
Where hast thou thy mines — but in their industry?
Thy bulwarks where — but in their breasts?[61]

The Volunteer Force was in very much the same tradition. Founded in 1859 and with a mainly working-class membership of some 200,000 by the 1870s, there is ample evidence that its backers saw its potential as a form of social control. When the establishment of the force was being considered, it was widely asserted that membership would lead to a moderation of political extremism, better standards of hygiene, and a greater sense of deference. The inculcation of punctuality, submission to authority and discipline was especially likely in those instances, reported from 'all over the country', where 'working men were entering the Force in financial and organisational dependence on their employers'.[62] Added to this was the fact that the Volunteers also provided a carefully regulated recreational outlet in the form of drill, physical training, shooting and music, all of which seem to have been among the main attractions to recruits.

Social control, however, was more than a matter of directing and influencing popular leisure: it involved also a battle for the mind, and here the relevant mechanisms were the press, religion and education. By mid-century, the increasingly influential provincial press was particularly important in spreading the values of contemporary bourgeois society. Bodies such as the Society for the Diffusion of Useful Knowledge and the Library of Entertaining Knowledge poured out material replete with similar ideals. They were sustained by periodicals such as Knight's *Penny Magazine*, which had a circulation of some 200,000 in mid-century, and Dickens' *Household Words*. Chamber's *Journal* addressed itself to 'the elite of the labouring community; those who think, conduct themselves respectably, and are anxious to improve their circumstances by judicious means'.[63] All served to strengthen the attack on political agitation, immorality and industrial strife, and to reiterate the benefits of social co-operation.

Very often such literature merely mirrored what was being read at school. There were two-and-a-half million names on the school registers in England and Wales by 1861. While the content of reading books had become less overtly religious in the course of the century, there was little change of tone or purpose. In one of the early books produced by the Society for the Propagation of Christian Knowledge, Watt's hymn found a place.

> In works of labour, or of skill,
> I would be busy too;
> For Satan finds some mischief still,
> For idle hands to do.
>
> In books, or work, or healthful play,
> Let my first years be past:
> That I may give of ev'ry day
> Some good account at last.[64]

There was little to choose between the sentiments expressed here and those which turned up in the later secular readers. Dunn and Crossley's *Daily Lesson Book, III* contained one lesson, for example, on the 'way in which labourer can improve his lot — increased skill — knowledge of best markets for labour — habits of forethought, temperance — economy'.[65] The evidence presented to the Newcastle commission on education by school inspectors stressed the success of schools in transforming working-class children into model citizens, refining their tastes, humanising manners, and teaching the truths of political economy — to which one inspector revealingly referred as developing their 'practical common sense'.[66] Kay-Shuttleworth, first secretary to the Board of Education, certainly saw his task in terms of social control. After the Plug Plot riots, he was to be found urging the home secretary to 'tame the working classes with education'.[67] The *Minutes* of the Committee of the Council on Education (1846) reveal the same concern with social stability. 'Supervised by its trusty teacher, surrounded by its playground wall, the school was to raise a new race of working people — respectful, cheerful, hard-working, loyal, pacific and religious.'[68] Similar influences operated among private educational benefactors.

When north-eastern coal owners were considering the provision of schools in the 1850s, Lord Londonderry's agent
wrote that pitmen's children were 'not likely to be instructed
morally or become even civilised unless we adopt some
energetic measures'.[69]

The same motives are evident in much organised Victorian
religion. The church offered a sober alternative to the public
house but fulfilled a similar function as a centre of fellowship,
singing and general recreational activity. What was taught,
however, had a strongly middle-class flavour. Although much
religious teaching in the nineteenth century had no specifically
social or political message, a survey of Anglican sermons of
the period 1830—80 indicates that clergymen did use the
pulpit to expound political and social values. Poverty and the
existing social structure were both justified on the grounds
that they were divinely instituted. It followed from this that
men should accept without question their station in life and
that submission to authority was a Christian duty.[70] In the
same way Sunday Schools have been widely seen as part of
the social control process. One commentator has described
them as 'among the principal channels through which the
middle and upper classes sought to impose their social ideals
upon the working class'.[71] As one Gloucestershire manufacturer put it in the early nineteenth century, they made
'children more tractable and obedient, less quarrelsome and
revengeful'.[72] Children's hymns certainly stressed such
virtues. Among Mrs Alexander's most popular hymns was
one which included the following verses:

> There's not a child so small and weak
> But has his little cross to take
> His little work of love and praise
> That he may do for Jesus' sake.[73]

Submission and obedience were paramount among the duties
necessary in order to gain a place in heaven.

> We must meek and gentle be
> Little pain and childish trial
> Ever bearing patiently.[74]

Religion, education, the press, temperance and improving

recreational institutions have been seen as the main channels of social control in the mid-Victorian period. At its most extreme, some of the writing on the subject has implied a degree of shared interest, consultation and cynical manipulation among the ruling social groups which is just unhistorical. Indeed, it has been recognised that one of the main obstacles to the reform and rationalisation of leisure, for instance, lay in the attitude of those members of the middle class who did not want their own pursuits refined, or who had no interest in using leisure as a means of securing class harmony. On the contrary, they turned to class-specific activities, such as mountaineering.[75] Even so, it has to be conceded that social control does not have to be consciously manipulative or cynical to be effective. While the intent of the school readers was quite evident, they were still capable of 'advancing the interests of the lower orders . . . [and] there was no evidence of selfish motives behind them'.[76] One of the leading temperance advocates, John Dunlop, was undoubtedly moved by the human plight of drunkards.

> I got no sleep except dozing all night, and dreamed of drunken women and boys, till I overhead myself groaning, so that I was afraid I might disturb those that slept in the room.[77]

Such genuinely held concern, harnessed to the temperance movement, became a potent force for social control. And if social control did not have to be consciously cynical in order to be effective, neither did it necessarily have to be the main or only impetus behind any particular institution. Few would doubt that the mechanics' institutes were seen by many contemporaries as a suitable vehicle of control, but equally it is true that each institute 'was an autonomous unit, subject to no central direction and under the sway of no dominating ideology. Each was brought into existence in a specific sociological setting, influenced by the social, economic and political pressures of the locality.'[78] Similarly, the new leisure patterns which emerged were not just a result of employers' efforts to secure social stability and pliable workforces. If this were so, then it would be difficult to explain the disappearance of some traditions from rural areas. While the period did see quite deliberate creation of public facilities such as parks, libraries and baths, other forms of leisure were the incidental by-products of technology – the ubiquitous railway excursion, for example.

Perhaps a more serious objection to the notion that social harmony was a product of social control is that it tends to see the mass of the population as passive recipients of whatever values thought desirable by the ruling cliques. Yet it must be apparent that most people remained unaffected by the various social control agencies. The only one with any major impact was the school – but even this is questionable since schooling ended relatively young for most children, and there was as yet no compulsion to attend. For the rest, membership of the Volunteers was about 200,000 in 1870; and the mechanics had a similar number in 1860, though the evidence suggests strongly that by this time the movement had little attraction to ordinary working men. As early as 1840 the Yorkshire union reported that only about five per cent of its members were workers. In the early 1850s only four of the thirty-two institutes in Lancashire and Cheshire had a predominance of working-class members: the bulk were professional and middle class.

The religious census of 1851 created such a stir precisely because it revealed the full extent of the church's failure to reach the mass of the population. In the industrial areas north of a line between Grimsby and Gloucester, only six out of thirty-seven towns reached the national average attendance of fifty-eight per cent. In the predominantly working-class parish of Bethnal Green, there occurred the worst attendance of all: 6.6 per cent.[79] Nor did the abundance of available improving literature have much mass impact. It was far more likely, it has been suggested, to find working-class boys with their noses 'buried deep in the weekly pages of some horror-soaked Lloyd publication' such as *The Black Monk*, *The Castle Fiend*, or *Varney the Vampire*.[80] The Lord's Day Observance Society, the main instrument of Sabbatarianism, was despised by many working men because it seemed to offer only church-going as an alternative Sunday occupation.

Temperance failed so signally that beer consumption

reached an all-time peak in 1876 of 34.4 gallons a head.[81]
Nor was this due to what temperance advocates liked to
think of as beer-bribed rowdies. Some working men, at
least, regarded the abstinence pledge as an unwarrantable
interference with individual liberty. It is perhaps significant
that the 1871 Licensing Bill was criticised by some working-
class spokesmen as an attack on the public house, 'every
Englishman's freehold'.[82] When the Club and Institute Union
(CIU) conducted an investigation into its failure to make
much impact among ordinary working men, the absence of
beer emerged as the main explanation, coupled with the
too obvious presence of the parson. More generally, the
improving institutions made so little impact because they
failed to make any provision for sexual mingling, which was
an important function of nineteenth-century leisure. As a
result, much popular leisure remained private and unorganised.

Such working-class support as did exist for the efforts of
the social controllers and the improving institutions came in
the main from the skilled artisans, and we are thus back with
a variant of the labour aristocracy theory, defined now in
cultural terms. This has produced the widely-held view that
the attack on old habits and values in the nineteenth century
is best understood not as the attempt of one class to impose
its own values upon another, but rather as a conflict between
two rival cultural systems — respectability v roughness,
industriousness v idleness, religiousness v irreligiousness.[83]
This was a clash which cut right across class, uniting middle-
and working-class respectables against the idle rich and the
undeserving, idle poor alike: a division perhaps symbolically
represented by the contrast between chapel and public house.
Yet even this explanation has its difficulties. For all that
many working men could perhaps be described as respectable
in the mid-Victorian sense, there was a marked element of
calculation and self-interest in their behaviour. Working-class
respectables, in other words, were not merely middle-class
cyphers. Sunday School attendance leapt upwards every year
just prior to the annual treat. In this sense respectability was
not so much an ideology as a consciously adopted role which
could be discarded as occasion arose.[84] In the same way,
working men were prepared to accept middle-class sponsor-

ship in the form of facilities or finance for as long as might be necessary, but showed little compunction about dispensing with it. Many might be attracted to a church by the possibility of playing football for a church team, but the links between church and team were often very quickly severed.

As early as the middle of the century, there was something of an upheaval within the mechanics' institutes movement against growing middle-class involvement. In Wolverhampton the re-formed management committee was so markedly proletarian in character that it prompted middle-class complaints in the local press about the restricted nature of its membership.[85] In similar vein, the annual report of the CIU for 1872—3 acknowledged that ordinary members 'are more and more anxious to dispense with pecuniary aid from other classes'. The Hackney branch, established in 1873, stated from the outset that members were determined to function without 'aid from any class of society outside their own'.[86]

Far from being middle-class agencies, Sunday Schools quite soon were predominantly working class in character.[87] Such working-class support as the Lord's Day Observance Society enjoyed was not just a matter of religious conviction. Until the extension of the Bank Holiday Act in 1875 and the gradual spread of the Saturday half holiday, Sunday was the only guaranteed day of rest for a good number of workers. In the same way, temperance secured some following among workers who saw drink as a main threat to security of both health and employment.

To some extent, then, working-class respectability was a matter of enlightened self-interest and calculation. Yet it did also embrace a corpus of ideas which marked it off from middle-class respectability. The aspiration to social and moral improvement was not the creation of the Victorian middle class *per se*; rather it was one interpretation of the common intellectual legacy bequeathed by ancient Greek and Old Testament Israelite alike, who between them had virtually shaped western culture.[88] What operated in Victorian England, therefore, was not the attempt of one class to impose its values on another, but rather two divergent versions of the same value system. To the middle class, respectability implied deference to one's betters, recognition of their superior virtues, and attempts to emulate them.[89] To the artisan, however, respectability entailed a rejection of patronage and an assertion of independence. The high value placed on independence goes far to explaining the general working-class loathing of the poor law and of charity. Asked why she was washing out some red flannel given her by a local charity, a Tysoe country woman replied sharply, 'I bin washin' the charity out on it.'[90] This independence did not mean the Smilesean self-help philosophy preached by the middle class: it meant the mutual assistance of the trade union, the friendly society, and the co-operative society. In artisan eyes, membership of such bodies was the reward for character, not the means of achieving it.[91] Working-class espousal of temperance can be seen in the same light. The original aim of moderation had little appeal to working men at all, but what caught the artisans' imagination was the total abstinence movement, pioneered by workers and tradesmen in the north. This, it has been suggested, 'transformed temperance from a code of social behaviour, prescribed by one class for the moral elevation of another, to a participatory ethic of self-help and self-denial'.[92]

Social control, it seems, can thus be added to the list of explanations which will not totally account for the relative social peace of the mid-Victorian period, simply because it does not seem to have worked. The bulk of the population remained impervious to the blandishments of the refiners, and those artisans who did seem to submit either had their own understanding of middle-class ideals or played a calculating role for what they could get out of it.

This belief that social control only touched a minority, and one which in any case cannot automatically be assumed to have exercised some kind of overall leadership within the working class, has led one author to develop a quite different explanation of social quiescence. In a brilliant study of the Lancashire textile towns, Patrick Joyce analyses the nature of the communities which grew up round the mills.[93] For most workers, he argues, life was dominated by the place of work. The factory was often the starting point for an outing or excursion and also provided the basis for many recreational outlets, for instance a works football team or brass band.

Whole communities, their amenities and institutions were dominated by employers whose paternalism went far beyond anything explicable in terms of simple, economic self-interest. There was much about this paternalism says Joyce, 'suggestive of times more antique than those of economic rationality'.[94] Their reward was a deference and even political support from the workforce, which was willingly, not fearfully given with connotations of servility. As one worker recalled, 'they were somebody that we were supposed to give a kind of reverence to. But at the same time we wasn't encouraged to do any bowing or scraping. But we was told these people were who they were.'[95] The whole relationship was symbolised in the spontaneous and frequently quite lavish celebrations organised by workforces when masters' sons came of age. Naturally there was some calculative element in such celebrations, but 'there is considerable evidence for the spontaneous character of workers' reactions.'[96] This picture of a society in which class existed without conflict is not likely to appeal to Marxists; and there must be some doubt, despite Joyce's valiant efforts to argue otherwise, as to whether the structure of Lancashire industry and the social relationships to which it gave rise were typical of the whole country.[97]

There remain the broadly economic explanations which see peace as the product of improved social and economic circumstance. Not that the period was one of general improvement in terms of wages and employment: on average nearly thirteen per cent of the population was in receipt of poor relief in each year between 1849 and 1880; and if the precise figures are perhaps questionable, the order of magnitude is significant.[98] It is possible that the general increase in price levels associated with the mid-Victorian boom reduced tension and conflict, because it lessened the conflict for income; but even for skilled workers it would appear that average aggregate wages rose no faster than in the preceding quarter century.[99] A number of important local studies suggest that most of the improvement that did occur came towards the end of the 1860s, rather late to explain a social transformation taking place from the 1850s.[100] Against this, however, must be set the improvements that featured in particular sections of the economy. In the thirty or so years prior to 1865, Britain had acquired over 13,000 miles of railway. Not only did the construction of this network afford a significant new source of employment, but its operation also generated many new jobs. For all that hours were generally long and discipline of a military tenor often imposed by the railway companies, these jobs had the great advantage of being more or less immune from the threat of serious unemployment, since the railway was not affected by slumps in the same way as manufacturing industry. Engineering, building, iron and mining were among the industries which benefited from the construction and operation of railways, both at home and abroad where British expertise was in heavy demand.[101] Still more important perhaps, the proliferation of this fast, bulk-carrying transport system helped to stabilise both the price and supply of food. Not for nothing had Ben Wilson, the Chartist, commented in 1847 (a year of high flour prices) that 'this was a good time to make politicians, as the easiest way to get to an Englishman's brains is through his stomach.'[102] Chartism had flourished on hunger, and it is thus significant that the last major outbreaks of food rioting in Britain took place in 1847.

Environmentally, too, conditions were improving, albeit slowly. In 1847, sixteen years after the agitation had first begun, John Fielden finally secured the passage of a bill restricting the hours of young persons and females in textile factories to ten a day. Subsequent measures blocked loopholes and extended protection to the same vulnerable groups in other industries. The Factory Acts (Extension) Act of 1867 led to the application of existing legislation to all factories employing more than fifty workers and also to certain specified places of work such as iron and steel mills, blast furnaces, and paper and tobacco works. In the same year the Workshops Regulation Act was passed, covering all establishments with workforces of under fifty. Enforcement of the law was difficult since there were so many of these small enterprises, but an act of 1871 made them the responsibility of the factory inspectorate. Similar slow change was occurring outside the place of work. Edwin Chadwick's *Report on the Sanitary Conditions of the Labouring Population of Great Britain* (1842) had made explicit the link between dirt and disease. Both epidemic and endemic illness, he asserted, were caused or aggravated

> by atmospheric impurities produced by decomposing animal and vegetable substances, by damp and filth, and close and overcrowded dwellings [which] prevail amongst the population in every part of the kingdom . . . the annual loss of life from filth and bad ventilation are [sic] greater than the loss from death or wounds in any wars in which the country has been engaged in modern times.[103]

Reform was slow, partly because ratepayers exhibited a marked reluctance to subsidise the general provision of amenities which in many cases they already enjoyed privately. The other obstacle was the lack of any suitable administrative structure to organise change. This was partially overcome by the 1848 Public Health Act which set up a central Board of Health to supervise such local health boards as various local authorities desired to establish. It was not, however, until the passage of the 1872 Public Health Act that local authorities were required by law to appoint medical officers, inspectors of nuisances, and the other functionaries of local health and sanitation, all under the general oversight of the newly-established Local Government Board. Prior to this, such improvements as had occurred owed much to local initiatives and philanthropic work. London, in particular, had benefited from the building of new sewerage schemes and efforts to improve the quality of working-class housing.

Yet, as a veritable army of social investigators was to discover at the end of the century, these reforms had little real impact. Nor did they come early enough to explain a shift of social attitudes from 1850. The chief explanation for the new atmosphere of co-operation and harmony must lie, therefore, in the simple passage of time. By the 1860s there were many fewer people who had direct, personal experience of the fundamental upheavals which had characterised the industrial revolution. The limits of industrialisation, urbanisation and technological change had by no means been reached, but as *processes* they were by now vastly more familiar. True there were efforts to preserve and even recreate some aspects of a society which, it was felt, had been lost. Rural traditions were transposed into an urban environment. Thus Saint Monday survived for a long time in some small-scale industries, and in mining it became the traditional day for doing routine maintenance work. When the railways began to run excursions from Birmingham in 1846, most of them ran on Mondays. Monday attendance (45,000 a year) at the Edgbaston Pleasure Gardens, opened in 1853, was greatly in excess of weekend visits.[104] In the same way, the traditional round dances of the pre-industrial village greens turned up in northern industrial towns as the annual whitsuntide walks. Despite these reminders of the past, there was no longer any concerted, broad challenge to the principle of change. Everywhere were indications of what the cotton unions' historian has called 'reconciliation with the new order'.[105]

The habit of urban workers seeking refuge in part-time rural work had begun to die out in the south of England as early as the 1830s, as labour became more exclusively town bred. The north was moving in the same direction by the 1860s.[106] If E.P. Thompson is right in seeing eighteenth-century food riots not merely as reflex actions against food shortages but as attempts to preserve an existing way of life and a particular value system, then the significance of the disappearance of food riots after 1847 is clear.[107] Studies of working-class poetry also point to this growing acceptance of the new social order. So, too, does the fate of millenarianism, which had lost much of its attraction. At least, the apocalyptic noises it had made were 'growing perceptively fainter'.[108] After the failure of O'Connor's land scheme, later appeals to the pre-industrial memory never again evoked such an enthusiastic response. Religious revivalism went the same way. Described by an eminent modern sociologist of religion as 'the attempt to re-establish agrarian values, to restore the advantages of stable community life to people who had lost all community sense', revivalism had little general impact after the early nineteenth century.[109] The outbreak which began in 1859 started in Ulster, and its influence was experienced mainly in peripheral areas such as Scotland and Wales.

Change in the co-operative movement also reflects this growing acceptance of modern society. Its first phase had been dominated by Owen, whose vision had been for communities in which competition was to be replaced by co-operation. After some initial reserve, he adopted the idea of raising the necessary capital from the profits made on co-operative trading and manufacturing. By the early 1830s there were some five hundred societies of this type in existence, with an estimated membership of about 20,000. All were committed, in the words of the 1832 London Cooperative Congress, to the view that the 'grand ultimate object of all cooperative societies, whether engaged in trading, manufacturing or agricultural pursuits, is community on land.'[110] Round about the 1850s, however, by which time the last of Owen's experiments (at Queenswood) had failed, a change of emphasis set in. Under the influence of the Redemption Society, the Christian socialists and the Rochdale Pioneers, the community builders of the first part of the century were transformed into little more than shopkeepers within a capitalist economy. The decision to pay dividends on purchases proved fatal to the original idea, for it implicitly recognised that trading surpluses belonged to individuals, not to the society. It was also a tacit admission that members needed such inducements to belong, the ultimate vision of community having evidently lost its drawing power.

The same process of acceptance is applicable to the new police force, resistance to which had been one of the influences out of which Chartism had grown. Although protest continued as the provincial police forces were established, its nature changed. By the 1860s no one seems seriously to have believed that it would be possible to get the new force abolished altogether. Protest now centred on more specific objectives, such as getting particularly officious officers removed or stopping police intervention in industrial disputes.[111] A local study of the Black country indicates that, despite the financial difficulties involved, the working class there made considerable use of the laws of prosecution — further evidence that they accepted the broad legitimacy of the new order and its institutions.[112]

None of this is to deny that tension and conflict were still very much in evidence in mid-Victorian society. However, contemporaries certainly believed, and it is argued here, that its nature had somehow changed. What was in question now

was no longer the nature of the game, but rather the precise
rules under which it was to be played.

5

Trade Unionism and Socialism, c. 1875-1900

The legislation of the early 1870s, like the earlier repeal of the Combination Acts, created a climate conducive to union growth. The spread of unionisation, especially among previously unorganised groups of workers, was encouraged mainly by the boom conditions which characterised the first half of the decade. The immediate spur seems to have been the long and successful strike conducted in 1871 by north-eastern engineers to secure a nine-hour day. It triggered off an astonishing response. Unions of unskilled labourers appeared in the Liverpool and London docks. Transport workers also began to stir. The Amalgamated Society of Railway Servants (ASRS) came into being in 1871 with the assistance of the wealthy brewer, M.T. Bass; and there was a major agitation among Liverpool tram workers in 1875. Tinplate workers organised, and the coal industry saw the emergence of new institutions catering for those who were not hewers — hence the Durham Colliery Enginemen and Boiler Minders Mutual Aid Association of 1875, for example. Strikes in the heavy woollen districts of Yorkshire resulted in still further organisation, this time with substantial female involvement.

The most spectacular development of all, however, occurred among rural workers. Little progress had been made since the time of the Tolpuddle Martyrs, although incendiarism and other traditional forms of protest had been almost endemic in parts of East Anglia since the 1830s. Now unions began to appear — in Kent in 1866 and another centred on Leicester, though neither was very successful. More significant was the North Herefordshire and South Shropshire Agricultural Labourers Improvement Society of 1871, which at its peak claimed a membership of 30,000 spread over six counties. A

second Kentish organisation gained enough support to withstand a major attack from farmers in 1878–9, and it entered
the 1890s as one of the country's ten largest unions, though
by this time it had taken in urban workers and was officially
classified as a general union. Much better known, however,
was the union launched under the aegis of Joseph Arch in
1872. It is true that Arch succeeded in building up membership
of the Warwickshire-based National Agricultural Labourers
Union (NALU) to 86,000, but a series of internal policy disputes and a very costly strike in the eastern counties reduced
this to slightly over 4,000 by 1889. Arch was certainly a
major personality and much in demand as a speaker, to which
art he brought all the fervour of his Primitive Methodist
convictions. It has been suggested, however, that the Kent
union was more successful than the NALU because Alfred
Simmons, its main leader, displayed personal qualities which
Arch lacked, in particular 'skill and sagacity' in organisation.[1]
Simmons certainly appreciated much earlier than Arch the
need to provide friendly society benefits, both as a way of
maintaining support and also of freeing labourers from their
dependence on village paternalism. Arch added to his own
difficulties by rejecting the help of other trade unionists and
following a very militant policy. The eastern counties strike
cost his union £24,000 in strike pay for the six thousand men
involved. But personality will not explain everything: Arch's
union was national, at least in aspiration, and thus much
more vulnerable to strike-breaking activity than the Kentish
organisation, whose sphere of operations was relatively
isolated and homogeneous.

The most frequent demands made by the new agricultural
unions were for better housing conditions and higher wages.
For most of the nineteenth century, working conditions on
farms had remained poor. Interviewed towards the end of the
century, one farm worker recalled that

> in his young days wages for horsemen used to be down to
> 9s. a week, and for daymen 8s., when the weather allowed
> them to be earned. During the Crimean War bread cost
> him a shilling a loaf, and other food a proportionate price.
> He stated that for months at a time he had existed on
> nothing but a diet of bread and onions . . . These onions

he ate until they took the skin off the roof of his mouth, blistering it to whiteness . . . They had no tea, but his wife imitated the appearance of that beverage by soaking a burnt crust of bread in boiling water. On this diet he became so feeble that the reek of the muck which it was his duty to turn, made him sick and faint . . . 'Things are better now', he added.

Well, things are better now; indeed, it is scarcely too much to say that in many cases today, the labourer has more than his share of the rather plumless agricultural cake. But with such a record behind him, knowing what his fathers suffered, is it wonderful that he should strive to drive home the nail of opportunity, and sometimes to take advantage of the farmers who in the past too often were so merciless?[2]

By the last quarter of the century, real incomes generally were rising as cheap imports of food pushed down basic costs; and we are told that as early as 1868 the Penrith Savings Bank held some 260 accounts worth nearly £10,000 from farm labourers.[3] However, in the 1880s average rural wages were still only about fifty-five per cent of industrial ones. Income was also being squeezed from new directions. Those parents who sought to take advantage of the 1870 Education Act and permit their children some schooling deprived themselves of a potential source of income and until 1891 had also to pay fees. As the century progressed, the opportunities for labourers to earn extra income diminished. Machinery replaced hand labour and, once depression began to bite in the wheat-growing areas especially, many farmers were unwilling or unable to pay for extras such as weeding — which was often left undone. Yet by themselves low wages could not have stimulated trade unionism in the countryside. After all, rural wages had always lagged behind, and in any case there was very little organisation in either the best or the worst paid counties.

Trade unionism among agricultural workers was largely the result of changing social relationships within the industry and of the growing integration between urban and rural areas. The demand for farm labour had been generally buoyant through the mid-Victorian years and the labourers' position had been further strengthened by continued improvements in transport which made it easier for them to respond to booming labour demand in the towns and indeed abroad. Better transport and communication served also to weaken the isolation of some regions; and it seems, for example, that in some centres the spark to organisation was provided by news of the successful nine-hour agitation.[4] Again, in Kent and East Anglia many of the labourers' traditional perks had been whittled away during the preceding years, and the ensuing resentments had been further stoked by the farmers' prosperity during the golden age of high farming. It is noticeable that unionism did best in those areas where men and masters had grown farthest apart. It had relatively little impact in the north, where many farm servants continued to live in, thereby strengthening the bond between farmer and labourer. The predominantly pastoral farms of the north also had much smaller labour requirements, and this also appears to have inhibited organisation, which was a feature of areas where a high proportion of farmers employed more than ten men each.[5]

Elsewhere, traditional relationships were disrupted by the effects of agricultural depression. The dominant groups in rural society were normally much more homogeneous than their urban equivalents, but the depression caused the interests of farmers and landlords to diverge. This weakened the solidarity of the front they put up against trade unionism, while financial constraints made it less easy for them to dispense the patronage which had given them such a hold in rural communities.[6] In East Anglia this process was assisted by the impact of the Methodist revival in the 1860s. Not only did this give many labourers valuable practical experience of administration — 134 of 154 active trade unionists in Lincolnshire, for instance, were Methodists — but it also provided them with a new sense of personal dignity and worth, a biblical concept of social justice. It was unlikely that new converts would resort to the violence entailed in traditional protest, such as cattle maiming or rick burning — hence the appeal of trade-union organisation.[7]

Yet rural unionism needs to be kept in perspective. It captured only about twelve per cent of the agricultural labour force, though rather more in Suffolk where about twenty-five per cent was involved. After its initial success, employer resistance hardened; and rural workers generally were not well placed to undertake lengthy stoppages. The onset of major depression in the arable sector of British agriculture after about 1873, and its subsequent spread to the pastoral sector, had an adverse effect on the demand for rural labour and weakened the unions. Further, it seems that they had not yet learned to cope with basic administrative problems. For example, only about half of local branch monies ever reached the NALU's Leamington headquarters, instead of the required three-quarters.

This pattern of rapid growth followed by contraction was repeated among many other groups which made their first substantial progress in the early 1870s. The period thus appears as something of a false dawn, with serious setbacks occurring after about 1875 preventing the consolidation of some organisations. The tinplate workers collapsed in the mid-1880s, while the Welsh slate quarrymen lasted for only three years after their foundation in 1874. Older unions, too, were affected by the onset of depression. The Northumberland and Durham miners' union lost fifteen thousand members in six years after 1874. That this was part of a general trend can be seen from the fall in total union membership, reckoned to have been about a quarter of a million, once the boom gave way to depression. Yet the period between 1875 and 1888 was not entirely moribund. The early 1880s witnessed the birth of new organisations for sailors and dockers at Hull and Liverpool respectively, while in 1886 unions for card and blowing room operatives in textiles and for smelters in the steel industry were set up. The previous year, the predominantly female labour force in the Dundee jute industry had established a union which by the end of the decade had spawned several independent offshoots. Increasingly as women were introduced to a wider range of semi- and unskilled jobs, male unionists were compelled to rethink their exclusive attitudes. The National Union of Boot and Shoe Operatives (NUBSO) thus agreed at their 1884 conference that 'all women working at the shoe trade be admitted into the association upon the same terms and entitled to the same rights as men'.[8] Despite falling numbers, most of the miners' unions survived, often by accepting sliding scale wage agreements whereby the level of wages fluctuated in accordance with the selling price of coal. The craft and cotton unions were not too badly affected by the depression. Not all of the unions first established in the early 1870s disappeared: by 1888 the ASRS had grown to 15,000 and the NUBSO had 19,000. Even more significantly, the National Union of Elementary Teachers (renamed NUT in 1889) had 14,000 members by this date, indicative of the growing interest in trade unionism being shown by white-collar workers.

White-collar workers had remained unaffected by unionisation in the first half of the century. Shop assistants worked in small, isolated units for paternalistic employers, as did clerks. Teachers aspired to professional status, and most white-collar workers regarded themselves as a cut above manual workers and, therefore, above trade unionism. Once again, however, interest in organisation was stimulated by changes in working relationships. The revised code gave school managers a block grant based on pupil attendance and performance in examinations. Teachers were left to strike their own bargains with the managers, but in effect they were being paid by results. This deprived them of a certain amount of classroom independence. The 1870 Act provided new masters for the teachers in the form of school boards whose members frequently knew little about education. This threatened the teachers' independence and also their aspirations to professional status, at the same time as their bargaining power was being weakened by the rapid expansion of the teaching labour force. The answer to these threats was believed to lie in organisation, and the NUET statement, issued in 1870, indicates quite clearly the body's trade-union mentality. Among other things, it demanded adequate salaries not based on results, stringent entry requirements for teachers, and their registration.

Similar pressures were coming to bear on clerical workers. In 1851 when there were only 91,000 male clerks and 2,000 females, unemployment was naturally very low, pay good, and prospects for advancement favourable. By 1891 these figures had grown respectively to 449,000 and 26,000, an expansion which threatened job security.[9] Further, the paternalism of the old small counting houses was progressively eroded by the growing scale of commerce and industry. As the size of employing units increased, so it became necessary to administer personnel in a bureaucratic fashion in which employees were no longer treated as individuals but as members of groups or categories. It was no coincidence, therefore, that the most significant developments in white-collar unionism took place in large-scale enterprises such as the railways and the post office.

The developments of the period 1875–88 were nothing compared with what followed. As in the early 1870s, it was an upswing in the trade cycle that formed the background to the most spectacular expansion seen since the 1820s and 1830s. It was dominated by existing unions, such as the engineers whose numbers rose from 53,000 to 71,250 in 1891. By 1900 such unions remained dominant, a situation often obscured by the rapid advances taking place among the so-called new unionists from the end of the 1880s. The spark came appropriately enough from a strike among girls at the Bryant and May match factory, which gained the interest and support of the influential intellectual, Annie Besant. In March 1889 Will Thorne successfully organised the London gas-workers and gained a three, rather than two, shift working system for members employed at the South Metropolitan Gasworks. As the demand for gas normally fell off in the summer months, numbers of gas workers were laid off. They commonly sought temporary employment in the docks, and it was here that the new unionism received its most significant impetus in August 1889 with a major stoppage which paralysed the port of London.

As we have seen, unionism among unskilled workers had already made some progress, mainly outside London, before 1889; but this strike in the capital, attracting international attention and the intervention of Cardinal Manning, came to symbolise the unskilled workers' struggle of this period. The issues at stake between the management and Ben Tillett's tea operatives were several but ultimately came to focus on what John Burns colourfully christened 'the full round orb of the docker's tanner'.[10] The men's victory in an industry where conditions of work and recruitment procedures were extremely degrading was the signal for a rash of new organisations among similarly placed workers. The dock strike leaders, Tillett, Burns and Tom Mann, became national figures almost overnight, and their assistance was eagerly sought. Group after group struck for reductions in hours, for wage increases, or for an eight-hour day. On Merseyside and in Glasgow the National Union of Dock Labourers (NUDL) flourished. General labourers flocked into the Tyneside-based National Amalgamated Union of Labour (NAUL). Havelock Wilson continued his drive to organise merchant seamen. In Swansea schoolboys struck, while a letter in the *South Wales Daily News* urged housewives to join the Amalgamated Society for Distressed Wives in order to protect themselves against drunken and negligent husbands. The response is not known, but one feature of the union fever sweeping the country was the involvement of women who were freely recruited by the general labour unions. Even when strikes were unsuccessful, there were sometimes beneficial knock-on effects. After worsted workers in Bradford's Manningham Mills were beaten in a long strike in 1890–1, the total number of trade unionists in the West Riding rose by some 10,000. 'Dyers, enginemen, trammen, busmen, drivers, labourers . . . and others,' commented the *Yorkshire Factory Times*, 'saw the weak position of the Manningham strikers and prepared for defence in their particular trade.'[11] Altogether the number of trade unionists in Britain doubled in the two years between 1889 and 1891.

John Burns, himself a member of the older ASE, contrasted the old and new unionists in physical terms. The old, he said, were physically much bigger and looked like 'Respectable city gentlemen'. The new, on the other hand, 'looked workmen: they were workmen'.[12] George Howell picked on another difference in his book *Trade Unionism New and Old* (1892). He attacked the militant strike policy of the new unions, their demands for state intervention in labour affairs, and their promotion of what he called 'a bastard socialist propaganda'.[13] The Webbs commented on similar lines, characterising the new unions as militant, socialist, general unions, catering for low paid, unskilled workers unable to afford to pay for the sophisticated benefits offered by the older societies. Like most generalisations, this hides more than it reveals.

It would certainly be futile to contest the characteristic of violence normally attached to the new unions. In his memoirs, Will Thorne recalls with evident glee the ambush he organised on blacklegs brought in to break the Leeds gas strike.[14] It is important to note that violence tended to persist only in industries such as shipping, where it was relatively easy to introduce scab labour. Elsewhere it was not long before union leaders began to realise the practical benefits of peaceful negotiation. In Liverpool the collective reputation for violence amongst new unionists rests entirely on the activities of the seamen and dockers in 1889 and 1890. The city's other new unions adopted a much more pragmatic stance. In Cardiff, the coal trimmers used the peaceful but effective tactic of playing off the two employing interests, shippers and owners, against each other. Nor did the London dockers resort to violence in 1889, though embittered employers did accuse Burns of intimidation, and there were some downriver clashes with strike breakers. On the whole, however, it was the dockers' very moderation that caught the eye. Since the 1860s the east end had been viewed as a potential source of social unrest, a feeling that had grown in the 1880s with a housing crisis, unemployment riots in which Burns himself had played a prominent part, and a great deal of socialist propagandising. The well-organised but essentially peaceful dock strike came as 'a cathartic release' from such fears.[15] As one involved contemporary, H.H. Champion, said,

> As soon as it became known that 1000's of the strikers had marched through the City without a pocket being picked or a window being broken . . . the British citizen felt that he might go back to his suburban villa . . . with full confidence that his warehouses would not be wrecked in the night, and that he could afford to follow his natural inclination and back the poor devils who were fighting with pluck, good humour and order against overwhelming odds.[16]

Apart from a tendency towards militance, the new unions had two other features in common. One was the emphasis they placed on state intervention in labour matters. This was because they were in the main organising workers who were not yet strong enough to gain their ends through controlling the labour supply as craft workers did. They were also distinguished, and this was missed by most contemporaries, by the very high proportion of their income spent on administration. The NUDL accounted for a staggering eighty-one per cent of its income in this way, the gas workers fifty-four per cent, as against the average of only twenty-six per cent spent by the largest hundred unions in the country.[17]

Otherwise, however, the new unions had few common traits. It is not true that they all eschewed benefit functions. The seamen and the NAUL paid accident and funeral benefit from the start, while others found it expedient to introduce benefit schemes in order to encourage members' loyalty. Thus the dockers added funeral benefit to their provisions in 1891. Again, there was no uniform structure. Some were general unions straddling several different industries. The gas workers, for example, recruited among labourers in the Yorkshire woollen industry and among oncost workers in the Welsh mines. Others, like the seamen, were organised in industrial unions, embracing all the employees within one industry. Other unions catered for particular groups within an industry, such as the builders' labourers. Finally, it is not really accurate to suggest that the new unionism involved only poorly paid, unskilled workers. Real wages generally were rising by this time anyway, but many new unionists earned more than the national average adult male wage of 25s. a week in 1890. Seamen could earn between 28s. and 33s., while a London gas worker might get as much as 45s. E.J. Hobsbawm has suggested very plausibly that many of the new unionists did have skills of a sort which gave them some bargaining power, especially when risks were pooled by joining with different types of workers in a single organisation. Gas men were skilled in the sense that they required considerable strength and stamina to stand the strain of constantly shovelling coal into the retorts. Dockers were casual workers who served no apprenticeship; but their job also required strength and stamina, as well as the knack — not acquired overnight — of handling heavy weights. It was this sort of skill, coupled with the rapidly rising demand for labour, that enabled such workers to establish permanent footholds in their industries for the first time. Between 1881 and 1901, the numbers employed in gas, water and sanitary undertakings increased in England and Wales from 25,000 to 68,000; in docks and harbours from 43,000 to 100,000. The number of carmen and carriers more than doubled to reach 273,000.[18] Where labour had any political influence, as it did in the person of John Burns in the London County Council, pressure could be exerted on local authority employers to recognise unions and their demands.

Many have suggested that socialism was a characteristic, even a cause of the new union upsurge, and socialists were certainly prominent in some industries and some areas, particularly London. This was hardly surprising, since the sort of individual likely to come to the fore in the London trade-union movement was also likely to have come under the influence of the secular socialism which so coloured the capital's numerous radical clubs. Thus Burns, Mann and Tillett were or had been members of the Social Democratic Federation. Eleanor Marx of the Socialist League helped Thorne, also of the SDF, to organise the gas workers. Edward Pease of the Fabian Society was involved with the National Labour Federation. In the provinces, however, socialist influence was patchy. The local branch of the Socialist League gave valuable assistance to the Leeds builders' labourers, while the gas men were backed by a whole range of local radicals. In Liverpool, by contrast, there was no direct socialist influence at all; and in the country at large trade-union leadership was predominantly liberal in its sympathies. Even where socialists were active in strikes, their precise influence is questionable. Except in Leeds and perhaps in London, there is little evidence of any broadly-based working-class support for them. Indeed, Champion reckoned that they were accepted in spite of, rather than because of, their views. Socialism did little to break down sectional rivalries between different groups of workers, probably because the leaders of the most active socialist body at this time, the SDF, were generally very dubious as to the value of diversifying their energies into trade-union agitation at all. At most, therefore, it might be said that socialism channelled the new trade unionism in some places. It was, however, neither a cause of it nor a characteristic.

The SDF was the first real fruit of the socialist revival which occurred in Britain in the 1880s. Interest was stimulated by Henry George, whose *Progress and Poverty* went into many editions, and who visited Britain three times between 1881 and 1884, on each occasion attracting huge crowds. His proposals for a single tax on the incremental value of land and for land nationalisation struck chords in the minds of those nurtured in Chartism, the Land Nationalisation Society, and the Land Reform Union. Along with Ruskin, Carlyle and the later writings of Mill, George did much to break the hold of classical economics on the minds of thinking working men in Britain. When W.T. Stead conducted a survey among Labour MPs in 1906 to find out which writers had most influenced their political thought, George, Ruskin, Carlyle and Mill were by far the most frequently mentioned.

Marx's ideas had a rather more restricted influence, but by the 1870s many of the London clubs, long centres of radical activity in the capital, were coming under his sway. Although the *Communist Manifesto* had been translated into English in 1850 and published in the *Red Republican*, it had been pretty well forgotten, and Marx's other works were not available in English until the 1880s. Yet Marxist theory was being discussed in the work of academic economists such as T.D. Woolsey and Albert Schaffle, and also in the various writings of E. Belfort Bax. It was also familiar to the various continental socialists who had settled in London to escape persecution.[19] The link between these socialist influences and the London artisans was provided by the Soho-based Manhood Suffrage League, founded in 1874, to which several prominent British trade unionists belonged. It was the league which kept alive the idea of independent, working-class political activity when the TUC seemed almost to have abandoned it in the 1870s. The league also became one of the main constituents of the Democratic Federation when it was set up in 1881. The immediate inspiration behind the federation came from H.M. Hyndman, who was deeply concerned that while the Liberal party professed to represent the people, 'at the last General Election . . . a vast number of members were returned to the House of Commons who represent any interest in the country but that of the working class.'[20] Hyndman had read Marx in French and borrowed many of his ideas, without acknowledgement, for his own *England for All*, which was distributed to all those attending the Democratic Federation's inaugural meeting. In 1884, under Hyndman's guidance, the organisation changed its name, becoming the Social Democratic Federation (SDF), and adopted a socialist programme.

With his Cambridge background and silk top hat, Hyndman was an unlikely revolutionary, but he soon gathered round him a group of able supporters: J.L. Joynes, who had been a master at Eton and who was to translate *Wage Labour and Capital* in 1886; H.H. Champion, who placed his Modern Press at the party's disposal; and the distinguished scholar, William Morris. John Burns brought to the federation not only his powerful oratory, but also a much needed proletarian element, for the leadership was overwhelmingly middle class. It had this in common with the other socialist body established in 1884, the Fabian Society. While the Fabians included some of the leading intellectual luminaries of the day, such as the Webbs, George Bernard Shaw, and Graham Wallas, they were at this stage wedded to the idea that socialism would be achieved by permeating the existing political parties. They thus had little in common strategically with the SDF, which in the main saw its task as one of developing the proletariat's class consciousness in order to build up support for working-class, socialist parliamentary candidates.

To this end vigorous open-air propaganda was a permanent feature of SDF work. This was backed by a newspaper, *Justice*, a venture only made possible by a generous financial subvention from Edward Carpenter. The advent of a general election in 1885 provided the first opportunity to test the state of the water by putting up candidates. The results were hardly encouraging. All three were beaten heavily, the best showing being by Burns at Nottingham where he obtained 598 votes. The following year the federation achieved considerable publicity when it organised demonstrations of London's unemployed which ended in rioting in the west end. Hyndman, Burns, Champion and Jack Williams were all arrested, though they escaped the charges of seditious utterances and conspiracy. Still greater notoriety came in 1887 when the federation directly challenged the Home Secretary's decision to close Trafalgar Square to public meetings. Bloody Sunday, 13 November, saw a major riot ended only by the intervention of troops. Both Burns and the radical MP, R.B. Cunninghame Graham, were arrested and imprisoned.

Yet barely was Burns out of prison than he began to move away from the SDF. Like others, notably Champion, he felt that the federation was making little progress. Tom Mann, who was working as an SDF organiser in Lancashire, admitted to Burns his doubts as to whether the 'S.D.F. as an organisation will ever develop to considerable proportions. I confess it looks horribly slow work. I can't see much headway that's been made . . .'[21] The dissidents all believed that Hyndman's insistence on the doctrine of class war was leading socialism into a blind alley and causing it to lose touch with the working class. To Burns, the trade-union movement seemed to offer a much more realistic vehicle for securing the election of working-class candidates to Parliament. Together with Champion, he lent his support to the TUC's Labour Electoral Committee which had been set up in the wave of enthusiasm following the passage of the 1884 Reform Act. They adopted a policy of supporting all candidates who were favourably disposed towards labour demands, and pushed their line in the *Labour Elector*.

This was by no means the first or the last rift that was to sunder the SDF. Although many of the clashes owed something to the resentments engendered by Hyndman's determination to have exclusive control of the party, they also centred on some basic contradictions within contemporary socialist ideology. As early as 1884, William Morris had quit to form the Socialist League, since he did not share Hyndman's belief in the efficacy of political action and parliamentary campaigning. If, as Marx predicted, capitalism was going to collapse anyway, what was the point of supporting palliative reforms to patch it up? This, argued one later dissident, was 'futile, reformist and careerist'.[22] Yet a party desirous of winning support for its parliamentary candidates had to put up a programme; otherwise it would be left, as some members of the SDF were, 'completely satisfied with preaching Socialism. They had no real desire to accomplish

any change.'[23] Even among those who were committed to
the idea of social reform, however, there were disagreements
about tactics. Hyndman's primary concern was to preserve
his socialist purity. Burns and Champion were prepared to
work with anyone if it would produce social progress and a
working-class presence in Parliament. The SDF, commented
Burns privately, must 'be remodelled not to say merged with
other bodies 'ere it does good work.'[24] Following his own
advice, he succeeded in getting himself returned, with the
backing of an alliance of local radical and labour supporters,
as the MP for Battersea in the election of 1892.

Londoners returned another independent working-class
MP in this election also, in the person of James Keir Hardie,
who won West Ham South. Hardie had for years been ad-
vocating working-class independence and had burst upon
the labour world with a fiery speech at the 1887 conference
of the TUC, in which he had attacked the secretary, Henry
Broadhurst, for supporting Liberal candidates. Subsequently
he had contested the mid-Lanark seat in a by-election in
1888 and then, breaking with the LEA, had established the
Scottish Labour party. Its policy, however, was very much
that advocated by Champion: putting up candidates in those
cases where existing ones were unacceptable because of their
views on labour questions. Hardie had hoped to carry the
TUC along this line, but in 1888 his 'independent' amendment to the TUC resolution on labour representation was
heavily defeated. Broadhurst and his pro-Liberal stance still
dominated.

Hardie was soon to become a major figure in the most
significant of Britain's socialist organisations, the Independent
Labour party. Its immediate genesis lay in the Manningham
Mills strike in Bradford, the defeat of which seemed to
strengthen the new unionists' arguments in favour of working-
class political action. During the strike, the local council had
clamped down strongly on allegations of intimidation and
broken up strike meetings with some force. The local socialist,
Tom Maguire, demanded how long working people in the
town were going to 'return people to the Council who, when
returned, use the force of the town against the working
classes?' He predicted that the Liberals would soon 'get such

a knockdown blow as they would never recover from'.[25] The *de facto* alliance of socialists, radicals and trade unionists which had supported the strikers then established a Labour Union in Bradford. With the active backing of Robert Blatchford and his influential paper, the *Clarion*, similar bodies were established in other, leading northern cities. In the autumn of 1892 a preliminary conference was held for people interested in turning these unions into the nucleus of an independent, socialist political party. Burns, the major figure in the labour movement at this time, did not bother to attend. He was unwilling to get involved in what he feared might turn out to be nothing more than a northern version of the sectarian SDF, and his own background made him suspicious of a socialism couched in terms of the New Testament. In his absence, Hardie took the chair. His presence guaranteed that the conference roused considerable interest, and his position as an MP enabled him to provide the new party with an important national focus. Early in 1893 the foundation conference of the Independent Labour party was held, its name decided upon, a constitution settled, and a socialist programme adopted.

For many of those who attended this inaugural conference or otherwise espoused it, socialism was more than just a political creed: it represented a new philosophy of life. As Hardie put it in 1907, socialism satisfied man's basic longing for both 'fraternity and the spirit of beauty'.[26] For men like Rev Stewart Headlam, socialism grew out of religious convictions. After reading Henry George, Headlam transformed the Guild of St Matthew, originally established to combat secularism in London, into a socialist body. For others, socialism had a strong ethical content. The Fabian Society emerged out of the Fellowship of New Life which, although totally overshadowed by its more illustrious offspring, continued for some time to propagate its own brand of ethical socialism in the magazine *Seedtime*. Undoubtedly the greatest exponent of socialism in this sense was William Morris. He viewed it as far more than a political and economic system. It was the means by which all people might 'have the utmost possible freedom to live the fullest and happiest lives'.[27] Similarly, Annie Davison recalls that her ILP father

and his comrades 'wanted their children to learn that socialism
was a good way of life'.[28] This was why he sent them to the
local Socialist Sunday School, which — along with John
Trevor's Labour Church movement — did much to foster and
express this broader understanding of socialism. The army of
lecturers deployed by the ILP frequently presented their
case in New Testament language, and this was not simply out
of deference to their own or their audiences' broadly non-
conformist backgrounds. Rather it was because socialism *was*
tantamount to a religion, representing a crusade for a new
moral basis of life and relations between men. Nowhere was
this better illustrated than in Blatchford's *Merrie England*
which so inspired the public with visions of a country of
widely-streeted towns, 'detached houses, with gardens and
fountains and avenues ... public parks, public theatres,
music halls, gymnasiums ...' that it sold three-quarters of a
million copies in a year.[29] It was Blatchford who did most in
a practical way to try to harness socialism to all that was
good and wholesome in nature. To this end he founded the
Clarion Scouts in 1894 and also the Clarion Cycling Clubs.
'Springtime is here,' enthused one Clarion cyclist, 'and once
again we turn our minds to wheels and sprockets and our
backs on smoke town, let out on the open road, like true
Bohemians casting off the shackles of conventionality.'[30]

In the space of ten years or so, the socialist movement in
Britain apparently made a considerable impact. A vast
amount of preaching (both written and spoken) had been
undertaken, newspapers flourished both nationally and
locally, and numerous branches of the main socialist bodies
had been founded. For all this, the effort was not really
matched by the achievement. 'Movement' perhaps implies
a degree of brotherly solidarity that was not always very
evident. Both the main socialist parties were prone to internal
wrangling. The SDF had two major splits by the 1890s, and
the ILP was by no means immune. Blatchford wrote in despair
to a friend about internal factions within the party, asking
'Are these creatures worth fighting for: are they fit to fight
alongside of? By God, Alec, I feel ashamed. I do. I feel
degraded. We cannot win battles with such a rabble rant.

Neither friends nor enemies are clean enough to spit upon.'[31] Again, the movement's two main national figures, Hardie and Burns, did not get on well in Parliament. Beatrice Webb, who knew them both, attributed this to Burns' jealousy, saying that his hatred of Hardie 'reaches about the dimensions of a mania'.[32] While there was some truth in this, there were also genuine political differences between the two. Burns had found in the London County Council that it was fruitful to work within the procedural rules, and he found Hardie's repeated parliamentary gaffes intensely annoying. Furthermore, Burns believed in co-operation with politicians of other pursuasions in the pursuit of common ends. Hardie's commitment to the principle of independence made him highly suspicious of this approach. To Burns this suspicion looked uncommonly like that same, narrow sectarianism against which he had rebelled in the SDF. In 1894, therefore, he lent enthusiastic support to moves initiated by conservative trade-union leaders to curb ILP influence within the TUC by alterations in the standing orders. Finally, there were marked differences of emphasis and tactic between the ILP and the SDF, well symbolised when the ILP ended its founding conference to the strains of *Auld Lang Syne*, rather than the *Marseillaise* favoured by the Social Democrats. Tillett touched on the main difference when he told the ILP conference that they wished to capture the unions for socialism and that the party consisted of practical socialists, not harebrained chatterers and magpies. Largely for this reason, the delegates rejected the proposal to include the word 'socialist' in the party's title, fearing that it would unnecessarily limit their appeal. Hardie made the same point to Engels, telling him on one occasion that the ILP was 'not given to chasing bubbles . . . we are more concerned with the realisation of the ideal than in dreaming of it'.[33] It was Hardie who resisted most fiercely the various proposals made in the 1890s for socialist unity. He knew that trade unionists had little time for the SDF.

On top of all these internal difficulties besetting English socialism, there were clear indications by the middle 1890s that the revival was running out of steam. When Tom Smedley, editor of the *Nottingham Socialist Echo,* committed

suicide in 1898, his final note reflected his despair at this
waning of socialist fortunes: 'If Socialism was not going to
sweep all before it, life had nothing to make it attractive.'[34]
With the death of local leaders like Smedley and Tom Maguire
and of national men like Morris, the ethical voice of
socialism was muted, and increasingly it became identified
with party politics. Even there, however, the prospects were
gloomy. By the middle 1890s the SDF had been washed into
a backwater by its own intransigence, while many ILP
branches vanished almost as soon as they were established.
ILP influence within the TUC had been curbed by new standing orders in 1895 which permitted only *bona fide* working
trade unionists to attend as delegates and also introduced
block voting, thereby strengthening the hand of the larger
and generally less radical unions. Nowhere was there any
indication that socialism was gaining anything like a mass
following. Fabian Society membership was a few hundred
and restricted to a limited circle of intellectuals. The SDF's
strength was concentrated in the east end of London and one
or two provincial centres such as Burnley and Northampton.
While the party had succeeded in publicising unemployment
in the 1880s, little permanent support had resulted because,
as *The Times* put it on a later occasion, 'the class which will
walk in the processions is traditionally ungrateful, and it
seems that it will throw the SDF overboard as soon as it may
be convenient.'[35] The ILP had attracted a somewhat greater
following, perhaps some 10,000, especially in the northern
industrial areas. It was more popular than the SDF among
skilled workers, but even so analysis of party membership
based on the shareholders in various party publishing enterprises reveals a disproportionately high number of professional
men and clergy. As was the case with the SDF, semi- and
unskilled men were poorly represented.[36] In one sense, of
course, this was hardly surprising — since all political parties
had relatively small active memberships. Yet mass support
was more crucial to socialist parties, since it was the only
means by which they were likely to acquire sufficient funds
to fight elections and finance propaganda work. Elections
were still very expensive affairs. With official expenses and
requests for patronage, Rider Haggard reckoned that a county

election campaign in 1895 cost him over £2000. Requests fell on him 'thick as leaves in Vallombrosa' and he was even asked 'to supply voters with wooden legs!'.[37] In the absence of wealthy backers even a single by-election, such as that at Barnsley in 1897 which cost the ILP over £500, seriously strained meagre financial resources.

Yet even when candidates were put up, there was little sign of any electoral breakthrough. The SDF had four candidates in 1895. Hyndman made the best showing at Burnley, getting almost 1500 votes out of the 11,000 cast. The average SDF vote was about 8.5 per cent of the total cast in the constituencies which they fought.[38] Every one of the twenty-eight candidates fielded by the ILP, including Hardie, was beaten. Worse, they all finished bottom of the poll and only half of them got into four figures. Burns alone remained in Parliament as the only authentic, independent working-class voice; but his socialism was by now in question and in any case he was not affiliated to any labour group, save his own Battersea Labour League. It might be argued that such a poor showing was a reflection of the limited nature of the franchise; for the 1884 Reform Act, while it had extended the vote, had not produced universal male suffrage. It is estimated that about two-fifths of adult males were still denied a vote.[39] Even so, the socialist parties generally only put up candidates in constituencies whose predominantly working-class character was thought to give them a chance of success. The truth was that, even in areas like these, not only was there a strong, working-class, Liberal sentiment but often a strong, working-class, Conservative vote as well — particularly in some of the poorer districts of London and also in the Lancashire cotton constituencies.[40]

Social control springs readily to mind, indeed too readily to some minds, as an explanation for the failure of socialism to make any lasting general impact in the late nineteenth century. With the introduction of compulsory attendance in the 1880s and the partial abolition of fees in the 1890s, elementary education now had a wider-reaching impact than previously, and its intent remained as deadening as ever. Charles Booth observed of one London board school which he visited that it was full of 'ragged little *gamins* [who] run quietly in harness, obedient to a look, a gesture of the teacher in command'.[41] By 1908 about a third of local education authorities in Britain were providing systematic moral education in their schools, often as a substitute for religion.[42] Religious education, with all its connotations of social quietism, still baulked large on the curriculum and was reinforced by the work of the Sunday Schools, still widely attended by working-class children at this time. Their combined influence was apparently widespread. In his novel *The Ragged Trousered Philanthropists*, Robert Tressell tells of the annual outing of the building firm of Rushton and Co. On the return journey, he writes, hymn singing began in the coach carrying the employers. The workers, he goes on, 'also sang the choruses. As they had all been brought up under "Christian" influences and educated in "Christian" schools, they all knew the words.'[43]

There are also those who see the dead hand of the social controllers behind the growing commercialisation of leisure and sport in the period.[44] The music hall, then in its heyday, has been described as much less an expression of working-class attitudes than a shaper of them. Certainly J.A. Hobson claimed that the halls were 'a more potent educator than the church, the school, the political meeting, or even the press'.[45] Hobson also observed that no social revolution was likely to come from a people 'so absorbed in cricket and football', and there can be no doubting the popularity of sport among working-class people.[46] Kipling even attributed the nation's poor showing in the Boer War to the fact that her menfolk were obsessed with 'the flannelled fools at the wickets' and the 'muddied oafs at the goals'.[47] At the north-eastern miners' annual picnic in 1910, one irate miner complained bitterly that while in the previous April 'thousands of people' had been caught up with the excitement when Newcastle beat Barnsley in the Football Association cup final, 'that very day a father of three children had gone out onto the moor and cut his throat because he had been out of work for 18 months . . . yet the thousands were more interested in the football match than they were in one human soul who wanted their help and aid so much.'[48] Small wonder that one recent writer has suggested that football 'diluted the political energies of English labourers'.[49]

Commercialism was also becoming a more prominent feature of journalism by the late nineteenth century. The ending of the stamp tax, cheaper transport and communication, and a fall in the cost of paper had all encouraged older established papers to modernise their approach to the dissemination of news, some of them even adopting American techniques. Fresh styles of news presentation appeared, best exemplified in the work of W.T. Stead at the *Pall Mall Gazette* and collectively dubbed as the 'new journalism'. There is little doubting Stead's motives: he saw his task as that of 'director of the steps of His [God's] people . . . [and] the enlightener of all men'.[50] The real revolution came with the birth of *Tit-Bits* in 1881, destined 'to modify in the most profound degree, the intellectual, social and political tone of the Press as a whole'.[51] Potted, easily assimilated information, presented in a concise and lively fashion, proved enormously popular with a reading public expanding under the impact of rising real wages and more widespread education. Fifteen years later came the *Daily Mail*, conservative, imperialistic and anti-socialist in tone, reinforcing old values. The *Daily Express* was also militantly anti-socialist; and it is perhaps significant to find the editor, Arthur Pearson, giving strong backing to Baden Powell's scout movement. Though less overtly militaristic than the earlier Boys' Brigade, the scouts did stress similar virtues, such as loyalty, obedience to authority, and discipline, while the emphasis was on national rather than class pride. The Boys' Brigade and the scouts were probably the most significant of the several uniformed youth organisations founded at this time, and they have been rightly described as 'important institutional vehicles' for the transmission of the middle-class value system.[52]

As an explanation for the failure of socialism, social control runs into the same problems which we discussed in a different context in the previous chapter. Press coverage was limited. While *Tit-Bits* achieved a circulation of 900,000 within three months of its first appearance, even this represented only some three per cent of the total population. In any case, most of the new publications were not aimed at the working class at all, but rather at the lower middle class. This was also

the case with the voluntary organisations. In 1917, the
Boys' Brigade attracted from the inner-city areas of
Birmingham and Manchester a mean membership of 5.5 per
cent of boys aged between twelve and seventeen. Even if other
organisations such as the scouts, Church Lads' Brigade, Jewish
Lads' Brigade, and army and navy cadets are included, the
figures rise only to ten per cent for Birmingham and 12.9
per cent for Manchester.[53] Furthermore, the organisers
frequently pointed out that most of those who joined were
not those who most needed what the movements could offer.
The schools were clearly much more comprehensive in their
coverage, but the discovery by the anxious middle class
of a 'youth problem' at the end of the century, frequent
truancy from school, and the evidence of popular hostility
towards movements such as the Boys' Brigade all suggest that
these particular social control agencies were still relatively
ineffective.

Secondly, social control explanations ignore the commercial elements evident in the growth of professional sport
and entertainment. Granted that entrepreneurs can to some
extent encourage public consumption of their goods by careful marketing and presentation, it remains true that their
interest in profit ensures that they provide what people want,
not what is politically expedient. Finally, the explanation
does not take into account that calculating element in working-
class life which we noted earlier, for there is abundant evidence
that social control institutions were still being taken over by
working men and shaped in accordance with their own particular interests and desires. Thus working-class involvement
in chapel life cannot be taken as indicative of any general
acceptance of nonconformist *mores*. In many late-nineteenth-
century communities, the chapel remained as the focus of
social as well as spiritual life. It was often the only source of
entertainment facilities, and it was quite possible for people
to be attached without sharing chapel values. Thus the ILP
pioneer, J. Bruce Glasier, recalled that long after his adolescent
faith passed away he continued to attend meetings of the
Young Men's Christian Association at the local nonconformist
chapel.[54] As the century drew to a close, working-class and
Liberal nonconformity increasingly diverged. With some

honourable exceptions, many middle-class nonconformists remained indifferent or hostile to Hardie's assertion that the pulpit would only become relevant if it developed a political and social conscience. Fred Jowett's warning — if the church opposed the labour movement, they would establish their own church — bore fruit with the establishment in 1893 of the Labour Church, which drew its strongest support from precisely those areas where Liberalism was least sympathetic to labour's claims. The CIU was another social vehicle which was reshaped by its working-class members in this period. Older radicals were dismayed to find political and educational activities increasingly discounted in the interests of more entertainment. Thus the CIU's *Journal* for June 1891 referred to the 'unsatiable thirst for amusements', lamenting that the 'educational side of club life is quite forgotten'. It was regrettable, it went on, that able lecturers could hardly get an audience while 'the comic singer and sketch artiste, however lacking in real ability, can always draw a hall full'.[55] In the same way the working class was imposing its own imprint on football. Originally seen by middle-class popularisers as a means of encouraging controlled exercise or as a carrot to foster church attendance, many of the church-based teams soon rid themselves of their ecclesiastical ties, while many of the new professional teams were initially founded by working men themselves. Cutlers established Sheffield United, munitions workers at Woolwich formed Arsenal. With this came a new approach to the game, based on team work and discipline, aptitudes more akin to those required in daily working life. When Blackburn Olympic defeated Old Etonians in the 1883 cup final, it was observed by one sporting journalist that the professionals had gone in for 'wide crossing, whilst their opponents stuck to the close dribbling game'.[56]

Generally, then, there is little in the suggestion that socialism in Britain was stunted by sophisticated forms of social control. The explanation is much less sinister. For most Englishmen life was bounded by their own immediate locality and daily concerns, not by broad political issues or the vision of some future utopia. This is why most of them were not swayed by jingoistic sentiment at the time of the Boer War. It was not that they were pro-Boer: on the contrary, they were generally indifferent about what seemed a very remote affair.[57] For music hall audiences, socialism was often the butt of their amusement. Little Tich had a famous sketch in which he claimed that 'my brother's in the gas trade . . . in fact he travels on gas. He's a socialist orator.'[58] For others socialism was a matter of yawning apathy, well summarised in Robert Roberts' boyhood memories of Salford. 'Hyndman Hall, home of the Social Democratic Federation, remained for us mysteriously aloof and through the years had, in fact, about as much political impact on the neighbourhood as the near-by gasworks.'[59] In a perceptive essay, Gareth Stedman Jones has shown how in the late nineteenth century the London working class (especially the artisans), far from accepting an imposed middle-class culture, developed its own based on the pub, the sporting paper, and the music hall.[60] *Sporting Life*, *Sportsman*, and the *Sporting Chronicle* had circulations in excess of 300,000 by the late 1880s; and the evidence suggests that the volume of betting was rising steadily. It was a reflection of a mentality that had no long-term past or future, only short-term memory and immediate anticipation; a culture of consolidation which accepted the present role of the working class in an apparently inevitable social hierarchy.

Max Weber has argued that the bulk of everyday actions are a matter of almost automatic responses to habitual stimuli. This perhaps explains why political allegiances, once formed, are very hard to shift, unless some major interuption in the stimuli pattern occurs. Viewed in this light, therefore, it could be argued that supporting socialism, even voting Labour, in the late nineteenth century was tantamount to an aberration in political behaviour, a breaking of habits long moulded by economic, family and working circumstances.[61] The factory frequently shaped the political sympathies of its workers. One Liberal manager observed as early as 1868 that 'each individual operative comes to identify with the mill at which he works, and if he be not troubled with convictions of his own, readily accepts its political shibboleths.'[62] The same point was made by Sir George Elliott, who attributed his defeat in 1874 to the fact that there had been an 'extremely rowdy election in which the workmen employed by the various candidates fought in their employers' campaigns'.[63]

For others, traditional behaviour was reinforced by economic insecurity. Generally the late nineteenth century was a time of rising living standards in Britain. Food prices fell under the combined impact of cheap foreign imports, cheaper methods of mass production, and the spread of multiple retail outlets taking low profits on high turnovers. Sugar and tea consumption doubled between 1860 and 1910, while mass-produced jam, margarine and even chocolate all became more familiar items in working-class diet. The expansion of the popular press and commercial entertainment were other indicators of rising standards. Yet the aggregate statistics can tell us little about the distribution of these benefits of falling prices. It came as an enormous shock when, at the turn of the century, social investigators such as Charles Booth and Seebohm Rowntree showed that significant proportions of the urban working population were living on or precariously near their definitions of subsistence. The belief in laisser faire was still very firmly entrenched at all levels of British public life and government responded slowly and reluctantly to the growing clamour from trade unions, philanthropists and others for state intervention to tackle the problems of poverty caused by old age, sickness, unemployment and accident. Another main cause of the poverty uncovered by the social investigators – low wages – could, it is true, be partially offset by high regularity of employment and long working hours. Against this must be set evidence that rising incomes were frequently dissipated on drink, which remained an integral part of working-class life and was a habit which responded only slowly to economic change.[64] Again, much of the potential benefit to be derived from falling food prices might have been lost because of a lack in many working-class homes of adequate cooking facilities or culinary expertise. On the whole, despite some progress with slum clearance in the bigger cities, housing remained poor. Even the revelations made by Andrew Mearns in 1883 produced little in the way of concrete progress.[65] Thirty years later another social investigator, Maud Pember Reeves, found housing so bad in Lambeth that her bi-weekly visit was like 'a bi-weekly plunge into Hades'.[66]

Extrapolating from Booth and Rowntree, Edwardians

believed that about twelve million people were living in or very near to poverty. It is small wonder that for such people political behaviour generally remained a matter of unthinking habit, and visions of a socialist millennium seemed remote. 'If I were to work ten hours a day at work I despised and hated,' wrote Morris, 'I should spend my leisure, I hope in political agitation, but I fear in drinking.'[67] Tressell noted this same stubborn indifference to new political ideas among the building workers who form the subject of his novel. Some of those who accepted pamphlets from the socialist hero, Owen, 'afterwards boasted that they had used them as toilet paper'.[68] In the absence of much welfare provision, other than the despised Poor Law or charity, this constant struggle for survival turned many inwards to their own families. Many commentators have drawn attention to the increased centrality of the family in late-nineteenth-century working-class life, a phenomenon observable in the work of some of the northern dialect poets, and also in music hall favourites such as *My old dutch*, originally sung to a backcloth depicting the work-house with its separate entrances for men and women. The family itself, it is argued, was another powerfully conservative stimulus, reinforcing traditional behaviour patterns.[69]

Almost certainly, however, the biggest conservative obstacle to socialist progress was the trade-union movement itself, a lesson brought home forcibly to the ILP at the time of the Barnsley by-election in 1897. Barnsley was the headquarters of the Yorkshire Miners' Association (YMA), the most powerful constituent of the Miners' Federation of Great Britain (MFGB). Four members of the MFGB executive, including Ben Pickard, the president, were members of the YMA. In deciding to fight the election, the ILP was appealing to the miners to go against their leaders in what Hardie regarded as the very heartland of official Lib-Lab'ism. Pickard had established his strong personal following in the area by his dedicated and often militant espousal of the miners' grievances, but he combined industrial militancy with political Liberalism. Notwithstanding the fact that the Liberal can-didates in the by-election was a colliery owner, the YMA officially supported him against the ILP nominee, Pete Curran. Pickard was virulent in his condemnation of the

ILP, suspecting that its real purpose was to get access to the union's funds, currently standing at some £30,000. In the event Curran was heavily defeated, taking only about 1100 votes in a poll of 11,300. The conclusion drawn by the historian of this campaign is that where trade unionism was of relatively long standing, it had usually shown itself to be a suitable vehicle for achieving working-class ends, which were primarily concerned with daily matters affecting working lives. Because it was of long standing, it had also tended to form political attachments with the Liberal party which few trade unionists could see the sense of breaking. The ILP only made real headway in areas such as Bradford where it emerged at the same time as a strong trade-union movement. This was also the conclusion reached by Hardie. Barnsley, he told David Lowe, was 'the worst thing we have yet done'; and thereafter he set out to forge an alliance with the unions, rather than encouraging the ILP to stand in its own right.[70]

As it happened, the circumstances were propitious for such a strategy, since the idea of working-class representation was making some progress. This had something to do with the growing physical and social isolation of the working class. As industrial concentration and merger spread, small businesses declined in importance. Employers became increasingly remote from their employees, and the continued disintegration of sub-contracting destroyed the hopes of those workers who had aspired to become their own masters. Those who made progress in the larger concerns tended to be drawn from the clerical grades rather than from the shop floor. The white-collar sector was by now one of the fastest growing occupational groupings, and its intermediate position placed yet another barrier between workers and employers. The 1870 Education Act may not have been terribly successful as a form of social engineering; but the introduction of compulsion in the 1880s served to heighten a sense of both common identity and social isolation among working-class children, since they were now all exposed to the deadening curriculum designed, as H.G. Wells observed, 'to educate the lower classes for employment on lower class lines'.[71] At almost the same time opportunities for secondary education were severely curtailed when the Public Schools Act of 1868 replaced the free places for the local poor with a system of open, competitive examinations, which naturally favoured those who could afford coaching. Transport developments accelerated the process of social segregation. Ease of movement prompted the building of better class housing in suburban areas, leaving city centres and other well-designated sectors for the workers. There was considerable middle-class resistance in London to proposals for extending the cheaper transport services available by the end of the century, on the grounds that this would expose middle-class districts to working-class invasion, spoiling them 'for ordinary residential purposes'.[72]

The gap between the classes was further widened by the accelerated erosion in the later part of the century of many traditional skills. In a host of industries such as engineering, boot and shoe manufacture, iron moulding, woodworking, plumbing and watchmaking, semi-skilled youths and women were introduced to work new machines detrimental to the status of skilled men. This had the effect of more thoroughly proletarianising the workforce. Of course this should not be exaggerated; for, as Robert Roberts points out, the working class itself remained riddled with internal divisions and distinctions. Nowhere, he writes, was this more apparent than at the theatre. 'Shopkeepers and publicans in the orchestra stalls and dress circle, artisans and regular workers in the pit stalls, and the low class and no class on the "top shelf" or balcony. There in the gods hung a permanent smell of smoke from "thick twist", oranges and unwashed humanity.'[73] Even so, the greater isolation and internal cohesion of the working class served to give the argument for political independence some extra import, especially when it was becoming ever more apparent that the Liberal party, particularly at local level, was indifferent to the interests of a class which it traditionally claimed to represent.

Francis Schnadhorst, secretary of the Liberal Central Federation, reacted very coolly in 1890 when the Metropolitan Radical Federation asked him to withdraw fifty Liberal candidates so that they could be replaced by MRF-sponsored radicals. Within a couple of years the Fabians had become so exasperated by the Liberal attitude that they had come out strongly in favour of creating an independent party. At

Attercliffe in 1894 the Liberals were divided when Labour put up its own nominee, Frank Smith. The local Liberal boss, Sir Fred Mappin, was resolute in his opposition, however, never even considering that Labour might have a moral claim on a predominantly working-class constituency. The Liberals took the seat, but one by-product was that a certain James Ramsay MacDonald applied for membership of the ILP. 'Liberalism,' he wrote, 'and more particularly, local Liberal Associations, have definitely declared against Labour, and so I must admit that the prophecies of the I.L.P. relating to Liberalism have been amply justified . . .'[74] In the same way, A.G. Symonds of the National Reform Union told C.P. Scott that working men would not attend Liberal ward meetings because 'they appreciate fully the fact that the money is in the hands of a few men who wd. refuse to subscribe for the election expenses of a working man.'[75] Nor was the Liberal cause much helped by the 1893 Featherstone massacre, when striking miners were killed by soldiers whose intervention had been authorised by the Liberal Home Secretary, H.H. Asquith.

The Featherstone massacre was one of several incidents which marked out the period 1893–1898 as one of bitter industrial conflict in which the unions suffered heavy losses. To some extent this was a result of the unions' own unrealistic aspirations. As early as December 1889, John Burns had warned lest enthusiasm 'degenerated into recklessness', but the tide of new unionism then seemed irresistible.[76] Many of the new organisations thus ran into difficulties because their ambitions outgrew their strength. In the main, however, the union setbacks were the result of noticeable hardening in employers' attitudes. Their counter-offensive had the support of some quite dogmatic anti-union organisations, such as the Liberty and Property Defence League, and was attributed by Havelock Wilson to a simple desire to ' "get" the men'.[77] Its main driving force came from the economic difficulties to which employers were being exposed by rising foreign competition and the falling profits associated with twenty years of economic depression. The heavy metal trades were affected by American and German competition especially. The employers' answer was the introduction of new, cheaper technology. Thus iron moulders found themselves under threat from metal moulding machines which could be worked by upgraded labourers. In engineering, capstan and turret lathes, milling machines and radial drills appeared, as did efforts to increase the speed of production through payment by results. Round about the turn of the century, new wood-working machines were also adopted, once more capable of operation by unapprenticed labour. In coal, owners were faced with falling prices. Yorkshire coal, for example, at 8s.3d. a ton in 1890 had plunged to 6s.10d. by 1893. Labour was by far the biggest, single cost item in the industry; so owners intent on restoring profit margins were headed directly for conflict with unions like the Yorkshire miners, who had no intention of surrendering the forty per cent wage increase they had secured since the 1880s. Even transport under-takings were in difficulty. Legislation in 1894 had bound the railway companies to charge the freight rates operative in December 1892. Since another act of 1893 also limited the hours which an individual railwayman could work, the companies found themselves in an effective economic strait-jacket, with little room to meet wage demands. Local transport men found wages and jobs threatened by the move from steam to electric trams and the replacement of horse cabs by motor-driven ones, while metropolitan railwaymen had also to face the threat posed by the advent of the new electric train. In the woollen industry, manufacturers had to meet foreign competition head on. Since their main markets were in the United States and Europe, they could not take the option open to other branches of the textile industry of retreating into relatively safe empire markets.

The result of all this was not only to push skilled and unskilled closer together, as we have already suggested, but also to set the stage for a series of industrial clashes whose severity was perhaps only marginally tempered by continued rising real wages for most of the decade. The number of working days lost each year through industrial action between 1892 and 1898 averaged 13.2 million compared with 2.3 million between 1899 and 1907.[78] Much of the conflict during the heady days of the new unionism had centred on the issue of employers' rights to hire and fire labour. The unions' ability to keep out blacklegs had been an important factor in their success. The Leeds gas strike, for instance, had been won because the council's gas committee found it impossible to protect the strike-breakers whom it had imported. It was on this same issue that the employers now concentrated their counter-offensive. The Employers' Shipping Federation grew out of a meeting organised to protest at the government's failure to protect non-union labour. It established offices in most of the ports, issued tickets to men willing to work with union and non-union labour alike, and then gave them preferential treatment when taking on labour. Using this system, they were able to defeat with comparative ease strikes in the London docks in 1890–1 and at Hull in 1893. The shipping companies and some of the smaller railway enterprises also utilised William Collison's National Free Labour Association, which specialised in providing semi- and unskilled workers as strike-breakers. It has long been assumed that this organisation, which also ran a newspaper and held annual conferences, was permanently subsidised by the shipping companies. Few of its records survive, however, and there is no direct evidence that employers ever did more than pay for specific services rendered at particular times.[79]

The employers' counter-offensive implied not merely an assertion of their right to control employment against labour's; the right was being asserted equally against government. The 1890s witnessed a number of changes in the organisation of the Board of Trade, one of which involved the creation of a new labour department. Using the provisions of the new Conciliation Act, the department sought to foster the idea of conciliation, which had emerged (as we have seen) in the 1860s. By 1904 it had assisted in the creation of 162 joint negotiating boards in different industries. But the Board of Trade's attempts to intervene directly in some of the major disputes at the end of the decade – the 1897 engineers' strike, the stoppage in the South Wales coalfield, the dispute in the Penrhynn quarries – were rejected by employers. Lord Penrhynn replied typically that such mediation would constitute 'a precedent for outside interference in the management of my private affairs'.[80]

The long engineers' strike was probably the most dramatic event in the whole saga. One important outcome was that the

TUC accepted a plan, which it had rejected in 1895, to establish a general federation as a form of mutual insurance against the heavy financial burdens of unduly long strikes. H.D. Lloyd touched upon a sensitive nerve among British workers when he warned at about this time that employers were taking 'the opinions of American lawyers as to the American way of dealing with labour troubles'.[81] Certainly it must have seemed that way, for the decade saw a number of legal cases which posed an immediate threat to union freedom. Lyons v Wilkins (1896 and 1899) led to the conviction of a striker for picketing, while in Trollope v London Building Trades Federation (1895) the publication of a list of 'blacked' employers was judged to be a conspiracy to injure.

Together these various pressures were enough to convince a growing number of trade unionists of the need to possess a more effective and independent political voice. In 1898, for example, the newly established federation of South Wales miners laid down as one of its objectives the provision of 'funds wherewith to pay the expenses of returning and maintaining Representatives to Parliament . . . to press forward by every legitimate means all proposals conducive to the general welfare of the members of the Federation'.[82] Miners of course had sufficient financial resources and voting strength to be able to return their own nominees to Parliament. For the rest, however, co-operation was necessary. In 1899 Hardie's years of ceaseless campaigning finally bore fruit. Although there were still those like Ben Pickard who believed that labour's best interests could be served from within the Liberal party, the delegates at the TUC carried a resolution summoning a conference to discuss the establishment of an independent, working-class political party.

6

The Emergence of Labour, 1900-21

The foundation conference of the Labour Representation Committee gathered at the Memorial Hall, Faringdon Street, London, in February 1900. It was attended by representatives of about half a million trade unionists, the main socialist parties, and a few assorted mavericks like Burns. Despite the fact that the SDF was soon to withdraw in protest against the new organisation's refusal to recognise the doctrine of class war, the socialists still gained an influence out of all proportion to their numerical strength. The twelve-man executive was composed of seven union nominees and five from the ILP, SDF and Fabian Society. Since no one else appeared to want the task, Ramsay MacDonald of the ILP was elected secretary. After some disagreement about precise wording, it was decided to establish 'a distinct Labour Group in Parliament, who shall have their own Whips, and agree upon their policy, which must embrace a readiness to cooperate with any party which for the time being may be engaged in promoting legislation in the direct interest of labour'.[1]

These were fine sounding words, but it still took a final thrust from the employers to drive home Hardie's message. In 1901 the House of Lords upheld the claim made by the Taff Vale Railway Company against the ASRS for damages incurred by its members during a strike. The ruling immediately exposed all other unions' funds to similar claims. Within a fortnight a second case, Quinn v Leathem, saw judgement given against a union for organising a boycott against an employer. Together with the earlier Lyons v Wilkins which had made inroads on picketing rights, these decisions were seen as a direct threat to the unions' ability

198

to take industrial action. As the House of Lords was the ultimate legal authority, the verdicts could only be reversed by altering the law itself, a situation which gave added weight to the argument for independent parliamentary representation. As L.T. Hobhouse put it, 'that which no Socialist writer or platform orator could achieve was effected by the judges'.[2] Trade unionists were by no means unanimous in their response to the Taff Vale decision. It was appreciated in some circles, for example, that the verdict was not simply an example of judicial hostility but a logical development of the legal device of the representative action. Some unionists saw in legal liability a way of encouraging responsible behaviour or limiting rank and file militancy. It also followed that if unions could be sued as corporate entities then they could also enter into legally binding contracts, especially with employers; and to some union leaders this was quite an attractive proposition. On the whole, however, those major unions which had already gained recognition from employers preferred to keep the law out of industrial relations. By 1903, therefore, several of the larger ones, including the engineers and Lancashire textile workers, had decided to affiliate to the LRC, thereby helping to raise party membership to 861,000 from only 375,000 in 1901. Very promptly the LRC committed itself to work with the TUC and GFTU for a complete reversal of the Taff Vale judgement.

This accretion of support was certainly welcome, as the party had made a very poor showing in the general election of 1900 which came barely six months after the Memorial Hall meeting. Of fifteen LRC candidates only two, Richard Bell of the ASRS and Hardie, had been victorious. This seemed to confirm the lesson of the 1890s: namely that, except in very peculiar circumstances, working-class political action without Liberal support was likely to be ineffective. Hardie and MacDonald drew the appropriate conclusion and entered into long negotiations with the chief Liberal whip, Herbert Gladstone, to get some agreement on the allocation of seats. The Liberal hierarchy — already divided over several important policy matters — was anxious to marshall all progressive forces under one banner and was quite confident of being able to contain the LRC. The process of accommodation was aided by the emergence of a number of important political issues on which there was little real difference between Liberal and Labour. Since both parties had strong non-conformist attachments, it is not surprising that they found the 1902 Education Act distasteful. Not only did this measure replace the old school boards, in which non-conformist influence had been quite strong, with local education authorities, but it also appeared to be subsidising Anglican and Catholic religious education out of the rates. Liberal and Labour alike were also outraged by the importation of cheap Chinese labour into the Transvaal. The objection was partly moral, partly economic; in that the employment of the coolies was seen as the first stage of a process that would end, in Lloyd George's dramatic phrase, with Chinese coolies on the hills of Wales. After 1903 Chamberlain's proposals for tariff reform further cemented this growing empathy, for Labour shared the Liberal commitment to free trade.

Victories for Will Crooks at Woolwich and Arthur Henderson at Barnard Castle in 1903 gave a boost to the LRC and seemed to confirm the wisdom of Gladstone's strategy, as both were barely distinguishable from orthodox Liberals. Not all local Liberals shared his enthusiasm, however, for when a general election came in 1906 eighteen of the LRC's fifty candidates had Liberal opponents and all were beaten. Isaac Mitchell, a trade unionist of such modest views that he was condemned by the local branch of the ILP, failed to win Darlington, for instance, prompting the conclusion that 'even the Labour label was enough to deter many middle class Darlington Liberals, despite the moderate views of its wearer'.[3] Elsewhere, though, the electoral pact held. In ten double-member constituencies, Liberal and LRC candidates ran successfully in harness. All told, twenty-nine LRC candidates were returned, no fewer than twelve of them in Lancashire.

The election produced the famous Liberal landslide, but for many contemporaries the first significant appearance of the LRC (soon renamed the Labour party) was almost as noteworthy. Arthur Balfour, the defeated Unionist Prime Minister, observed in his usual languid fashion that 'we are face to face (no doubt in a milder form) with the socialistic

difficulties which loom so large on the continent.'[4] The editor
of the *Daily Express*, Ralph Blumenfeld, was much more
direct. The new party, he claimed, was nothing more than an
amalgam of 'the unsuccessful, the unfortunate, the discon-
tented, and the lazy . . . with the ill-balanced dreamer of
dreams'.[5] Blumenfeld was one of those Unionists whose fear
of socialism verged on paranoia – he played a leading role
in the establishment of the Anti-Socialist Union in 1908 –
and it is small wonder that J.R. Clynes, the new Labour MP
for North East Manchester, could later recall that he and his
colleagues had been widely condemned as 'red tie fanatics'.[6]
Yet nothing could have been further from the truth. The
new party's representatives were an elderly and highly respectable group. Their average age was well over that for the
House of Commons as a whole: over two-thirds of them
were trade-union officials, while the majority claimed some
link with temperance and non-conformity. Further, there
were just twenty-nine of them. Even with the addition of
J. Johnson, who left the Liberal benches soon after the
election, a dozen or so miners' MPs, and those trade unionists
returned as Liberals, there were still only about fifty representatives of labour in the House – hardly sufficient to
threaten an overall Liberal majority of 130. Labour was
even still outnumbered by the other minority party, the
Irish Nationalists.

Yet the labour press was just as taken as its national
counterpart with the LRC's success, and by the end of 1906
its enthusiasm did not seem all that misplaced. The government had dropped its own proposals to deal with the Taff
Vale judgement in favour of the Trades Disputes Bill, a much
more radical measure produced by the Joint Board of the
Labour party, TUC and GFTU, conferring immunity on
unions against prosecution for damages incurred during
strikes. A new Workmen's Compensation Act was passed,
some of the harsher rules governing the administration of
the 1905 Unemployed Workmen's Act were relaxed, and
legislation also went through permitting local authorities
to provide meals for needy school children. At local level,
too, the party progressed, buoyed up by parliamentary
success. Representation on local councils grew and so did

party affiliation, though hardly at the rate suggested by
one panic-stricken Unionist, 'thousands of adherents every
week'.[7] Even so, for every Labour activist there were many
others who shared the cynical views of one of Tressell's
decorators. 'Look at them ther' Labour members of Parliament — a lot of b-----rs what's too bloody lazy to work
for their livin'. What the bloody 'ell was they before they
got there? Only workin' men, the same as you and me. But
they've got the gift of the gab.'[8]

Within a couple of years a similar cynicism was to be found
among the ranks of the faithful themselves. The first mutter-
ings of discontent were heard in 1907, a year in which the
party's lack of parliamentary impact, while in keeping with
its true insignificance, stood in marked contrast to the
achievements of 1906. Matters came to a head in the winter
of 1908—9, ostensibly over the matter of unemployment
which reached serious levels at this time. Here it seemed was
a promising field for a Labour initiative. John Burns, in
charge of unemployment policy by virtue of his presidency
of the Local Government Board, had preferred to do very
little before the report of the Royal Commission on the Poor
Law was ready. A small grant of some £200,000 had been
made available to local authorities desirous of creating work
schemes for their unemployed, but Burns' parsimonious
handling of the money had only added to Labour anger. The
Joint Board had its own remedy to hand in the form of the
Right to Work Bill, which would have compelled local
authorities to provide the unemployed either with work or
maintenance. The bill had first been introduced in 1907 and
then again in March 1908. When unemployment began to
rise steeply in the autumn of 1908, therefore, the party was
left at something of a loss — as the rules of parliamentary
procedure did not permit a measure to be introduced twice
in one session. Victor Grayson, who had won the Colne
Valley by-election in 1907, was suspended from the House
in October when he tried to introduce the unemployment
issue during the committee stage discussions on the Licensing Bill. As he left the chamber, Grayson turned to condemn
the Labour members as traitors to their own class for failing
to insist on the primacy of unemployment. It was a criticism

which cut much deeper than the unemployed issue *per se*,
however. Grayson had won Colne Valley without the official
support of the Labour party, and had termed himself a 'clean
socialist'. By this he meant one who was not prepared to
compromise his principles for the sake of either tactical
advantage in the Commons or maintaining the ILP alliance
with the predominantly Liberal trade unions. Hardie himself
had expressed some doubts on this score, telling Bruce
Glasier in 1908 that 'there are times when I confess to feeling
sore at seeing the fruits of our years of toil being garnered
by men who were never of us'.[9] If Hardie and a group of
more radical party members were prepared to co-operate
with the Social Democratic Party (as the SDF became in
1908) in the National Right to Work Council in order to keep
up a lively agitation on behalf of the unemployed, they were
certainly not willing to see the labour alliance disrupted
fundamentally, even in the interests of 'pure' socialism.[10]

Grayson lost his seat in the first of the two general elections held in 1910, but it scarcely mattered as he was by now
a leading figure in the growing rank and file move to free
socialism from the labour alliance. All the political running,
it seemed, was being made by the government; and this was
a major source of discontent within the movement. After
Asquith replaced Campbell-Bannerman as Prime Minister in
1908, the new Liberals — with their commitment to using
state power to protect the individual — became more prominent within the cabinet. A spate of important social reforms
ensued, designed to deal with some of the chief causes of
poverty uncovered by Booth and Rowntree. Old age pensions
came in 1908. Five shillings a week for those over seventy
with no other substantial income was perhaps not much, but
it did provide a welcome buffer for the many elderly people
living on the margins of poverty. For such people, recalls
Flora Thompson,

> Life was transformed . . . At first when they went to the
> Post Office to draw it, tears of gratitude would run down
> the cheeks of some, and they would say as they picked up
> their money, 'God bless that Lord George!' (for they
> could not believe that one so powerful and munificent
> could be a plain 'Mr') and 'God bless, you miss!' and

there were flowers from their gardens and apples from
their trees for the girl who merely handed them the
money.[11]

The scheme was non-contributory and, partly to help raise
the necessary revenue, Lloyd George introduced a budget
in 1909 which contained a number of controversial proposals
to increase taxes on the wealthy few in order to benefit the
penurious many. It was eloquent of the disparities of wealth
taken for granted in Edwardian Britain that an outraged
House of Lords took the unprecedented step of rejecting the
finance bill, thereby precipitating a constitutional crisis with
the Commons, not fully resolved until 1911.

Two years previously the government had introduced legislation to improve wage bargaining and conditions for some of
the thousands working in the sweated industries. Unorganised,
predominantly female, and often working at home, this was
the part of the labour force most vulnerable to exploitation.
As Jack London wrote:

> Conceive of an old woman, broken and dying, supporting
> herself and four children, and paying three shillings per
> week rent, by making match boxes at 2¼d per gross.
> Twelve dozen boxes for 2¼d, and, in addition, finding
> her own paste and thread! She never knew a day off, either
> for sickness, rest or recreation. Each day and every day,
> Sundays as well, she toiled fourteen hours. Her day's stint
> was seven gross, for which she received 1s. 3¾d. In the week
> of ninety hours work, she made 7066 match boxes, and
> earned 4s. 10¼d., less paste and thread.[12]

Although of limited impact, the 1909 act established wages
boards in four of the most abused areas — ready-made clothing, chain, box and lace making. The same year saw the passage of another significant measure, the Labour Exchanges
Act, steered through by Winston Churchill but mainly the
brainchild of a rising young civil servant, W.H. Beveridge.
The object was to facilitate the flow of unemployed labour
to areas of labour demand, in this way reducing the amount
of time an individual might spend without work. Two years
later came the crowning glory of the social welfare state
which the Liberals had been erecting. The 1911 National

Insurance Act established a limited, contributory insurance system to protect some workers — those in heavy industry and some particularly prone trades — against unemployment, and to protect all adult male workers against loss of earnings due to sickness.

In all of these measures, Labour had little more than a consultative role. Even in the attack on the House of Lords it appeared as little more than an appendage of the Liberal radicals. True, union officials were consulted about details of legislation and expressed reserves about the limited scope of the reforms or about possible adverse implications. There was a good deal of suspicion about labour exchanges, for instance, since there was a widespread fear that they would be utilised as blackleg recruiting centres during strikes. What Labour generally and the parliamentary party in particular was failing to do was to make any policy initiatives. It was this which some of the movement's own members found so galling. In 1910 dissident members of the ILP produced the famous Green Manifesto, *Let Us Reform the Labour Party*. It was very critical of the moderate policies followed in Parliament and bitterly attacked the ILP leaders for abandoning the socialist position of independence from all other parties. The following year the rebels broke right away, merging with the SDP and the Clarion Fellowship to form the British Socialist party (BSP), which was led by that most durable of socialist virgins, H.M. Hyndman. By 1912 the BSP claimed a following some fifteen thousand, about half the strength of the ILP at its peak. Some ILP branches defected to the BSP, and others split over whether or not to join.

Yet there was much to be said for the strategy being followed by MacDonald, who had emerged as Labour's chief parliamentary tactician. For one thing, the party was making little electoral headway. In fourteen by-elections between 1910 and 1914, Labour candidates finished bottom of the poll on every occasion. Although parliamentary strength had been augmented as a result of the 1910 general elections, this was largely illusory and a result of the miners' decision to affiliate in 1908, thus handing Labour a dozen or so safe seats. Ever a realist, MacDonald knew that advance did not lie down the path of 'pure' socialism. Furthermore, the party could not afford to risk alienating the unions by becoming more radical, since it was in considerable financial difficulty. In 1909 the political levy with which the unions supported the Labour party was ruled illegal as a result of the Osborne case. Attempts to minimise the impact of this by organising voluntary contributions from union members proved singularly unsuccessful, further proof, if any were needed, of the tenuous foothold the party still had within the union movement. In 1911, therefore, MacDonald offered Labour support for the government's National Insurance Bill in return for a government pledge to introduce a measure for the payment of MPs. While this solved the immediate problem of maintaining Labour members, it did nothing to restore the flow of union money to the party coffers. This was only achieved by the act of 1913 which permitted the restoration of the political levy after a ballot among union members. Just how realistic MacDonald's moderation was is seen in the fact that in many unions there were sizable votes against the levy. Nearly 200,000 miners opposed it and 35,000 railwaymen; the carpenters supported it but only in the ratio of 13:12, weavers by 98:76, and engineers 21:13.

One conclusion which might also be drawn from these figures is that the bulk of trade unionists still believed that in the main their day-to-day problems were of a sort more usually amenable to solution through industrial action and negotiation. Blatchford had claimed in 1902 that just as a union was a 'combination of workers to defend their own interests' so the Labour party was the same thing in Parliament.[13] Once the Trades Disputes Bill was passed, legitimate questions were raised about the Labour party's value to the unions, doubts exacerbated by its persistent reluctance to draft a comprehensive political programme. From about 1901 there had been relative industrial peace in Britain. It is tempting to see this as a result of the various legal judgments passed round the turn of the century, and then to explain growing unrest after 1907 as the product of the freer conditions provided by the 1906 Trades Disputes Act. There is certainly an element of truth in such an interpretation, although — as the 1907 Belfast dock strike indicated — the meaning of the peaceful picketing permitted by the 1906 legislation could still be very narrow.[14] More importantly, however, the pattern of industrial relations in these years has to be seen firstly in terms of growing inter-union disputes arising from constant technological innovation and secondly in terms of the increasing inadequacy of conciliation schemes, for the most part set up in the 1870s, to cope with the changing economic circumstances of the first decade of the twentieth century. Many major industries such as mining, engineering and shipbuilding, had adopted procedures for the referral of disputes to central joint committees. By 1907 many of these central bodies were coming under severe strain. In the South Wales coal industry, for example, no agreement was reached in 231 of the 391 disputes referred to the conciliation board between 1903 and 1910.

The chief reason for this inadequacy was that both sides of industry were coming under increasing economic pressure. Real wages had been falling since 1900, and this for a generation which had known little but improvement in its general living standards. In specific industries, workers found themselves under particular pressures. Mining costs were rising, partly because of falling productivity, partly because of the costs incurred in implementing new safety legislation. The bill restricting miners' working hours to eight fell especially hard on the South Wales men who worked piece rates for longer hours than any other miners except those in Lancashire. It is not surprising, therefore, that South Wales was one of the most militant mining areas at this time. For those owners whose product was exported, the answer to rising costs could not be price increases, since this would adversely affect the sale of coal in foreign markets. Over half of Welsh coal was exported and thus again it is no surprise to find that the Welsh owners, led by Sir William Lewis, were among the most resolute opponents of the 1912 Minimum Wages Act. Effectively restrained from raising prices, they were looking to cost reductions, and the biggest cost in mining was labour. Similar tensions were present in the railways. As we have seen, freight rates were pegged at 1892 levels by act of Parliament. In face of rising costs which could not therefore be countered by raising prices, railway owners were not very sympathetic to demands for greater money wages to offset falling purchasing power. In some cases they attempted to meet their own difficulties by introducing larger engines and rolling stock. As a result, by 1907 many firemen were shovelling twice as much coal as the previous generation for no increase in pay.

After 1910 the rate of strikes accelerated in line with the more rapid fall in real wages. There were major stoppages on the railways and docks (1911) and in the coal industry (1912). The number of days lost through industrial action (which had averaged 2.7 million for each year between 1900 and 1907) reached ten million on 1911, forty million in 1912, and 11.6 million in 1913. Industrial militancy was encouraged by the low level of unemployment. The increase in trade-union membership from 2.6 million in 1910 to 4.1 million by 1914 certainly owed something to the unions' role as administrators of the new health insurance scheme, but it owed much more to the rising demand for labour which facilitated both recruitment and militancy. It was a condition similar to that which had prevailed during the last great period of growth and agitation in the 1880s and early 1890s.

Conciliation boards thus found themselves caught between employers set on lowering costs and unions intent on preserving living standards. The pressure merely highlighted the main defects of most conciliation schemes. Much wage negotiation was in fact conducted at local level where there was no formal mechanism for resolving disputes. These therefore had to be referred to the central machinery, which was often slow and cumbersome. Conversely, local negotiators often found themselves bound by the terms of national agreements over which they had had little say. The other main weakness was that the conciliation schemes covered only about seventeen per cent of the workers in that part of the labour force which the unions might have expected to organise. The bulk of the workforce thus had no formal means of expressing grievances. The general result in an economic climate of falling real wages and rising costs was growing frustration in the workforces of several key industries. Sir Charles Macara's attempt to head this off by launching a National Industrial Council in October 1911, consisting of representatives of unions and management, failed to make any progress because it rested on the facile assumption that conciliation could of itself remove the underlying economic causes of industrial tension. Local resentments were reinforced by the fact that with growing size many unions now had a leadership that seemed remote from the problems of ordinary shop-floor workers. This was doubly true in those unions whose general secretaries doubled as members of Parliament. Shop-floor frustration, therefore, was increasingly voiced through unofficial leaders such as shop stewards. The north-east engineers strike of 1908 was just such a case. Local demands for greater autonomy led eventually to the resignation of the ASE's national secretary, George Barnes, MP. Similarly, the Aberdare miners' strike of 1911 grew out of rank and file annoyance at executive committee inactivity over redundancies at Maesteg and the matter of non-union labour in the pits. 'I think it is the commencement,' commented one miner, 'of a new era, and I can find nothing but an expression of dissatisfaction at the methods adopted by our leaders . . .'[15] His prediction was not far wrong. Everyone involved in industrial relations in these years commented on the growing incidence of unofficial action. The government's chief industrial troubleshooter, George Askwith, wrote, 'Official leaders could not maintain their authority. Often there was more difference between the men and their leaders than between the latter and the employers.'[16]

To some extent, too, this clash between official and unofficial leadership was a clash of generations. The older school of union officials had had their attitude moulded in the economically hazardous years of the great depression when conciliation was often the only way for unions to survive at all. They found it difficult to cope with a changed economic environment which was causing younger militants to demand an end to conciliation in order to protect incomes and to maximise labour's growing bargaining power.[17] In South Wales this difference between the generations was personified in the contrast between the staid officialdom of William Abraham and the Marxist militance of his young critic, Noah Ablett. Writing in August 1910 about 'Mabon', as Abraham was generally known, Ablett claimed that he 'tells us "with all due deference" that we are young and inexperienced. And you Mabon with equal deference — you are old — almost too old to hear the rising generation knocking at the door of progress.'[18] Another contemporary put the contrast into verse.

> You senior colliers kindly take
> A little hint from me —
> It isn't wise for your own sake
> That you're content to let things be . . .
> Tis yours to lead and not be led
> Nor leave the tail to wag the head.[19]

The unrest of this period was also characterised by a degree of violence which many contemporaries found alarming. Troops were called out on several occasions, most notoriously to Tonypandy in 1911. Contrary to popular Rhondda mythology, Winston Churchill as Home Secretary generally exercised a restraining influence on their use, for all that on occasion he was so exasperated by what he saw as union intransigence that he was 'in a shoot 'em down attitude'.[20] Violence in industrial relations was hardly novel, but what made it seem so ominous was that it coincided with the drift towards civil war in Ireland, the militant campaign being waged by Mrs Pankhurst's suffragettes, and the growing bitterness of inter-party hostility over the powers of the House of Lords. The great French historian, Halévy, believed that all these movements were symptoms of a general rejection of classical liberalism. Later writers have generally eschewed the notion of any underlying connection between these several protests, perhaps because Halévy did not really explain why they took a violent form. Beatrice Webb reckoned that in each case the issue really boiled down to a question of whether men were to be 'governed by emotion or reason. Are they to be governed in harmony with the bulk of the citizens or according to the fervent aspirations of a militant minority in defiance of the will of the majority?'[21]

Her diagnosis seems particularly apposite to industrial relations, because it was widely feared that at the root of the strike wave lay the revolutionary doctrine of syndicalism with its emphasis on direct and, if necessary, violent action. The general tenor of this ideology was, as one important contemporary publication had it, that 'the old policy of identity of interest between employers and ourselves be abolished, and a policy of open hostility installed'.[22] There were several sources of syndicalist influence in Britain. In South Wales an influx of Spanish workers had brought with them syndicalist ideas, and there was even a branch of the Spanish Socialist Workers party in Dowlais. The Socialist Labour party, centred mainly in Scotland, had broken away from the old SDF in 1903 and in the search for an alternative revolutionary strategy had been much influenced by Daniel De Leon's ideas of trade-union reorganisation to buttress the work of a revolutionary political party. De Leonist influence was also strong in Ruskin College, a small residential Oxford centre which provided further education for working men. In 1908 the principal and a number of the students demanded a restructuring of the Oxford syllabus to permit the teaching of Marxist economics and sociology. Faced with refusal, the rebels quit and set up their own Labour College in London with the backing of the Plebs League. Both the college and the league did much to spread Marxist ideas through their educational work. The other main syndicalist organisation was the Industrial League, which rejected the De Leonist emphasis on political action, preferring straightforward industrial warfare. Its policy, therefore, was one of infiltrating and influencing existing trade-union structures. Finally, there were a number of charismatic personalities who held syndicalist views. The most important were probably James Connolly and James Larkin, whose combined efforts came closer than any other to breaking down the age-old sectarian barriers which divided the working people of Ireland. In England Tom Mann was the most significant individual.

Mann had come under syndicalist influence during his travels in Europe and the United States. His was the charisma and his the journal, the *Industrial Syndicalist*, which served, albeit briefly, to pull together these somewhat disparate elements. The establishment of the National Transport Workers Federation in November 1910 represented a step towards his aim of creating a single union for each industry. In Wales the Unofficial Reform Committee issued an important pamphlet, *The Miners' Next Step*, which called for a policy of class war as a prelude to a takeover of the coal industry by the miners. Yet syndicalism did not really have the wide influence contemporaries sometimes feared. For one thing, it began to show signs of fragmenting after 1912. The failure of a Transport Workers Federation strike in London in that year led to the loss of a quarter of the membership. Similarly, the emergence of syndicalist influence in the South Wales coalfield was accompanied by a fall in membership of the SWMF. Nor was the establishment of the Triple Alliance between transport workers, railwaymen and miners a move towards the syndicalists' ultimate aim of one big union: it was merely a pragmatic alliance. Since a stoppage in any one of the industries concerned usually involved lay-offs in the others, it made sense to reduce the costs of strike pay by co-ordinating wage demands. Again, in the majority of strikes in this period it is difficult if not impossible to detect the syndicalist hand. While there was a tremendous increase in strikes in the textile industry, for example, they were born of economic, not ideological circumstances.[23] More appealing perhaps to British trade unionists, in whom ideas of parliamentary government and constitutionalism were deeply ingrained, was guild socialism. This was the brainchild mainly of A.R. Orage and S.G. Hobson, journalists on the *New Age*, whose plans for workers' control of industry and workers' guilds did not involve any form of drastic industrial confrontation. Even so, if syndicalism was overrated by contemporaries, it did represent an important phase in working-class history. It saw the clearest polarisation to date between the preponderant advocates of labourism, moderation and gradualism on the one hand and the militants on the other, who believed that fundamental social change was necessary and that it could only be achieved through violence.

The whole scene was changed quite dramatically by the outbreak of war in August 1914. Everywhere, it seemed, the disharmonies of the late Edwardian period were transformed in the enthusiasm for the conflict against Imperial Germany. Lengthy queues of working men formed outside the recruiting stations to such an extent that for nearly two years Britain was able to fight the bloodiest war in its history using volunteer servicemen. In the first seven months alone, 200,000 miners, nineteen per cent of the coal industry's labour force, enlisted.[24] Although there were those in the labour movement who opposed British involvement, most notably Keir Hardie and Ramsay MacDonald, they were a minority. One reflection of the general support for the war was the immediate issue by the TUC of a statement encouraging the hasty settlement of industrial disputes. In December 1914 the number of working days lost in strikes (three thousand) was a startling contrast to the 100,000 lost in the last full month of peace.

Yet the euphoria did not really last long. As war distorted the normal pattern of supply and demand, prices rocketed. Within two years food prices had more than doubled, forcing a Liberal administration to compromise with its laisser-faire principles and appoint a food controller, along with local committees to ensure fair distribution. Rents also shot up as workers poured into the centres of strategic war industry. Eventually the government was impelled to intervene after a well-organised rent strike on the Clyde in 1915 which threatened to interfere with the invaluable output of the area's engineering and munitions industries. The resultant Rent Restriction Act pegged all rents at prewar levels. In the protest that produced such measures, organised labour played its full part. The War Emergency Workers National Committee (WENWC), representing the unions, the Labour party, and the co-operative movement, was established very early on in the war. It offered advice and formulated policy over a whole range of issues from food control to disability pensions. Its suggestions were remarkably prophetic in the resemblance they bore to actual government policy, especially after Lloyd George became Prime Minister in 1916. Labour MPs who supported the war were taken into the government in the interests of national unity and performed valuable roles both as administrators and as bridges between government and labour. For what the war revealed as never before was the crucial role played by labour in the modern industrial economy. Trade-union co-operation was deemed vital in smoothing the introduction of new production techniques made necessary by the emergency of war; similar co-operation was essential when government itself took over responsibility for major industries such as the railways and mines. Thus when it was decided that manpower shortages in munitions and engineering could only be met by diluting skilled workers with unskilled, union officials were fully consulted at the Treasury Conference of 1915. Thereafter they were given places on the advisory committee established to oversee dilution. Unions were also directly involved in administering the trade card scheme whereby certain skilled workers were given exemption from military service, once conscription was introduced. It was perhaps in response to this growing involvement in public administration that Harry Gosling, the TUC president, argued in 1916 that 'we must not be satisfied until organised Labour is as important in its greater and more national aspects as any of the Departments of State, with its own block of offices and civil service . . .'[25] This seemed an ambitious vision in wartime for an organisation which had only appointed its first full-time secretary and clerical assistant some dozen years before, but shortly after Gosling's speech a staff development committee was established with a view to recommending organisational changes.

Locally, too, trade unions were incorporated into new administrative machinery set up to cope with wartime dislocation. The tribunals created to administer the Derby recruiting scheme were supposed to contain labour representatives. About one in eight of the places on local food control committees were allocated to labour (as against twenty-seven per cent to private traders and farmers).[26] Such involvement frequently opened the eyes of local labour leaders to their real economic significance. Thus the secretary of the Hereford Trades Council pointed out that his organisation

> has had an uneventful career for several years until 1914, when the circumstances arising out of this war brought into prominence the workers . . . making it the medium for pressing [their] interests forward before the various authorities and by its means the trade unions have secured representation on War Committees.[27]

While much of the information used by local union organisations in such war committee work came from central bodies like the WENWC, there is plenty of evidence that local and national union representatives did not always work in total harmony. The main vehicles of local involvement tended to be the trades councils, since they contained all grades and types of workers. Very often the councils, which in any case tended to attract more active and radical workers, found their role unsatisfactory; sometimes because they disagreed with the policies they were asked to implement; sometimes because they considered their representation inadequate. Thus one trades-council secretary – while admitting that the war had brought substantial benefits to organised labour, particularly 'the wholesale recognition of Trade Unionism by the State, the entrance of labour into the Cabinet, and the admission by the Government of our rights to representation on public bodies' – added that nevertheless there remained 'a suspicion that the total results of all is that the governing classes and capitalistic interests have but tightened their grip on labour . . . Samson has been lured and shorn of his strength.'[28] As war weariness grew after 1917, the trades councils became increasingly critical of the war effort, clashing more frequently with both government and central trade-union authority. One commissioner on the 1917 inquiry into industrial unrest in South Wales took the view that the councils had 'become centres of social and political activity more potent, perhaps, than any other of the social movements in the community'.[29]

The main source of friction between national and local trade-union leadership was government intervention in the labour market. When war broke out, nothing was done to stop skilled men enlisting. By July 1915, therefore, nearly a fifth of male engineers and a quarter of skilled explosives workers had joined up, leaving a diminished labour force to cope with rapidly rising demand. Labour unions and employers were unable to agree on measures to meet the shortage or to raise output, mainly because the latter reckoned that the answer lay in the suspension of restrictive labour practices. Vickers Armstrong, for example, estimated that this would enable them to increase output by at least twenty-five per cent. The unions, however, were unsympathetic, knowing that skilled men would object to any such threat to their status, especially if there was no guarantee that normal conditions and procedures would be restored after the war. 'There is a rooted feeling among . . . the intelligent working class,' wrote Beatrice Webb, 'that the governing class is using the opportunity of the war to alter the institutions of the country so that any kind of resistance against industrial oppression can be put down.'[30] Faced with the inability of labour and capital to reach any voluntary resolution of this problem and spurred on by a munitions crisis on the western front and the disruptive effects of strikes, the government itself intervened. A Ministry of Munitions was created to step up production. The first incumbent was David Lloyd George, who also presided over the 1915 Treasury Agreement by which unions agreed to suspend many traditional working practices in return for a government promise of their later restoration and also of an attack on profits. But this satisfied no one: profits were not adequately controlled, prices continued to rise, and union officials did little to press the rank and file to abide by the agreement's terms. Nor did employers find that there was much improvement in the supply of labour. This general discontent paved the way quite soon for legal controls, and most of the points of the Treasury Agreement were incorporated into the Munitions of War Act. Strikes were declared illegal, restriction of output became a criminal offence, and safety regulations were put in abeyance. In addition, unions were to accept the dilution of skilled work. The act also introduced what were thought to be more effective controls on profits.

Within two weeks of the act's passage the government was challenged by the miners of South Wales. On 21 July 1915, 200,000 of them struck work, threatening supplies of the raw material out of which toluol explosive was made and also supplies of vital naval coal. Despite threats from Lloyd George, who was dispatched to end the strike, it was clearly impossible to implement the Munitions Act and imprison so many strikers, and arresting ring leaders would merely have antagonised local resentments. Always a realist, Lloyd George put pressure on the owners (who had anyway been making enormous profits), and the miners secured nearly all their demands.

Quite quickly, however, the focus of attention shifted to

the Clyde engineering industry. So great was the demand for labour in that area that in the early part of the war unemployment among trade unionists had fallen to 0.06 per cent, and it is reckoned that about an eighth of Clydeside's industrial capacity was unused because of labour shortage. With its provision for dilution, the Munitions Act came as a major threat to the power and earning capacity which such a favourable labour market had conferred upon skilled engineers. Clyde workers had a long history of militance and also of hostility to England. Both were encouraged by the presence of a sizable Irish element in the population. Marxism was relatively strong, and John McLean provided Scottish workers with arguably the most outstanding Marxist agitator of his time. His resolute opposition to the war ensured that Glasgow remained virtually the only city in Britain where anti-war speakers could get a hearing. The SLP was well established in the area, and it was this party which provided most of the important personalities on the Clyde Workers Committee which organised opposition to the Munitions Act. This body was chaired by Willie Gallagher, and most of his lieutenants were shop-stewards whose importance had been generally growing even before the war as rank and file experienced growing remoteness from the national leadership. This feeling was certainly exacerbated during the war, when national ASE officials condoned the Treasury Agreement and then the Munitions Act. In the pay strike of February 1915, national ASE officials had aided government efforts to get the men back to work; and leadership of the strike had naturally devolved upon the shop-stewards' committee. Even after that strike was settled, the committee continued to meet informally, and it now emerged to lead the opposition to the Munitions Act. So alarmed was the government by this threat to its proposals to solve manpower problems that Lloyd George was once more sent to charm the workers, as he had so often done in the past. This time, however, he failed. Feeling on Clydeside was already inflamed by the chronic housing shortage, and on Christmas Day 1915 Lloyd George was howled down at a rowdy meeting in Glasgow. When he agreed to meet a deputation from the CWC, he was presented with demands for a government takeover of engineering, a greater degree of shop-floor participation in management, and more stringent controls on dilution. The SLP's paper, *Forward*, was closed down, while leading shop-stewards were arrested and deported to other cities. Deprived of leadership, the spontaneous protest strikes which erupted soon petered out and dilution was made more effective in the area.

There is little doubt that the government was determined to pursue its manpower policies as ruthlessly as necessary, but it is misleading to see the suppression of the CWC as part of a sustained campaign conducted by the Ministry of Labour against a quasi-revolutionary movement.[31] The civil servants most involved, Beveridge, Askwith and Llewellyn Smith, were all progressive men who had worked in the years before 1914 preparing welfare legislation or (in Askwith's case) in industrial relations, in a genuine effort to shift the balance of economic power more in labour's favour.[32] Further, it should be remembered that the Munitions Act in the main incorporated proposals to which most union leaders had agreed at the Treasury Conference. Nor is there much evidence that the mood of workers on the Clyde was revolutionary. It is true that some of the dilution commissioners on the Clyde believed that the CWC itself was a revolutionary body; but while several of its leaders espoused syndicalist views, the committee itself did little to raise people's aspirations above the level of immediate trade-union or economic grievances. Nor did they ever seek to organise a national stoppage, although there were other engineering centres — notably Sheffield and Barrow — where shop-stewards became equally significant and militant during the war. There was little prospect of success had they resorted to any action like this, since there were no parallel movements in other industries. Miners, for example, walked out of the Treasury Conference and did not regard themselves bound by it. They did not, therefore, feel the same sense of betrayal as did rank and file engineers, and existing union agencies seemed adequate enough as channels for their grievances. When the committee did take the initiative in calling a national conference in 1917 to link up various shop-steward movements, they were paralysed by their own commitment to decentralisation and suspicion of centralised leadership. It is doubtful, too, if there was any widespread support in the Clyde area itself for a revolutionary platform. There was plenty of discontent about housing and wages, but the CWC never effectively harnessed growing war weariness. Its main support came from those trade unionists whose fears it articulated, namely conservative craftsmen, fearful for their skilled status. That is why the shop-steward movement made most progress in those engineering centres where technology had remained relatively backward and old craft traditions survived. There was very little support for it in the newer engineering districts of the south midlands, where modern technology had been introduced right from the start and craft traditions already breached.

War finally ended in November 1918. It appeared that a new form of struggle was about to begin in Britain itself, however. Within a week of the armistice, Walter Long began sending alarmist memoranda to Lloyd George, predicting that 'there will be some sort of revolution in this country . . . before twelve months are past'.[33] The secretary of the Liverpool Trades Council caught the mood well when he warned that 'there is evidence, from every quarter, that the harassed, worried and exploited people are determined that they will no longer be the tools and victims of the employing class'.[34] Another trades-council official claimed that 'trade unions will no longer be merely defensive organisations against the encroachments of employers and capitalists but are directing an offensive against the very citadel of capitalism itself'.[35] Small wonder that J.A. Hobson commented in 1919 that, for the first time in British history, 'property is seriously afraid'.[36]

The immediate cause of such fears was the rash of industrial unrest which developed as war came to an end. In the last two years of fighting, the number of working days lost was nearly twice that of the first two years. The first full year of peace saw the loss of nearly thirty-five million days (as against five million in 1918). As early as January the CWC had 70,000 engineers out in Glasgow, and later in the same year provincial policemen struck (as their London colleagues had done in 1918) in protest at not being permitted to unionise. In January the miners demanded a six-hour day, a thirty per cent increase in wages, and nationalisation. Their threatened industrial action was only averted by the appointment of the Sankey Commission, whose report in favour of nationalisation diverted the miners' energies into a totally barren political campaign. In September railwaymen organised a national strike to resist wage reductions. The following year was no better. Strikes accounted for 26.5 million working days, and the Triple Alliance was reactivated as the miners persuaded the railway and transport workers to support their claim for fresh increases. The government, which had taken over control of the mines during the war, once more averted trouble by offering a six-month temporary increase. Despite the onset of depression and growing unemployment from mid-summer onwards, 1921 was marked by the loss of another eighty-five million days. The most serious stoppage was in the coal industry. The industry had always been noted for its bad industrial relations record. Perhaps this was because mining workforces were often very self-contained and homogeneous, with the result that work grievances could easily become communal grievances; or perhaps it was that in mining the contrast between wealthy capitalist and physical labourer was so starkly represented. Safety legislation had done much to improve working conditions in the pits, and the period of wartime government control had produced substantial advances for the miners; but as the British industry was still basically a matter of picks and shovels, working conditions were still appalling. The gradual adoption of mechanical cutting made little difference in this respect. One cutter said,

> Sometimes you're on your knees at the coal face, but I've seen men work on their belly. There was one place at Ravenhead where it was raining harder than you've ever seen on top, and never stopped — the colliers were up to their knees in water ... When you were cutting you couldn't talk to each other. If the day wageman wanted to say anything, he'd wave the lamp.
> Sometimes the roof would break off the coal and sink down a bit. Sometimes I've seen it fall, then you'd get squashed. I've seen one or two buried with falling roofs and get very injured.[37]

With the ending of the wage subvention, the government decided to hand the problems back to the coal owners by advancing the date of decontrol to March 1921. For their part, the owners believed that they could only counter foreign competition in their labour-intensive industry by heavy wage reductions. This the miners contested. On 31 March, the day of decontrol, they were locked out. Railway and transport workers agreed to launch a sympathetic strike, but shortly before it was due to start the railwaymen pulled out, ostensibly because the miners had refused to participate in fresh talks. Lacking their support, the miners were eventually starved back to work after a bitterly fought six-month strike. Thereafter the number of stoppages and days lost fell away as depression began to bite.

Government policy during the period of post-war industrial tension was essentially one of prevarication, designed to keep the parties talking, stalling strikes where possible, but all the time quietly preparing adequate defences in case of a major confrontation between labour and capital. Thus the passage in 1920 of the Emergency Powers Act gave government powers to act to maintain essential services in the event of major unrest. The establishment of the Sankey Commission was interpreted in some quarters as an example of government stalling. Ernest Bevin, who as national organiser of the dock workers was now beginning to rise to prominence, made the same assessment of the government's motives in calling a National Industrial Conference at beginning of 1919. This meeting of union officials, employers, politicians and civil servants set up a sub-committee which in five months produced a substantial programme for reforming industrial relations practice. Nothing was done, however, though Bevin's claim about the government's motives was probably unfounded. Lloyd George was absorbed in the Versailles peace negotiations and in his absence industrial policy was increasingly dominated by his Conservative coalition partners, temperamentally much less sympathetic to labour than the Prime Minister.

The real stumbling block, however, was that there was little genuine interest in conciliation. It had been the same immediately before the war and also during the war, when the Whitley Committee proposed the establishment of national and local committees in industry to discuss wages, conditions, general problems of management and efficiency. The seventy-three Whitley Councils in existence by 1921 received most enthusiastic support either from neutral observers or from those in industries such as pottery and printing which had some successful experience of such experiments. Although Whitley Councils were to become a feature of government departments such as the post office, there was little progress in major private industries as the unions were against them. In the aftermath of war, then, there was little genuine interest in industrial conciliation *per se* and certainly not at the expense of more fundamental economic priorities. Conciliation could never remove the underlying economic causes of industrial conflict.

Prices had risen enormously during the war. Aggregate wage figures show a parallel increase of about one hundred per cent. Within this average, however, skilled workers' wages had declined, certainly until 1917, and most of the improvements had gone to unskilled labour. Flat-rate increases and the importance conferred upon unskilled workers by insatiable labour demand destroyed many of the old differentials. Under the National Building Agreement of 1919, builders' labourers were confirmed at not less than seventy-five per cent of the craftsman's rate as against the sixty-six per cent common before the war. Prior to 1914 all engine drivers had earned at least twice as much as porters; by February 1919 they were only sixty per cent above the porters. Engineering labourers in 1920 were paid eighty per cent of the fitters and turners' rates as opposed to the fifty-nine per cent of 1914.[38] Unskilled men were naturally determined to hang on to these gains which had done so much to lessen the extent of primary poverty in Britain. Skilled men were equally set on restoring lost ground. Both were also affected by the rapid increases in the cost of living which accompanied the postwar boom, and both sought to benefit from the relatively high employment levels which prevailed until the middle of 1920. On the other side, owners and employers, especially in the export sector, were faced with the tasks of re-establishing markets lost during the war or of competing with newer sources of supply. Either way the pressure was on them to keep wage costs as low as possible.

The likely severity of any confrontation between labour and capital in the postwar period was enhanced by several other considerations. One concerned the standing of employers. They emerged from the war more highly organised than before. The Federation of British Industry was established in 1916 to promote the interests of British industry. More directly involved with industrial relations was the British Employers Federation of 1919. The creation of such organisations probably increased popular suspicion that business had done rather well out of the war, and also that business interests were mainly responsible for the non-appearance of the many social reforms which had been promised to sustain falling civilian morale in the last year or so of war. Mention of reform, particularly in housing and education, had created high expectations among the population; and J.H. Thomas, the railwaymen's leader, said that postwar discontent was a product of the frustration of 'age-long expectations accelerated by the developments of the war'.[39] In March 1922 the *Daily News* reported that an ex-soldier from the Royal Field Artillery was living with his wife and four children in London under a shack of tarpaulins, army groundsheets, and bits of tin and canvas. 'If they'd told me in France that I should come back to this,' he said, 'I wouldn't have believed it. Sometimes I wish to God the Germans had knocked me out.'[40] The House of Commons returned in the coupon election of 1918 contained 265 members with business interests, and there were many who shared J.M. Keynes' view that reform prospects were killed off in Parliament by hard-nosed businessmen who saw in social reform expenditure the certainty of falling profits and economic disaster.[41] It was, after all, a businessman, Eric Geddes — one of the many drafted into high administrative office by Lloyd George during the war — who was responsible for preparing the savage cuts in government expenditure in 1921. The Geddes axe fell particularly heavily on health and education, as the government sought to restore foreign confidence in Britain by balancing the budget.

Labour came out of the war much more homogeneous than it had been in 1914. A Ministry of Labour memorandum on the shop-stewards movement commented on this process of consolidation, referring to 'the increasing tendency for the trade unionists of one shop, works or small district to act together, irrespective of their division into crafts or occupations. What is called "class consciousness" is obliterating the distinction between those who follow different occupations in the same works.'[42] In a way this process had been symbolised by the creation of the WENWC, which united labour in its three functions as producer (the unions), consumer (the co-operative movement), and citizen (the Labour party). As we have seen, war eroded wage differentials, thereby deepening the process of proletarianisation which had been a feature of the prewar period. The erosion of differentials was also a major cause of the drastic reduction in poverty after the war. The continuation of some rent controls, a major item in the expenditure of poorer households, and a reduction in the average family size of unskilled workers also served to narrow the gap between unskilled and skilled workers – a gap which had been very marked in Edwardian times. Psychologically perhaps the gap had been reduced when the ease with which dilutees had picked up the skills of engineering craftsmen suggested that those skills were not in fact all that difficult. This conclusion is reinforced by the failure of many apprenticed engineers to pass union entry tests to army artificer units. In Walter Greenwood's famous novel, *Love on the Dole*, Harry Hardcastle (a young engineering apprentice) is told by a time-served man that in the Great War women had 'picked up straight away what Marlowe's and the others say it takes seven years' apprenticeship to learn'.[43] Working-class homogeneity was also fostered by the weakening of local ties during the war. Military and industrial requirements resulted in the wholesale disruption of long-established communities. Older towns such as Burnley lost population, while strategic centres like Coventry expanded rapidly. The impact was particularly marked, as one might expect, in rural communities. Flora Thompson writes that in her Oxfordshire village in 1900 'boys were being born or growing up . . . expecting to follow the plough all their lives, or at most, to do a little mild soldiering or go to work in a town. Gallipoli? Kut? Vimy Ridge? Ypres? What did they know of such places? But they were to know them, and when the time came they did not flinch.'[44] Local loyalties were also undermined in a different way as local variations in earnings diminished. With the introduction of compulsory arbitration in 1915 and the government itself taking a controlling hand in vital industries, national wage settlements were increasingly the order of the day – on the railways in 1915, in the mines in 1916, and in the engineering industry in 1917.

The unions themselves were much stronger in 1918 than they had been in 1914. It is true that once depression set in membership began to decline, but it also remains true that by 1918 twice as many people had had direct experience of union membership, perhaps for the first time. The enormous increase in labour's bargaining power during the war, coupled with the shift of labour into trades with relatively long traditions of organisation, contributed to a significant increase in membership, which reached eight million by 1920. In addition, war brought expansion to the white-collar sector and to women's organisations. For instance, the Workers Union had only five thousand female members in 1914. By the end of the war this had risen to almost 80,000, a quarter of the union's total membership and more than any other general union. Altogether it is estimated that some two million women directly replaced men in the labour force, though many were themselves replaced when war ended and there was little real change in the actual status of women's jobs.[45]

Organisationally, too, the unions were stronger in 1918. The appointment of the Staff Development Committee in 1916 coincided with growing Labour party criticism of the old Joint Board, mainly on the ground that the presence of the TUC and the GFTU conferred dual representation on the unions. Further impetus to find a more appropriate structure came out of the transport workers' strike of 1919. As a result of their experience in establishing a co-ordinating committee to run the strike, the transport workers suggested that the functions of the Parliamentary Committee should be extended to make it the effective central co-ordinating body for the

trade-union movement. The details of the subsequent reorganisation owed much to the inspiration of Ernest Bevin
and G.D.H. Cole. There emerged a thirty-strong General
Council and a system of committees, each serviced by its own
specialist officials. This generally accentuated the authority
of the TUC among its constituent members and also gave it
sufficient technical expertise to evolve sophisticated policies
on a range of important social and economic issues. A number
of joint committees were established with other labour
bodies. Of these, the committee organised in conjunction
with the National Federation of Trades Councils in 1922 was
one of the most significant, as it enabled the TUC effectively
to control the aspirations of militant trades-council members
to turn their own national federation into a rival focus of the
union movement.

None of these developments of themselves made industrial
conflict any more likely. What they did was to make the
division between capital and labour more clear-cut and also
make it probable that any conflict between the two would be
more far-reaching in its effects because of the greater strength
and solidarity of the two sides. The prospects for industrial
harmony were reduced still further by the general European
background of revolutionary upheaval. The Russian revolution
had been generally welcomed in Britain, not least by organised
labour. As the true nature of Russian communism slowly
revealed itself, however, a spate of anti-Bolshevik propaganda
appeared. Much of it came from older organisations such as
the Anti-Socialist Union and the British Empire Union.
Others, such as the Economic League (1919), were founded
specifically to oppose 'all subversive forces whatever their
origin or inspiration, that seek to undermine the security of
Britain in general and of British industry in particular'.[46]
Trade unionists anxious to remedy economic grievances were
obvious targets for organisations such as these, intent as they
were on finding suitable bogeymen to explain the current
industrial unrest. Many of these groups had links with the
Conservative party, and one survey shows that they contained a significant proportion of company directors.[47]
Unfortunately, they seem to have believed their own propaganda and the warnings of alarmists like Field-Marshal

Wilson who warned the cabinet that 'a Bolshevik rising was likely'.[48]

To be fair, however, there were superficial signs which appeared to lend credibility to such claims. Because the government itself had taken control of several key industries, labour unrest in such sectors could quite easily be represented as a threat against the state itself. Reference could be made to the statements emanating from the Leeds meeting of 1917 summoned by the United Socialist Council to consider the Russian revolution: the Bolshevik success was given a hearty welcome, demands made for the establishment of workers' and soldiers' soviets in Britain, and delegates were agreed that the Russian example should generally be followed. In 1920 came more signs of apparent sympathy with Bolshevism. Dockers refused to load a ship with arms destined for Poles fighting in the Ukraine against the Bolsheviks. The dockers' stand was endorsed by the TUC and the Labour party, who established a National Council of Action to organise opposition to any Allied intervention in Russian affairs. This council and the three or four hundred local equivalents which were also set up were regarded as potentially subversive by the government. Their activities were covered in the Home Office's regular reports on revolutionary organisations. Even more grist to the anti-Bolshevik mill was provided by the establishment of the Communist party itself. Most members of the Labour party, trade-union leaders, and the patriotic, pro-war wing of the BSP, led by Hyndman, had quite quickly rallied to support Britain's involvement in the war; but within both the ILP and the BSP were quite significant minorities who had not. Together they formed the United Socialist Council in 1916, and it was this body which took the initiative in instigating talks with other leading socialist groups to consider setting up a revolutionary political party. The major area of disagreement was over the matter of affiliation to the Labour party, and Sylvia Pankhurst's Socialist Workers Federation soon dropped out of the unity talks because of its opposition to affiliation. The SLP was divided on this issue, and only a portion of the party actually joined when the communists held their unity convention in 1920. By the time of the 1921 conference, most of the main groups of British Marxists had come in. The main exceptions were some left-wingers in the ILP.

For all that the Communist party of Great Britain (CPGB) involved, at its inception, only a few hundred people, it was important because it was the first major political party in Britain to ground a revolutionary strategy in industrial action. Yet the party remained small and, since it was more heavily dependent on Moscow than any other member of the International, it was easily portrayed as the puppet of Russian ambitions and designs. It attracted very little support from British workers, and it is clear that the fears of the anti-Bolsheviks were ill-grounded. The call made at Leeds in 1917 to follow the Russian example was virtually meaningless, because wartime censorship meant that few people had any real idea of what was actually taking place inside Russia. Further, the activities of local workers' and soldiers' soviets which were called for by the delegates hardly warranted any comparison with their Russian counterparts. Their whole role was concerned with the mundane details of life within the existing social system — how to exploit food shortages and to secure pensions for war casualties, for example.[49] Nor did the welcome given to the revolution by British workers spring from any underlying political sympathy. On the contrary, the revolution seemed to open up the possibility that a new Russian government would pursue the war much more effectively, while it also freed Britain's social democratic labour movement from the embarrassment of fighting a war in alliance with a country whose Czarist system it had been criticising for years. For those in Britain who opposed the war, the collapse of Russia was seen as improving the prospects for a negotiated peace. In the same way the establishment of councils of action in 1920, while it had the support of Bolshevik sympathisers, represented the wish of the majority to avoid the threat of another war. War weariness, not Bolshevism, was the main impetus for the councils, which specifically rejected any communist participation.[50] Even so, the appearance of the CPGB and the favourable reception afforded to the Russian revolution in Britain, whatever the motive, did much to heighten the atmosphere of fear and suspicion which clouded industrial relations in the immediate postwar years.

7

Triumph and Defeat,
1921-27

The year 1921 was the high water mark of postwar industrial conflict. In the face of deepening depression and rising unemployment, shop-floor militancy declined. Unions were increasingly forced back onto the defensive. One device to which many of them resorted was amalgamation, a technique made simpler by the passage in 1917 of the Trade Union (Amalgamation) Act. The initiative for this measure had come from John Hodge, the Minister of Labour. Since he was himself a steel worker, it was appropriate that the first important amalgamation should occur among the steel unions with the establishment of the British Iron, Steel and Kindred Trades Federation in 1917. In 1921 the old ASE disappeared, merging with some smaller engineering unions to form the Amalgamated Engineering Union. The next three years saw the establishment of what were to become the largest general unions in the country. The Transport and General Workers Union (TGWU) appeared in 1922, the General and Municipal Workers Union (GMWU) two years later. Such was the extent of bureaucratic reorganisation taking place that, while total union membership was falling off, the number of full-time officials was actually increasing, thus further weakening the influence of the militants.

By the time the GMWU was formed, Britain had had its first taste of Labour government. It was produced by an electoral deadlock in 1923 and lasted for less than a year. Nevertheless, the fact that the Labour party was now in a position to form a government, even a minority one, represented a major advance on the situation prevailing before the war. As recently as 1911, Philip Snowden had written that 'it is doubtful whether we shall have in this country within the next generation an avowed Socialist Party . . . which will be sufficiently strong to take the reins of government . . .'[1] Yet he was wrong. The replacement of the Liberals by Labour in the country's political structure stands as one of the major themes of early-twentieth-century working-class history. The causes of the change remain one of the major controversies among twentieth-century historians. The issue has been neatly expressed in T. Wilson's metaphor.

> The Liberal Party can be compared to an individual who, after a period of robust health and great exertion, experienced symptoms of illness . . . Before a thorough diagnosis could be made, he was involved in an encounter with a rampant omnibus (the First World War) . . . A controversy has persisted ever since as to what killed him. One medical school argues that even without the bus he would soon have died . . . Another school goes further, and says that the encounter with the bus would not have proved fatal had not the victim's health already been seriously impaired.[2]

Among leading practitioners of the first school, which may conveniently be labelled 'inevitablist', Dr Pelling has argued that the supplanting of Liberalism by Labour was inevitable, due to long-term social and economic changes which were simultaneously uniting Britain geographically and dividing her in terms of social class.[3] Certainly, the appearance of a new, radical party — committed, in Snowden's words, to applying 'collectivist principles to the treatment of every question' — presented a serious threat to a party based on laisser-faire.[4] The response of some Liberals was to produce a new, progressive philosophy based on the assumption that individual and collective freedoms were inextricably bound together and that the good of one implied the good of the other. This New Liberalism was translated into a practical programme of social reform by men such as Herbert Samuel, Leo Chiozza Money, Churchill and Lloyd George. This attempt to retain electoral support by a popular programme of social reform was almost certainly misplaced, since ordinary working people seem to have been very suspicious of it. Some, however, feared that the programme threatened the internal unity of the party itself. 'Though we are not socialists,' John Morley told Henry Campbell-Bannerman, 'many of our friends live next door, and the frightened people will edge off in the opposite direction.'[5] There was little justification for Morley's fears, certainly at parliamentary level. Statistical analysis of Edwardian division lists reveals no solid, coherent bloc of radicals opposed by a constant Whig group.[6]

There were indications at local level, however, that the Liberals were losing frightened members and also voters. Of course it might be objected that local elections were not of any major significance, being decided mainly on local issues; but turnout was usually high, even though the local government franchise was only enjoyed by about twenty per cent of the population, and the elections usually fell in periods of general political quiescence. A detailed study of local government election results in Bradford, Brighton, Wolverhampton, Norwich and Reading points to the conclusion that Liberals were finding it increasingly difficult to keep a hold on local politics before the war.[7] A fuller study of several major industrial towns in the midlands and north confirms the impression of Liberal decline.[8] In his study of rural workers in East Anglia, Alan Howkins has shown that before 1914 their traditional support for Liberalism was transferred almost totally to the local ILP which had stood by them in a strike. 'Industrial conflict,' he concluded, 'produced a switch to an independent working class position.'[9] If this was generally true, one could perhaps expect to find that the roots of Labour's future rise to power were nourished in the industrial tensions of the period 1909–14. It is true that the party's municipal election performance in those years was, superficially at least, quite impressive. More than a hundred candidates were returned each year between 1911 and 1913, while Labour's municipal vote rose from 170,000 in 1906 to 233,000 in 1913.[10] Yet there is little evidence to suggest that industrial troubles did produce any general switch of the sort postulated by Howkins. In North Wales, for example, industrial troubles may have caused local slate workers to lose faith in the Liberals as far as their industrial problems were concerned; but the depressed state of the industry and declining union membership made union leaders reluctant to abandon a party from which tangible gains could be expected in favour of one which at that time could offer only hope.[11] The historian of modern Wales remarks that the effects of the industrial troubles affected voting patterns only very slowly.[12] Furthermore, the figures of Labour's progress have to be kept in proper perspective. By November 1913 there were still only ninety Labour councillors in fourteen of the most important industrial boroughs, as against 427 Conservatives and 297 Liberals. Progress was very uneven, the gains of one year frequently being lost the next. While there is evidence that Liberals were losing ground at local level, there is good reason to assume that the beneficiary was the Conservative, rather than the Labour party.

Whatever was happening at local level before 1914, there is no suggestion of any general swing from Liberalism to Labour in parliamentary elections. True, there was often friction between the two parties over their claims for candidatures. By 1909 the Midland Liberal Federation was complaining that local Labour party officials were 'willing to receive much and concede little'.[13] After a major row over who had the right to nominate the candidate for Enoch Edwards' Hanley seat in 1912, *The Times* correspondent made the accurate observation that 'there may be a loose coalition in the House of Commons; there is none at all in the country.'[14] Insofar as the Labour party was set up to increase working-class representation in Parliament, such conflict was inevitable and no Liberal policy, however attractive, would prevent the party from putting up its own candidates. As Brougham Villiers noted in 1912, the basic division between Labour and Liberal 'is upon the independence of Labour, not upon any economic or political doctrine in any ordinary sense at all'.[15]

In this sense it could be argued that the failure of the Liberals to accommodate this desire for working-class representation before 1900 made the formation of the Labour Representation Committee (LRC) inevitable. It does not follow from this that Labour would inevitably supplant the Liberals. Indeed, Labour candidates successful in the general election of 1906 were returned without Liberal opposition under the terms of the Gladstone-MacDonald pact. In fourteen by-elections between 1910 and 1914 all four Labour-held seats were lost, and Labour finished bottom in every three-cornered contest. Where it is possible to compare Labour's performance in any one seat at a general and a by-election (as at Holmfirth, Crewe and Leith), there does seem to have been a general increase in the party's vote of about twenty-five per cent, though it is possible that this represented nothing more than the anti-government vote normal in by-elections. A better guide is perhaps provided by the voting patterns in constituencies which had several by-elections in the prewar period. There were not many of these; but the results at Keighley, where by-elections occurred in 1906, 1911 and 1913, indicate that Labour had reached a ceiling of about thirty per cent. This was sufficient to embarrass the Liberals but not enough to suggest that Labour was likely 'to win further seats in its own right'.[16] It appears, too, that in areas such as Wales and Lancashire Liberalism held its own. It has been powerfully argued that in Lancashire politics had already taken on a national, class aspect even before 1914 and that working-class voters remained faithful to Liberalism.[17] It is worth noting, however, that it was the New Liberalism which prevailed here. In Wales by contrast it was the traditional variety, reinforced by the nationalism and non-conformity with which it had long been associated. Since there also existed in Lancashire a strong and peculiar form of working-class Toryism, Wales may have been more representative of the nation as a whole. Yet it was precisely this form of Liberalism which was most vulnerable to the effects of the First World War, which saw a significant weakening in the hold of nonconformity and also a progressive whittling away of laisser-faire ideology.

The implication of all this is that despite some weaknesses the Liberal party was holding its own against Labour and that the war was primarily responsible for its demise. The erosion of non-conformity was the erosion also of the faith which had done so much to give Liberalism its passion and its principle. To some Liberals the very notion of war was abhorrent; others were alienated by the methods used in its conduct. Bit by bit Liberal values were compromised in the search for victory. The potential for internal division was increased, it is alleged by some historians, by the ambition of Lloyd George who, egged on by Tory press barons, plotted successfully to unseat Asquith and himself become Prime Minister. Whether explanations in terms of personal ambition and plot are realistic or not, Lloyd George emerged as leader of those Liberals who were prepared to give priority to winning the war at the expense, if need be, of Liberal principle. Equally damaging, perhaps, was the withdrawal from active party life of those who believed that the party had been betrayed by its leaders. The two Johns, Burns and Morley, were perhaps no great loss, but among Liberals who joined the Labour party during or immediately after the war were some able men such as C.P. Trevelyan, C.R. Buxton, and Arthur Ponsonby.

Against this it might be argued that the war also produced schisms within the Labour party even more serious than those which befell the Liberals. Apart from some minor resignations in 1914 and the activities of pacifists who worked in E.D. Morel's Union of Democratic Control, leading Liberals were generally agreed on the need to fight. The divisions which developed subsequently were over matters of leadership and how best to pursue the war. The split in Labour's ranks, however, came right at the beginning of the war and was over the fundamental issue of whether to fight at all. Several Labour MPs were so committed to the war that they at one time attached themselves to Victor Fisher's British Workers' League. Some of Labour's best-known national figures – Hardie, MacDonald and Snowden – all opposed British involvement. So, too, did other prominent labour leaders such as George Lansbury. Yet if it was in this sense more fundamental, the Labour split was more temporary in its impact, healing once peace returned. The Liberal split persisted for much longer because the principle at stake, laisser-faire, had equal application in peace as in war.

The war also contributed to the Liberals' eclipse in a second, less direct way. The existing franchise and registration systems were both based on stability of domicile and property occupation. The considerable population movements occasioned by the war rendered both lists completely out of date. It was not practical in wartime to compile a totally new register or even to construct one on the basis of occupation lists dating from July 1914. Thus although the government itself was not particularly anxious to change the franchise, a radical simplification of voting qualifications was called for. The act of 1918, therefore, conferred universal male suffrage over the age of twenty-one and also gave women over thirty the vote for the first time. Thus the electorate of 1918 was very much bigger than it had been in 1914. There is no need, therefore, to postulate a massive switch of political allegiance as the cause of the Liberals' fate. Modern research suggests that once party allegiances are formed they are not easily changed. Although by 1918 a significant number of Liberal politicians had transferred to Labour, there is little evidence to suggest that voters made a similar move. On the contrary, the Liberal vote continued to rise, reaching an all-time peak in 1929 of 5.3 million. What the act of 1918 must have done, therefore, was to enfranchise for the first time a vast pool of hitherto untapped Labour support. Prior to 1918 the vote had been denied to paupers (472,000 in 1910), living-in servants in England and Wales (205,000 in 1910), bachelor sons living with parents without exclusive use of their own room, lodgers in unfurnished rooms worth less than £10 per annum, and nearly all serving soldiers and sailors. Almost forty-four per cent of the adult male population did not have the vote. By definition nearly all those in the excluded categories, except perhaps the first two, must have been adult, working-class males. This is confirmed by the fact that the English and Welsh boroughs had much lower levels of registration than the counties, the lowest levels of all being recorded in working-class areas of big cities. These were the people who now, it seemed, gave their newly acquired vote to Labour.

Why should the bulk of new voters have opted for Labour rather than the Liberals or even the Conservatives, particularly — and this is often overlooked — as the act enfranchised nearly twice as many women as men, and women are and were thought generally less likely to vote Labour? After all, it has been suggested that in prewar Lancashire the Liberals did best in the most highly enfranchised constituences, so there was evidently no inherent link between a high level of enfranchisement and a Labour vote.[18] One possible answer is that Labour MPs now had some experience of office in wartime coalition governments and had disproved the common charge that they were untried and therefore dangerous. Probably much more significant, however, was the greater sense of working-class homogeneity created by the war. As argued above, one of the main causes of this was the enormous expansion of trade-union power and membership. The Labour party had been the creation of the unions, and it is possible that the experience of union membership enjoyed by many during the war for the first time was important in influencing voting habits among the new voters. This seems even more likely in view of the Liberals' total inability to find a meaningful industrial relations policy in the postwar years. Their involvement in predominantly Conservative coalitions, which sanctioned the use of troops during strikes, delaying tactics such as commissions of inquiry, and the passage of the Emergency Powers Act in 1920, did considerable damage to their credibility as the party of the working class. So, too, did their concentration on the propagation of an anti-socialist platform. Not until the middle 1920s did it dawn on Liberals that this was done much more effectively by the Conservatives. By the time the search began for a more constructive policy of their own, it was probably too late to recover the ground lost to Labour.[19]

If, as was argued earlier, voting patterns are largely determined by tradition, the social upheavals and wider horizons created by the war must also have made it easier for Labour to stake a claim on voters' loyalties. Soon after the start of the war the vicar of Southwold was told by his gardener of the latest war news: 'Them Jarmans have took Berlin.'[20] The isolation of this community as revealed by the gardener's comment was soon to be broken down by successive influxes of troops drawn from all over the United Kingdom — Lincolnshire Yeomanry, Royal Sussex Rifles, Bedfords, Montgomery Yeomanry, and Welsh Fusiliers. It was a pattern repeated in many other areas. Lancashire may have been an exception, but generally it was the Great War which made Britons out of people whose social horizons had previously been bound by the street, the village, or the neighbourhood.

Yet the Liberal eclipse was not only a matter of policy and franchise extension, but also of party organisation. Liberals had, so it is argued, an essentially rationalist view of politics which assumed that elections were won mainly by an appeal to issues, rather than by good organisation of the electorate. Party organisation had never been particularly good, and it had grown flabby in the complacency induced by the victory of 1906. Even then, however, wealthy individuals, alarmed by the party's growing radicalism, were quitting. A further brake on party income was applied by the internal dissensions during the war, although Lloyd George developed his own methods of rectifying the deficiencies. By the end of the war, many local organisations were in total disarray. Given that the newly enfranchised masses almost certainly had a lower level of political awareness than the prewar electorate, organisational weakness was a crucial drawback to the Liberals. It was made doubly significant by the fact that the Labour party had reorganised itself, particularly at local level, in such a way as to reap the maximum benefit from a wider franchise. As early as May 1912, MacDonald had encouraged acceptance of schemes for the regular appointment of local agents to be controlled by head office and for the provisions of financial assistance to local parties. Henderson's reorganisation programme of 1918 strengthened local influence still more by reserving five places on the national executive for the nominees of local parties. For the first time, too, party membership was made available to individuals, who no longer had to join through a trade union or a socialist affiliate. This opened the way for more middle-class sympathisers to join the party, a development welcomed by Henderson and MacDonald who both felt that hitherto it had been 'too short of brains'.[21]

If the Labour party was now better organised, both nationally and locally, it had also a distinctive programme of its own. The new constitution of 1918 committed the party for the first time to an explicit socialist objective. Sidney Webb's policy document, *Labour and the New Social Order*, laid down a programme of practical social reform which was half way between Marxian socialism and Lloyd Georgian social reform, and which appealed to the mass of the people whose expectations had been raised by the war. It included a commitment to achieve a national minimum standard in wages, hours and conditions of work; the democratic control of industry; the use of heavy taxation to subsidise comprehensive social services; and the use of any national surplus to improve educational and cultural opportunities for ordinary people.

Moreover, this programme was being put forward by a united party which appeared to have been only marginally associated with the conduct of the war. The Liberals, whether Asquithian or Lloyd Georgian, had been deeply involved in the decision to go to war and had still not resolved their differences. It is true that Henderson had been given Labour's blessing in joining the coalition in 1915, and it is also true that most Labour MPs supported the war effort wholeheartedly – though younger elements in the ILP were increasingly restless as the fight dragged on. In 1917 Henderson visited Russia. What he saw there convinced him that democratic socialism could only survive if the Russians were permitted to leave the war immediately. Accordingly he took the view that a crippled Russia, ruled by men sympathetic to the Allies and to liberal democracy, was preferable to a Bolshevik state which would sue for peace on any terms at the first opportunity. He therefore decided to attend the Stockholm conference of European socialists to discuss the prospects for a negotiated peace. Since German delegates were also to be present, Henderson's decision caused considerable misgivings in the cabinet. In the famous 'doormat' incident, Henderson was kept waiting for a long time outside the cabinet room while his colleagues considered his position. This gave him the opportunity to resign from the government. His visit to Russia had also convinced him that if socialism was to be achieved by peaceful means in Britain, then the Labour party needed to be reorganised. This he proceeded to undertake.

When the armistice finally was agreed in November 1918, a special Labour party conference decided that the party should formally withdraw from the coalition and assert its independence. J.R. Clynes obeyed with some reluctance, but George Barnes and a few others stayed in, thereby forfeiting their party membership. When the first peacetime election took place under the new franchise, Labour contested nearly 400 seats. Only fifty-seven were taken, but more significant was the second place secured by seventy-one Labour candidates in three- or four-cornered contests. This was perhaps cold comfort, since coalition candidates swept the board and most of Labour's experienced men were beaten. MacDonald and Snowden went down because of their anti-war record, and Henderson was also defeated though he won a by-election in 1919. It was 1922 when the real breakthrough came, by which time the euphoria of peace had worn off, expectations of social reform had been dashed, and the country had had four years of persistent industrial unrest. It was noticeable that the ILP (which had taken only three seats in 1918) this time won thirty-two, doing particularly well in Scotland where the Clyde area returned a strong contingent of very able ILP men, such as Emanuel Shinwell, James Maxton, and John Wheatley. Altogether Labour won 142 seats, and all the old stalwarts (except the unfortunate Henderson) came back. Substantial strides had been made in areas where the party had previously performed badly — London, the north-east and Yorkshire. Further gains came in 1923 when Stanley Baldwin dissolved Parliament and went to the country on the tariff reform issue. While the reunited Liberals won 158 seats, Labour moved further ahead to 191. As the Conservative platform had been decisively rejected by a majority of the electorate and they had only 258 seats, not enough for a clear majority, the King asked MacDonald to form the first-ever Labour administration.

It was not a particularly memorable government. MacDonald went outside the party to fill some offices and acted as his own foreign secretary. Nor did it achieve very much, hardly surprising as it was dependent on Liberal support and lasted only for nine months. Its most noticeable piece of legislation was the work of Wheatley, the only Clydeside militant in the cabinet. His Housing Act provided a government subsidy for local authority housing and was important in stimulating the building industry. On the foreign front, MacDonald had some success in building bridges with France, but his efforts to cement friendship with the Soviet Union appeared to confirm the allegations made at the time of the 1923 election that he was unduly responsive to left-wing pressure. The *Saturday Review*, for example, had accused him of regarding 'the war merely as a bridge to the world revolution . . . He and his fellows have infected Trade Unionism with the Bolshevik influenza; in all their plans they stipulate for relations with Soviet Russia.'[22] As the Conservatives were at this time playing the anti-socialist card for all they were worth, it is not surprising that MacDonald's decision to drop the prosecution for sedition of J.R. Campbell, a Communist publisher, gave them extra ammunition when a fresh election was held in 1924. Superficially perhaps, the charge of communist sympathies could be made to appear credible since MacDonald and many of his colleagues had been present at the Leeds conference in 1917, had been pacifists during the war, and had supported the councils of action in 1920. Shortly before the 1924 election, the *Daily Mail* published a telegram purporting to come from Zinoviev, President of the Third International, giving the Communist Party of Great Britain (CPGB) explicit instructions for undermining the British constitution.[23] 'Anyone who voted for Labour tomorrow,' thundered Lord Curzon in response, 'was voting for handing this country over to the Communists and to Moscow.'[24] In fact the Labour party had consistently tried to dissociate itself from extremism. Conference had rejected the CPGB's application for affiliation in 1924, and individual communists could not get endorsement as official Labour candidates. When the election results were in, Labour was seen to have lost forty seats, enough to oust the government but small enough to suggest that the Zinoviev telegram had little influence on party support. The real victims in the election were the Liberals, who lost 118 seats. If people were genuinely swayed by the anti-socialist scare, then it was clearly a waste to vote for a party which could not even put up enough candidates to secure a majority. Thus if the 1924 election brought to an end the life of the first Labour government, it also ensured that for the foreseeable future Labour would be the natural opposition to the Conservatives. 'To vote Liberal,' it has been observed, 'was already beginning to seem a luxury . . .'[25]

One feature of MacDonald's leadership in the early 1920s was his apparent reluctance to work closely with the TUC. The joint Labour party–TUC committee, for instance, remained in almost total abeyance; and trade-union membership of MacDonald's cabinet had been relatively small. Trade-union leaders in the postwar period tended to ignore politics and to concentrate on industrial affairs. It was no longer common for union secretaries to sit in the house and at least one union, Bevin's TGWU, regarded Parliament as a suitable pasturing ground for retired officials. This had an unfavourable effect on the quality of the union contribution to the Labour party and also lessened the degree of effective co-operation and co-ordination between the two wings of the labour movement. This was particularly unfortunate when the movement was shortly to face its greatest test in the shape of the general strike of 1926.

With the Conservatives back in office at the end of 1924, the Treasury and Bank of England officials persuaded the Chancellor of the Exchequer, Winston Churchill, against his better judgement to return to the gold standard at the pre-war parity. As this made no allowance for sterling's declining value since 1914, the result was to overprice British exports. Among the hardest hit was coal, already facing foreign competition and challenged by oil and electricity. This over-pricing coincided with the reappearance on world markets of German coal after the evacuation of the Ruhr by French and Belgian troops. In this situation, coal owners pressed for wage reductions, district settlements instead of a national wage agreement, and a return to an eight-hour day instead of the seven which had been standard since the end of the war. This was rejected by the MFGB. Their stand was supported by the general council of the TUC, which promised sympathetic action in the form of an embargo on the movement of coal if the government did not intervene. The government duly obliged with a wage subsidy to last for nine months while a commission under Sir Herbert Samuel considered the problems facing the industry. It is sometimes suggested that Baldwin took this step in 1925 because, in his own words, 'we were not ready'.[26] In fact Sir John Anderson had reported to the cabinet as early as July 1923 about the need to overhaul the machinery established under Lloyd George to deal with the effects of prolonged industrial action. Subsequent reports suggest that by the autumn of 1925 the government could have coped adequately with the threatened embargo on coal movements. Baldwin, whose own background was the steel industry where industrial relations were generally good, hoped that Samuel would produce a formula which would avert a crisis in the industry. When Samuel produced his report in March 1926, however, the owners wished only to talk of the short-term proposals for wage reductions, the miners of the long-term suggestions for restructuring the industry.

Negotiations were not made any easier by the personalities involved. Herbert Smith and A.J. Cook, the miners' leaders, were an oddly assorted couple. The mule-like Smith, in his famous flat cap, was a man of few words, the most important in the context of the impending coal strike being his insistence on 'not a penny off the pay'. Cook, secretary of the MFGB, was a former communist who talked in terms of class warfare, bringing to it all the eloquence which in his youth he had deployed from a Baptist pulpit. Lord Birkenhead considered these two the most stupid men in Britain – that is until he met the owners. Those owners who came from profitable coal fields such as Yorkshire and the east midlands tended to be moderate, but they were overshadowed by hard-liners like Lord Londonderry, D.A. Thomas of the giant Cambrian Combine, and W.A. Lee and Evan William, respectively secretary and president of the Mining Association of Great Britain. They all appeared to believe that the aim of the MFGB was to destroy private industry in Britain, and they negotiated accordingly.

Deadlock ensued. On 1 May 1926, a special meeting of trade-union delegates agreed by 3,500,000 votes to 50,000 to back the miners' case with industrial action from midnight on 3 May. Last minute peace talks were ended dramatically with the government claiming that printers at the *Daily Mail* had already committed overt acts in pursuance of the strike (they had refused to set up an editorial bitterly critical of the unions' stance). That the government took such a step led then and since to the conclusion that the strike was deliberately engineered by a pro-capitalist government, thirsting for all-out confrontation with the working class. 'By the early months of 1926,' runs one account, 'every element within the British capitalist class was convinced of the need for a major showdown with organised labour.'[27] When the Tories resumed office, says another, 'the stage was set for the offensive against the conditions of the British working class. Economic crisis was to be translated into political attack.'[28] The evidence for such assertions is thin, even if the doubtful premise is accepted that there was a united capitalist class pulling the strings of a puppet Conservative government.

There are no indications that either the National Council of Employers Organisations or the Federation of British Industry was actively seeking a confrontation. The Mining Association was prominent in its resistance to the miners because it existed to protect the individual colliery owners, many of whom could only meet competition by reducing costs, since their scope for increasing productivity was limited by the age of their pits. Other industrialists engaged in exports tended to support the owners. It is true that big business was among the most generous supporters of the various anti-socialist propaganda agencies – the British Empire Union received funds from brewers like Courages and Davenports and also from Austin and Morris, the car manufacturers – but it is a moot point as to whether this is the same as actively seeking confrontation. Nor is it as evident as is sometimes implied that the government as a whole was intent on conflict. Certainly establishment figures had flocked in 1925 to join the Organisation for the Maintenance of Supplies which was scheduled, in the event of a crisis, to be integrated into the government's own emergency machinery. It is true, too, that there were important politicians who were notoriously anti-union. At least four members of Baldwin's government – W. Ashley, W.C. Bridgman, Samuel Hoare, and Oliver Locker-Lampson – had been long-time activists in the Anti-Socialist Union. By 1926 the man designated as chief civil commissioner in the event of a strike, Sir W. Mitchell Thompson, had been on the ASU's executive for fifteen years. Lord Birkenhead was known for his anti-labour views as was Churchill, who had almost defeated an official Conservative candidate at a by-election in which he had stood as an anti-socialist. It is also true that the Conservative party as a whole was probably anxious to end the unions' privileged legal status; but Baldwin generally kept his hawks under control, and in 1925 he had even opposed a Tory private member's bill to end the political levy. This was consistent with his usually constructive approach to the coal crisis in 1925 when, as suggested above, he had genuinely hoped that Samuel could produce a solution. In the meantime, the preparations which he sanctioned were no more than any government worth the name would take to provide for contingencies that might never happen. The only significant difference between government arrangements in 1925 and 1926 was that by 1926 each of the twelve administrative regions into which the country was to be divided now had a permanent standing headquarters. At most, therefore, it would seem to have been a militant clique within the government which actively wished for a strike. On the day that the government finally broke off negotiations, Churchill had been to the offices of the *Daily Mail*; and the suspicion remains that he and other cabinet hard-liners had encouraged the editor, Marlowe, to write the editorial which so incensed the printers.

The strike began at midnight on 3 May. It lasted for nine days and took on something of a hybrid character, combining revolutionary sentiments with bank holiday atmosphere and rag day spirits. It was, suggested Beatrice Webb, 'little more than a nine days wonder, costing Great Britain tens of millions and leaving other nations asking whether it was a baulked revolution or play acting on a stupendous scale'.[29] There was certainly enough humour, much of it admittedly unconscious. Told in the middle of the night that the *Daily Mail* had ceased to function, George V's private assistant secretary, Eric Wigram, befuddled with sleep, replied, 'That's alright. We don't take the *Daily Mail*.'[30] Middle-aged men by the dozen flocked to realise their boyhood dreams of driving trains. One by-product was a significant increase in the number of rail accidents. The Marylebone Cricket Club (MCC) issued a statement to the effect that 'cricketers should be guided by a sense of public duty rather than by affection for their counties, but they strongly recommend that the best possible clevens should be put into the field against the Australians'.[31] Not even a general strike, it seemed, was to be permitted to interfere with the nation's cricketing honour. So

zealous were the members of the Typographical Association
in obeying the strike call that they refused to print much of
the material ordered by the TUC itself. A dash of rag day was
injected by student volunteers. The few who were members
of university socialist societies placed themselves at the
disposal of local strike committees. The majority, encouraged
in some universities by official assurances that their degree
prospects would in no way be harmed, joined the other side.

It is not easy to guage the impact of the strike at local level.
Many newspapers continued to appear, albeit in attenuated
form, but they are not unbiased sources. News was difficult
to get, reporters worked as printers, and most papers took a
pro-government line. Few union officials were willing to give
information or impressions to papers produced by blackleg
labour. The strikers often published their own local papers
though these, too, must be treated with caution. They were
often the work of activists who projected their own view of
the strike, and exaggeration was often necessary in order to
sustain morale. The same reservations apply equally to the
government paper, the *British Gazette*, and the TUC reply,
the *British Worker*. Nor are BBC reports above suspicion.
Nominally impartial, it did broadcast some information provided by the union side but also put out false reports of
numbers at work and refused to permit union leaders to
speak over the air.

Most contemporaries were struck on the first day by the
Sunday-like atmosphere of the city streets. Behind the
scenes, however, there was a great deal of feverish and often
chaotic union activity. The General Council's tactic was one
of progressively tightening the screw. To this end about
2,500,000 workers were eventually called out. Included in
the first wave were miners, printers, builders, transport, iron,
steel, chemical and paper workers. Distributive workers and
textile operatives were to remain at work, while engineers
and shipbuilders were stopped after a week. In the general
enthusiasm, though, many of those who were supposed to
work came out. Others found they could not get to work
because of transport difficulties or had nothing to do if they
did get in because raw material supplies had dried up. The
TUC further complicated matters by requesting the power

workers (the Electrical Power Engineers Association was not in fact affiliated to the TUC) to provide power for emergency and domestic use but to deprive industry, which was technically almost impossible.

The response to the strike varied considerably from trade to trade and region to region. NUR and ASLEF men were almost solid, though white-collar railway workers were less enthusiastic, only about seventy per cent of them staying away. The members of the TGWU and dockers also backed the strike call but Havelock Wilson's seamen ignored it. Local transport workers were not very well organised outside London; and their jobs, while relatively immune from unemployment, were easily filled by blacklegs. As a result, local transport services, especially private ones, tried to keep running, albeit at a token level. Local bus and tram services were probably the most frequent target of local pickets. Even London had a surburban bus service by the time the strike ended. The response of printers and road hauliers was patchy. Regionally, support was firmest in the more heavily unionised north, though strong engineering centres such as Clydeside were hampered by the inclusion of engineers in the second wave of strikes. The strongest support of all was in the coalfields of Wales and north-east England. In the south the *Gloucester Journal* could report that 'the general strike and its attendant discomforts still appear to have perturbed the normal life of Gloucester but little', even though there were some surprises.[32] Brighton was the most strike-bound town in the region, and even in a largely agricultural county like Devon trade unionists responded well. It is calculated that an average of ninety-six per cent of all the drivers, guards and firemen on the Great Western Railway joined the strike, and no freight trains ran in the Exeter division for five days.[33]

The TUC's organisation left much to be desired and its *ad hoc* arrangements contrasted strongly with the relatively smooth operation of the government's emergency plans. Both the General Council and national union executives issued directives, often contradictory, to their local representatives. The Swansea Trades Council was so confused by the welter of messages it received 'at intervals, cancelling one another and signed by leaders of different unions' that it was moved to ask whether the government was itself concocting 'telegrams to mislead Strike Committee'.[34] Locally, responsibility for organising the strike devolved on the trades councils, which had performed a similar function in the establishment of councils of action in 1920 and which were also the most representative, local union bodies. The councils moved quickly to deal with problems such as the difficulty caused when both the strike committee and the transport unions in a particular locality issued permits controlling the movement of supplies. In some areas, most notably the north-east and Lanarkshire in Scotland, food moved only at the behest of pickets. Occasionally heavily policed convoys defied efforts at union control, but other forms of pressure could be applied. In Chopwell, County Durham, one shop which received supplies from such a convoy was boycotted so effectively that within weeks it was forced to close and never open its doors again.

The organisational difficulties experienced by the unions sprang primarily from their general lack of preparation. This in itself is perhaps sufficient comment on the view that the general strike was a revolutionary movement. Right-wing elements such as the *Daily Mail* claimed that it was a revolutionary agitation 'which can only succeed by destroying the Government and subverting the rights and liberties of the people', but this can be dismissed as a near hysterical attempt to rally public opinion behind the government.[35] The strike was and is often viewed in a similar light by the left, who believe that it was betrayed by a reformist leadership. A leadership, however, can hardly betray something to which it has never been committed and few of the General Council even wanted a strike at all, still less one that might result in the downfall of the government. In 1925 the TUC had established a Special Industrial Committee to apply itself 'to considering the task of devising ways and means of consolidating the resistance of the trade union movement should the attack be renewed'.[36] Despite the efforts of Walter Citrine, the TUC secretary, nothing tangible was achieved as the dominant union figures, Thomas and Pugh, gave him no support. Once the strike began, most union leaders did their utmost to discourage violence. 'Allow no disorderly or subversive elements to interfere in any way,' said Thomas's message to railwaymen, 'maintain perfect order.'[37]

If the strike was not intended as a revolutionary movement, did it have revolutionary potential? In one sense there can be no doubt that it did, simply because of the numbers involved. The government's problem was well put in a Kensington strike bulletin. 'Sir John Simon says the General Strike is illegal . . . All strikers are liable to be interned in Wormwood Scrubs. The three million strikers are advised to keep in hiding, preferably in the park behind Bangor Street where they will not be discovered.'[38] But if we accept the view that revolution is the product of disaffection among small elites, while mass economic dissatisfaction will produce only riots and other short-lived protest, then there was little revolutionary about 1926.[39] Many of the oral reminiscences on which the claim is made come from those who were political activists and probably not typical of the anonymous masses.[40] The CPGB played up the strike's revolutionary potential, dispatching a number of executive committee members to assist local comrades in certain areas. Their influence was most noticeable in the trades councils, but the claims made for their importance have been grossly exaggerated. In Lanarkshire, it has been claimed that the seven communists organised and ran the forty-strong strike committee.[41] This was the heyday of communist activity, yet the party still only had about 10,000 members and most trades councils were quick to stifle their influence. Stalin himself was to say at Tiflis that 'the weakness of the British Communist Party played a role of no little importance in contributing to the failure of the General Strike'.[42] To suggest that strike committees were 'embryo soviets' is little more than wishful thinking.[43] Their work represented nothing more than an effort to ensure success in an industrial dispute by well-co-ordinated, sympathetic action. Most unions rejected proposals to establish their own defence forces, thus confirming the evidence of 1921 that few British workers were interested in overthrowing the existing order.

Revolution, of course, can often grow out of situations of violence, especially if government itself is weak. In fact government in 1926 showed itself to be extremely strong, and there was in any case little serious violence. To a large extent the incidence of violence depended on relations between police and strikers. At one extreme was the famous football match at Plymouth in which the strikers beat the police 2-1. At the other was the comment of the *Northern Light*, a strike bulletin produced by communists in Blaydon: 'The lowest aim in life is to be a policeman. When he dies he is so low he needs a ladder to climb up into Hell.'[44] In South Wales, where strike support was almost total and well organised, the police sensibly kept a low profile. Elsewhere, however, they were more in evidence. In Middlesbrough they were brought in to control a crowd of four hundred which had wrecked the railway station. In Hull they were complemented by naval ratings. Almost every major city saw some clash between pickets and police, and even Brighton and Devon saw baton charges. These incidents were no more severe than those which had often accompanied earlier industrial unrest; nor was the scale of the violence so great. In a strike involving some 2,500,000 men and their families, only 3149 prosecutions were brought: 1400 for violence, 1700 for incitement. Certainly many incidents must have passed unreported, but nothing can alter the impression of a low level of violence. There is only one report of shots being fired, and it is small wonder that Beatrice Webb referred in her diary to the view current on the continent 'that English working men were cowardly, that they cannot carry out a revolution because . . . they apparently accept the bourgeois regime so quietly'.[45]

With the government remaining firmly in control in most areas, the TUC General Council had to face the prospect of a prolonged strike. Not only did this raise the possibility that control would be lost to local militants, but TUC sources indicate that they were also afraid of strong legislation from the government, and that they were further influenced by indications that the workers' solidarity was weakening. Printers and railway clerks, for instance, were alleged to be returning to work. The union leaders thus welcomed the offer of mediation made by Sir Herbert Samuel and used it as an excuse to call off the strike on 12 May. The sense of shock among the strikers was profound. In protest more men came out, so that on 13 May more were on strike than at any time during the strike itself. Quite quickly, however, the drift back to work began, except among the miners. Facing wage reductions and longer hours in an industry which had sustained over 600,000 industrial injuries between 1922 and 1924, they had little to lose. In any case they more than anyone felt betrayed, as they did not accept that the TUC had any right to negotiate and accept terms on their behalf. The long coal strike which followed reinforced the miners' resentments. Conditions were appalling. That they resisted for so long was due partly to the action of the co-operative movement which provided extended credit underwritten by a union guarantee, partly to the fund for miners' wives which raised £300,000 for relief, and partly because Russian miners sent a million pounds. For several months they opposed the owners' efforts to introduce company unions in the north east, rejected the so-called Bishop's memorandum, and even survived Chamberlain's decision to abolish those boards of guardians which were in his view too generous in their dispensation of relief to strikers' families. Small wonder that the bitterness of the general strike has remained deeply entrenched in the miners' folk memory. Other groups had equal cause for bitterness. Despite official assurances to the contrary, there was a great deal of victimisation. Transport workers were especially hard hit. Even an interview with the general manager of the Great Western Railway did not enable the general secretary of the NUR to get back the job of Max Goldberg, an official of the Railway Clerks' Association, who was dismissed purely for his part in the strike. Men at the Southdown Motor Works in Brighton had a fairly typical experience, returning to find jobs barred to strikers and filled by non-unionists.

The Conservatives' Trade Union Act of 1927 did little to ease the bitterness. All through the crisis Baldwin had tried to restrain his militants and as late as 11 May had reiterated his intention not to sanction any alteration in trade-union law. Once the crisis was over he weakened, 'prostrated by the ordeal, experienced a kind of nervous collapse, and lost interest in placing his authority on the settlement'.[46] In the absence of firm, prime-ministerial direction, it was hard-line attitudes which shaped the act. Although the measure took its place in labour's demonology, its bark was much worse than its bite and many employers were critical of its modera- tion. The unions retained their privileged legal status. The clauses against sympathetic and political strikes were never invoked, and no strike was ever to be declared illegal under its terms. Nor was the new contracting-in clause for the political levy very effective. In the short term there was a drop in Labour party income, but astute union secretaries soon learned to include the relevant form among the many to be signed by new union members.

In an attempt to ease the feelings stirred up by the strike, Alfred Mond, a leading Conservative spokesman on industrial relations, took up an idea of Arthur Steel-Maitland's and suggested a series of meetings between the two sides of industry. This had some attraction for union leaders, who had had no real successes since 1920, whose membership had declined, whose wage rates had been cut, and whose finances were much strained. For their part, employer participation has to be seen as part of a general move to industrial rationalisation in the 1920s. New technology and new production methods could, it was increasingly recognised, only be successfully introduced with trade-union co-operation. Meetings began in 1928 and it soon became apparent that the objectives which emerged were similar to those of the non-political trade-union movement which had grown up in the midlands under the influence of George Spencer — rationalisation to maintain profits, negotiation to settle disputes, the separation of industrial and political issues.[47] Since Spencerism was very suspect to orthodox trade unionists, nothing very fruitful emerged from the talks. Some, like Cook, were opposed on principle to any talks with employers, while others were disappointed that neither the Trade Union Act nor the miners' Eight Hours Act of 1926 had been discussed. On the employers' side, small enterprises were unwilling or unable to abide by concessions made by representatives of major concerns who were themselves more involved in high industrial policy than with shop-floor negotiation. Since neither em- ployers nor union representatives had any mandatory control over their constituents, there was little real hope that the talks would produce much action. Their significance lay only in the fact that perhaps for the first time industrial relations were being treated as part of a general economic situation and not in isolation.

The general strike is often portrayed as a major turning point in trade-union history, because it was followed by the Mond-Turner talks, the repressive legislation of 1927, declining trade-union membership and unrest.'[48] It is also suggested that extremism diminished, and the idea of the general strike as an industrial weapon was finally killed off; but there is little in this. The Trade Union Act had little real impact though it may have inflamed feeling. Nor did the Mond-Turner talks produce any practical results. They can be seen simply as part of a recurrent pattern of efforts by moderates to rally centre opinion in times of high industrial tension. They were a direct descendant of the 1911 talks and the 1921 conference. The fall in trade-union membership after 1926 was certainly most marked among the unions most heavily involved, especially the miners, railwaymen, printers and transport workers; but general union membership had been tumbling since 1920 and the most dramatic losses occurred in 1921, not 1927. Nor was there much of a downward trend in strike activity. The extension of national, collective bargaining agreements after 1919 produced a series of important national stoppages and these persisted into the 1930s. While days lost in strikes in 1927 and 1928 were down to slightly more than a million, they rose again and the real turning point came in 1933. Measured by affiliation to the CPGB and the National Minority Movement, the vehicle through which the party hoped to capture the unions, extremism did not die away immediately after the strike. The NMM lost thousands of members but it did not formally go out of existence until 1933. Membership of the CPGB plummeted to 3,200 by the end of the decade, but this had little to do with any general rejection of extremism after the strike; rather it was the result of Stalin's abandonment in 1928 of the united front policy. Party leaders who resisted were overwhelmed and replaced by hard-liners at the 1928 conference. A class against class policy had little chance of success in Britain and was not even attractive to many Communists. If there was any turning point in industrial relations, it came not with the calling off of the general strike, but rather on Black Friday in 1921 when union leaders pulled back from supporting the miners. It was this which did most to discredit the appeal of a general strike, which was followed by the most significant decline of membership, and which saw also a marked diminution in the level of industrial unrest. In 1921 the union leaders went voluntarily to the brink, did not like what they saw, and pulled back. In 1926 they were dragged over the top by circumstances they could not control, and scrambled back to safety as soon as they decently could.

8

Depression and Apathy, 1927-39

Towards the end of 1927, J.C.C. Davidson of the Conservative central office warned Stanley Baldwin that the government appeared 'to be piling up a legislative and administrative record which is giving serious offence . . . which, when the General Election comes along, may well prove to be our undoing'.[1] By-election results certainly seemed to support this prognosis. Of the forty-six seats which the Conservatives defended between 1924 and 1929, sixteen were lost; and there was no sign of the customary swing back to the government as Parliament neared the end of its term. On the contrary, five Conservative seats were lost in 1928 and another five in the spring of 1929. Six of these were taken by Labour. When the general election came in 1929, the Conservative representation fell to 261 and the Liberals to a paltry fifty-nine, leaving Labour as the largest single party with 287 seats. After some hesitation Baldwin resigned, and MacDonald was invited to form the second Labour government.

Labour's performance in some ways was the fruit of good party organisation. By 1928 almost two hundred full-time agents were at work. While organisers were permitted a fair degree of discretion in their activities, annual staff conferences were held along with training and briefing sessions, and weekly reports had to be submitted to party headquarters. Perhaps as a result of this, the number of divisional-local branches and trades councils affiliated to the party had risen to 3,500, an increase of some five hundred since 1924. The local strength of Labour was further indicated by its growing intervention in municipal elections. The party's share of total local government candidatures was forty-four per cent in 1929, and the years 1926—9 saw an average of one hundred seats gained each year. The general election success was also and perhaps primarily a reflection on the Conservatives' record, as Davidson had predicted. Harold Macmillan was probably unduly critical when he suggested that only the passage of the Local Government Act in 1929 had enabled the administration to end 'on a constructive note', but it was true that several important interest groups had been disturbed by government policy.[2] Disarmament talks had progressed only slowly and relations with the United States were poor. At home, right-wing demands for expenditure reductions had been only partially satisfied, and the farmers' lobby had been alienated by Baldwin's refusal to remove the burden of the Agricultural Wages Act. Surprisingly, the Trades Disputes Act seems to have figured but rarely in the campaign, a result perhaps of the somewhat improved industrial relations picture of which the Mond-Turner talks were the main manifestation.

Unemployment, the dominant election issue, was of course one of equally pressing concern to working people, and one on which the outgoing government's record was less than impressive. In one sense this was to be expected since the problem was by now so enormous and its causes not fully appreciated. After the short postwar boom, whole sections of British industry had found themselves under pressure in world markets. Various combinations of slowly rising demand, over-capacity, old plant, over-manning, technological backwardness, and bad industrial relations had produced massive structural unemployment in the staple export industries of shipbuilding, steel, coal, engineering and cotton textiles. Matters had not been aided by a government financial policy designed to restore sterling's position as an international currency, and the return to the gold standard at prewar parity had further overpriced British exports. Unemployment policy itself had been slow-acting and really directed towards symptoms rather than causes. With unemployment averaging ten per cent of the insured population after 1920, it was deemed neither politic nor practical to extend poor relief, especially as the worst hit areas were generally those with the slenderest financial resources. In 1921 Poplar Borough Council refused to levy rates towards the upkeep of London County Council, the police and the Metropolitan Asylums

Board on the ground that wealthier west end boroughs
made no contribution towards outdoor relief, which was by
now Poplar's largest expense. Rather than pay, the thirty
councillors, led by George Lansbury, went to prison. The
whole episode made the government appear ridiculous, since
once in prison the councillors proceeded to organise the
other prisoners to demand their rights. The need to tackle
unemployment was deemed still more urgent in that it was
regarded, perhaps rightly, as a potential source of social
upheaval. Once the postwar boom broke, unemployment
reached unprecedented levels and fell particularly hard on a
workforce used to the high labour demands generated by the
war. By the end of 1921, more than a third of shipbuilders
had no work. A fifth of building workers and more than a
quarter of all engineers were similarly affected. During the
war the presence of the armaments firm, Vickers, had brought
prosperity to Barrow. By August 1922 almost half the
town's insured population was out of work.[3] Spontaneous
demonstrations broke out, soon to be channelled and organised
by the National Unemployed Workers Movement (NUWM),
led by Wal Hannington, a tool maker. Hannington had been
involved during the war in the shop-stewards movement and
was a communist. Mainly for this reason the TUC tried to
keep the NUWM at arm's length, though a joint committee
of the two did function between 1924 and 1927. Throughout
the winter of 1920–21, demonstrations occurred in several
major cities, confirming government fears that unemployment
would produce disorder.

In 1920 unemployment insurance had been extended to
cover the majority of the workforce, and a series of subsequent
measures extended the period over which benefit could be
drawn, and also changed the rates of benefit and contribution.
Most significant, perhaps, was the act of November 1921
which for the first time introduced *pro-rata* payments for an
individual's dependants. There remained, however, the problem
of those who had exhausted their rights to benefit under the
insurance scheme. For them the dole was instituted, an
uncovenanted benefit whose cost was, in theory, to be
recovered from the recipient when he resumed work. For
this purpose the Unemployment Fund was permitted to
borrow up to £30,000,000 from the Treasury.

But unemployment showed little sign of diminishing. The numbers claiming insurance benefit soared, as indeed did the number of those transferring to the dole. Increasingly, therefore, it was the Treasury that was coming under pressure, partly because it was responsible for the dole, partly because the Unemployment Fund itself had inadequate resources since the whole scheme had been predicated upon the existence of much lower levels of unemployment. In 1921 a seeking work test, really little more than a character test, had been introduced in order to discourage fraudulent claims. The Conservative Unemployment Insurance Act of 1927 retained this for claimants under the insurance scheme, but ended it for those on the dole. Apart from relief, a few feeble efforts were made to tackle the problem by increasing the amount of work or retraining the labour force. Industrial transference schemes had little impact, however, and the scale of local authority public works which the government permitted was too small to have any real effect on unemployment. Not surprisingly, therefore, unemployment remained obstinately high; and by March 1929 the registers showed 1,200,000 people out of work. Since the brunt of the depression was being borne by the old export industries, unemployment was regionally very concentrated, particularly in the north-east and the Celtic fringes. The implications of this were graphically portrayed by the Mayor of Merthyr in South Wales.

> When the works were in full employment, a number of elderly men were employed as watchmen, signalmen, gatekeepers ... if the works were still going they would still be in employment. Similarly, elderly men and women who had small shops ... have since had to close down because of the reduced purchasing power of the inhabitants ... Women who kept lodgers, or who went working days cleaning and washing for workers' families who are now unemployed, or parents who were dependent on sons or daughters who have removed from the area, are also in receipt of public assistance.[4]

When the election of 1929 was held, Labour's most substantial gains came in depressed areas such as Lancashire, Yorkshire and Cheshire, as well as those areas which were prospering because of rising new industrial enterprises such as vehicle manufacture and electrical engineering.

MacDonald's cabinet reflected not only the greater range of experienced talent available to him than in 1924, but also his continued wariness of both the unions and the ILP. At six, union representation was only one fewer than in 1924, but non-cabinet appointments to ministerial posts included only eleven trade-union representatives as against the seventeen contained in the first Labour administration. The ILP was virtually excluded altogether. After James Maxton replaced Clifford Allen as its leader, the ILP had grown increasingly critical of official Labour policy and had produced its own, often very radical alternatives which MacDonald, with one eye on the electorate, had done his best to suppress. His only concession to the left now was the inclusion of George Lansbury as First Commissioner of Works. For the rest, after some difficult dealing and bargaining, Henderson took the Foreign Office, Snowden the Exchequer, and Clynes the Home Office. Sidney Webb, by now elevated to the peerage as Lord Passfield, came in as Colonial Secretary. MacDonald also included as Minister of Labour Margaret Bondfield, the first woman to reach cabinet rank. It was an unenviable task, as the new minister's functions included responsibility for administering unemployment insurance whose viability was now in doubt. The job of finding policies actually to reduce unemployment was vested in a small committee consisting of Lansbury, two junior ministers (Thomas Johnston and Oswald Mosley), and presided over by the last of the Big Five, Jimmy Thomas, who was Lord Privy Seal.

The committee's efforts were all but barren. In part this was because of its unofficial status, but the main reason lay in deficiencies of both policy and personnel. Lansbury was an inspirational socialist and already in his seventies. Johnston and Mosley were only juniors and neither in the cabinet. Despite his undoubted flare for publicity, Thomas had hardly a single constructive idea in his head and lacked much understanding of economics. On one occasion, Mosley recalls, Thomas turned up to a meeting of the unemployment committee carrying a tin telephone box costing four shillings. He compared it favourably with the imported mahogany box then in use and costing fifteen shillings. What Thomas failed to comprehend in his desire to boost home industry was that twelve shillings of this covered the cost of the works inside![5] Increasingly Thomas was forced back on platitudes. 'All that Government can do, when all is said and done, is infinitesimal compared with what business can do for itself.'[6]

The truth was that Labour had no unemployment policy other than that of waiting for a revival of world trade, though this was not as unrealistic as might at first appear since the economic indicators for 1929 were quite favourable. Even so, the committee's failure was eloquent testimony to Labour's intellectual bankruptcy and indeed its failure to give the problem much serious thought since its last spell in office. Baldwin had been able to excuse his own inadequacies on the grounds that the first Labour government 'no more than any other Government, have been able to produce a panacea that would remedy unemployment'.[7] In 1929 only the Liberals, inspired by Lloyd George, had any far-reaching programme. With their closely integrated schemes of government expenditure and public works, the proposals in *We Can Conquer Unemployment* have been described by one modern authority as 'intellectually the most distinguished that have ever been placed before a British electorate'.[8] Labour's reply, *How to Conquer Unemployment*, was feeble in the extreme, containing no definite promises and 'totally devoid of the insights that lent distinction to the Liberal pamphlet'.[9] Although written mainly by G.D.H. Cole, it reflected the classical economic outlook of Philip Snowden whose shadow lay heavily across all Labour's unemployment options. The Chancellor was wedded to orthodox finance with all the conviction of one who had dealt with his own youthful poverty 'by the simple process of reducing his own wants'.[10] There was much truth in Leo Amery's comment to Thomas that in agreeing to tackle unemployment he was 'working with a noose round your neck and the other end of the rope ... in Snowden's hands'.[11] Strictly speaking, of course, the other end was in the hands of Snowden's Treasury advisers, but there was little danger of them pulling in any contrary direction. As Churchill graphically put it, 'the Treasury mind and the Snowden mind embraced each other with the fervour

of two long-separated lizards.'[12] The government's inability
to break out of the constraints of orthodox, budget-balancing
finance was largely responsible for driving out of office
Oswald Mosley, the one Labour man who did have a coherent
policy and the political energy to carry it through. Mosley
had drafted a scheme involving new administrative machinery,
long-term economic reconstruction, short-term work plans,
and a more radical financial policy. Snowden sat on the
committee of the cabinet which considered and rejected the
plan, whereupon Mosley resigned to seek remedies for the
nation's ills in other directions. One small outcome, however,
was that MacDonald, whose main concern had always been
in foreign policy, did now begin to take a more active interest
in unemployment.

The Prime Minister's personal intervention resulted in some
slight policy modification in the form of minor extensions of
government building programmes and the encouragement of
local authority works. The results were too negligible and
slow-acting to offset the financial crisis about to sweep over
the nation. On the left, the ILP was increasingly restless,
bringing forward its own budgetary proposals involving the
expenditure of some £200 million on the social services.
Early in 1930 the ILP moved to strengthen its position
within the Labour party, calling on all ILP men who were
MPs to abide by ILP rather than Labour party policy. In fact
only eighteen of the ILP's 140 MPs responded to this, but
even an incipient revolt was enough to add to the constraints
under which the government was working. By March 1930
the number out of work had risen to 1,700,000, greatly in
excess of official expectations. In July Margaret Bondfield
sought a further increase in the insurance fund's borrowing
power to £60 million — provoking a storm of protest in the
Conservative press about insurance abuse and work shy
scroungers. Retrenchment was the watchword of the attack,
as unemployment relief cost over £92 million in the year
1930—1.[13] The general Tory mood was summed up
in evidence presented by the National Confederation of
Employers to the Royal Commission on Unemployment.
Insurance, it was claimed, was 'insidiously sapping the whole
social and financial stability of the country' and preventing

unemployment from 'acting as a corrective factor in the adjustment of wage levels'.[14]

Yet the real burden on the Treasury was a product of Labour's own modification of the 1927 transitional benefit scheme. This had been designed by the Conservatives to cope with the problem of people whose working history had been too spasmodic to enable them to make the required thirty insurance premium payments over the previous two years. Transitional benefit was introduced and paid to those who had made eight premium payments over two years, or thirty at any time in the past. Though intended as a one year stop-gap, the persistence of heavy unemployment, much of it long term, had ensured that transitional benefit was continued. In 1930 the Labour government removed the stipulation that applicants for it should fulfil the 'seeking work' test, shifting the responsibility onto hard-pressed, local labour exchange officials to prove that applicants were not actively seeking work. The 1930 measures also transferred financial responsibility for transitional benefit from the insurance fund to the Treasury. As a result of these changes, the number of transitional beneficiaries doubled between March and May 1930, while in the first complete financial year transitional benefit cost the Treasury £19 million. As unemployment continued to rise through the winter of 1930–31 in the aftermath of the Wall Street crash in 1929 and the ensuing world depression, the insurance fund, even without the weight of transitional benefit, came under growing pressure. By March 1931 its expenditure exceeded income by £36,430,000 and it was some £75 million in debt.

At the beginning of 1931, Snowden – alarmed by the growing debt and the ammunition which it provided for the opposition – announced that he was establishing a committee under the chairmanship of Sir George May, secretary of the Prudential Assurance Company, to investigate the problems of national expenditure. The publication of the May report in the summer could not have come at a less auspicious time, for it coincided with a major world financial crisis following the failure of the Kredit-Anstalt in May. As the Kredit-Anstalt was the largest and most prestigious bank in Austria, its collapse threatened the solvency of the numerous domestic and foreign institutions which depended on it. The Austrian government froze all assets in order to stop the flight of money out of the country. Because a large proportion of these funds were German, the crisis was simply extended. In turn Germany, desirous of protecting its own banking system, prohibited the export of gold and foreign currency. As Germany's largest creditor, Britain now came under pressure from foreign investors seeking to protect their liquidity by withdrawing funds from London. Into this fraught situation May's estimates of a budget deficit of £120 million and an insurance fund debt of £105 million fell like a bombshell, shattering any confidence which Bank of England action might have instilled in foreign investors. Money poured out of Britain, as much as £60 million in the month up to 6 August. By all the canons of orthodox finance, May's recommendations for drastic economies in government expenditure were even more urgent if confidence in Britain was to be maintained. On 12 August the cabinet committee on national expenditure assembled to draw up a suitable programme of economies. It was over the details of this programme that the second Labour government stumbled and finally fell.

The committee pruned some of May's estimates, but when the full cabinet met Snowden still demanded substantial reductions in the pay of government employees such as civil servants and members of the armed forces. Teachers' salaries were also earmarked for cuts. The most contentious item, however, was the proposal to reduce unemployment insurance expenditure by £48,500,000. Such was the severity of Britain's position that any action to restore foreign confidence required not merely the support of the Labour party but also of Parliament as well. For Conservatives, however, Snowden's proposals did not go far enough; for some of his own party they were utterly unacceptable. The problem was that there was no way to reconcile the demands of the opposition, foreign financiers, and the bankers for a fully balanced budget with the social conscience of the Labour party and of the TUC.

After the general strike the unions (perhaps somewhat paradoxically) had grown in public esteem, probably because of their participation in the Mond-Turner talks. Ernest Bevin had by now emerged as a major figure, exercising considerable influence within both the TUC and the Labour party through his powerful Transport and General Workers Union. With the opening of Transport House in 1928, the TGWU became the party's landlord, and sharing the same premises as the party certainly gave Bevin speed of access if nothing else. He was also instrumental in revitalising the *Daily Herald* on sound commercial principles, so that in 1933 it became the first newspaper to achieve a regular circulation of two million. His talents found a perfect foil in the quiet but firm efficiency of Walter Citrine, secretary of the TUC. Citrine later wrote that he could not recall 'a single issue of first-class importance on which we seriously differed'. Certainly he and Bevin were at one in their ambition that the TUC 'would be regularly and naturally consulted by whatever Government was in power on any subject of direct concern to the unions'.[15] Bevin had served on several official committees and had some grasp of alternative economic strategies, embodied in the TUC's proposals for the present crisis. Although the unions had not yet broken through to the idea of deficit finance, their suggestions included increases in taxation, suspension of the sinking fund, and maintenance of wage levels. Reductions in wages and insurance benefits were rejected. Behind the TUC proposals, as yet indistinct and crudely articulated, lay an instinctive feeling that the right course of action lay in keeping up demand and creating employment.

With Treasury and Bank of England officials, not to mention the American government, all clamouring loudly for precisely the opposite approach, it is small wonder that MacDonald paid scant attention to the union proposals. Neither he nor Snowden had come from a trade-union background, and his relations with the TUC had never been particularly smooth. He had reduced union representation in his second government and had further ruffled TUC feathers by failing to consult it about the composition of the 1930 Royal Commission on Unemployment. Many of MacDonald's colleagues did owe their place in the labour movement to earlier trade-union activity. If some like Thomas did not allow this to influence them at this time of crisis, Arthur Henderson remained true to his union roots. When the Americans demanded as the price of their assistance a fully balanced budget and therefore by implication Snowden's economy cuts, Henderson led the cabinet dissidents. By twelve to nine, however, the restrictionists carried the day. MacDonald now faced a major political crisis with a cabinet almost evenly divided on a fundamental policy issue. It is possible that he and Henderson had been heading for a clash anyway over the latter's handling of projected negotiations on help for Germany in the financial crisis. This may well have marginally influenced Henderson's decision to challenge MacDonald's authority in the cabinet. Equally, it may well have encouraged MacDonald to abandon a party in which he had no real power base, certainly not one comparable with that of his foreign secretary. Having failed with an impassioned plea for unity MacDonald took the only course open to him and tendered his resignation, advising the King to form a national government. After some hesitation he himself acceded to widespread urgings that he should lead it. His immediate reward was expulsion from the party which he had led from obscurity to government. The news of his expulsion was conveyed to him in a very shabby fashion – a brief note headed 'Dear Sir' and signed with a rubber stamp over the national organiser's signature.

Whether or not the insult was calculated, MacDonald's defection produced a good deal of recrimination at the time and has continued to do so. Ever since 1931 he has in some circles been vilified as the leader in a long line of Labour traitors running from John Burns down to George Brown and Reg Prentice.[16] Ultimately all politicians are concerned with power, but the allegation that this was MacDonald's only interest totally discounts his unswerving pacifism – against party policy and public opinion – during the First World War. Some critics like Dame Margaret Cole find the suggestion that MacDonald had always planned to sell out the party 'not in the least incredible', but the concrete evidence for such a claim is dubious.[17] It is true that in the years before 1914 MacDonald was often to be found knee-deep with the Liberals, but this was hardly surprising for the leader of a small, strategically placed party which was heavily dependent on Liberal goodwill. Even when he formed his first government, MacDonald was dependent upon the Liberals for his very survival, and indeed could only find sufficiently able personnel by recruiting former Liberals to his cabinet. Nor should it be forgotten that MacDonald's political views had been forged in the late nineteenth century, when radicalism had Liberal rather than socialist connotations.

In turn, this makes nonsense of the oft-made claim that at the moment of capitalist crisis MacDonald and the Labour party failed to implement the genuine socialist solution. To be sure it was never very clear what this solution was, but in any case the Labour party owed nothing at all to Marxism or to any other revolutionary theory. It had been conceived as a constitutional party designed to operate as the political arm of the trade unions and within the framework of existing parliamentary procedures. Because of the existence of the Lib-Lab pact in the Edwardian period, the Labour party, mindful of the electorate, had generally selected candidates of moderate persuasions. The 1918 programme, for all that it committed the party to a thorough-going socialist platform, was designed to be implemented by parliamentary methods with compensation for those who lost either property or privilege. In short, neither the Labour party nor MacDonald was likely, either by temperament or background, to implement any radical solutions to the current crisis.

Intellectually MacDonald's dilemma sprang from his conviction that socialism would evolve out of successful capitalism. He was not therefore equipped to deal with a different scenario in which capitalism seemed to have failed. Eventually he moved towards the idea, also favoured by J.M. Keynes, of protective tariffs for British industry. Politically, however, this was unrealistic since it would offend not only the Liberals whose parliamentary support was essential, but also Philip Snowden. The Chancellor, it is true, was hardly the most loved or most powerfully supported member of the party, but he did have considerable public prestige and was too significant a figure for MacDonald lightly to contemplate his loss. This left the proposals of the TUC or the ILP. Apart from the fact that they were based on what were then highly suspect economic assumptions, MacDonald dismissed them as representing narrow sectional interests rather than those of the nation as a whole.

It is often assumed that MacDonald could have adopted Keynsian deficit financing as a way out of his difficulty. Various individuals such as Lloyd George and Mosley had proposed remedies which involved, *de facto*, the idea of the multiplier, and the TUC had instinctively leaned to the view that demand should be kept as high as possible. Such piecemeal attacks were not likely to break down the closed reasoning which underpinned classical theory. Only a fully integrated alternative system of economic theory could do this, and it did not come until Keynes published his *General Theory* in 1936. Until that time orthodoxy reigned supreme, firmly entrenched both mentally and institutionally in the Treasury and the City. Furthermore, its ramparts were defended by some eminently respectable academic economists, many with intellects as formidable as Keynes' own. It is in any case questionable that public works sustained by deficit financing would have made much impact on the unemployment figures, because the scale of government budgetary operations was still quite small and unemployment was structural rather than cyclical in nature. The corollary, direct control of investment, was a political and administrative impossibility. Devaluation was ruled out on the grounds that Britain's whole economic strategy since 1925 had been based on maintaining gold convertibility at the prewar exchange rate. So MacDonald was forced back on deflation, the human consequences of which were too awful for many of his cabinet colleagues to consider. When the crunch came and the decisions had to be taken, therefore, there were many who preferred to sacrifice their government rather than their conscience. While MacDonald cannot be exonerated entirely – he failed to find a *modus vivendi* between the opposing factions in his cabinet and arguably spent too much time on foreign affairs – it is fitting that he should emerge from his latest and fullest biography neither as a betrayer nor betrayed, 'not as a cold blooded conspirator pursuing a predetermined aim but as a prisoner of circumstances beyond his control, searching despairingly for a way of escape'.[18] Further, it is clear that the search took a great deal out of him personally. Nicholas Davenport, attending a dinner in MacDonald's honour in 1931, recalls that 'the poor man was mentally exhausted. He

mumbled and bumbled – no sentence was properly finished
. . . the words ended in an inarticulate jumble.'[19]

MacDonald was joined in the new National Government by
Snowden, Thomas and a handful of backbenchers. In the
election that followed, he was swept to victory on a safety
first programme. Thus in spite of being disowned by his
local party and every branch but one of the NUR in Derby,
Thomas comfortably retained his seat on the slogan, 'The
nation first and the nation always'.[20] Tactically, Labour was
placed at a considerable disadvantage. It was difficult to
claim that it represented the national interest as it was quite
overtly the party of organised labour. Alternatively, it could
assert the primacy of labour in the nation, though this was
equally difficult in view of the current national crisis and the
government's poor record. Furthermore, the defection of
MacDonald meant that much of the party's election literature
had to be hastily rewritten for the campaign. While by-election
results since 1929 indicate that the Labour government would
probably have been defeated anyway, it was the magnitude
of the losses in 1931 which was so stunning. Labour was
annihilated. All told, the party was reduced to fifty-two seats
as against thirty-three Liberal and 521 for the National
Government (Conservative 473: National Liberal 35: National
Labour 13). All the main parliamentary leaders went down,
and of the cabinet only Lansbury retained his seat. Three of
the Big Five were now regarded as traitors; though Henderson
and Clynes returned to Parliament in 1933 and 1935 respectively, neither was to play a central role in the party again.
Junior ministers like Clement Attlee and Stafford Cripps,
both of whom survived with the slenderest of majorities (551
and 429 respectively) were thus catapulted somewhat pre-
maturely to positions of prominence. Most of the surviving
backbenchers were trade unionists of little political weight,
though they were enlivened by young, articulate radicals
like Aneurin Bevan. Labour's parliamentary position was
weakened still more by the fact that the overlap between it
and extra-parliamentary bodies was much reduced. At one
time Lansbury was the only member of the National Executive
who was also an MP. Consequently, the executive fell even

more under the domination of the big trade unions, notably the TGWU, railway, textile, miners and municipal workers.

Although the election results were so devastating in terms of seats and personnel, Labour's vote held up surprisingly well, especially in the depressed areas. While it is apparent that many Labour supporters abstained rather than make the choice between MacDonald and the party, the real cause of Labour's defeat was the failure of the Liberals to contest many seats. In 1929 many Labour victories had been won on tiny majorities, forty-one per cent of their seats being taken on minority votes. In 1931 the anti-Labour forces united in name if not in policy, and only ninety-nine Labour candidates were opposed by both a Liberal and a Conservative as against the 447 in this position in 1929. Once the Labour abstainers returned to the fold, party fortunes recovered quite quickly. The local elections which followed hard on the heels of the general election saw a loss of 206 seats and only 149 successes. As early as 1932, however, the trend began to turn the other way, 458 Labour councillors being returned. More gains accrued in 1933 and 1934, when for the first time Labour won control of the London County Council. By 1935 the party had also won ten parliamentary by-elections.

This rapid recovery suggests that the 1931 election was fought in an atmosphere of panic and fear which subsided relatively quickly. Yet within the labour movement itself the events of 1929—31 produced some substantial re-thinking, not least on economic matters. Far from pushing Labour towards a Marxist position, the crisis pushed it towards Keynsian solutions, lending some credence to Kingsley Martin's view that the crisis changed the philosophy of a substantial number of Labour activists.[21] The party's lack of a realistic short-term programme had also been cruelly exposed, and George Strauss claimed that the whole crisis had been caused by 'the complete lack of a policy on the more important domestic questions'.[22] In much the same vein, R.H. Tawney argued that the Labour government had been the victim neither of 'murder nor misadventure but pernicious anaemia'.[23] This was quickly recognised by the NEC, which appointed a policy sub-committee at the end of 1931. After much discussion and amendment at conference, the *Immediate Programme* was ratified in 1937. Bevin's hand was clearly discernible in this document. Five years earlier. *Saving and Spending* had appeared, in which proposals to nationalise the joint stock banks had assumed a much greater degree of importance than the nationalisation of strategic industry, though this was very much a reaction to the feeling (naturally very strong in 1932) that the Labour government had been deliberately broken by a bankers' ramp. There were always those who had argued that any administration intent on fundamentally changing the distribution of power and wealth in Britain would be opposed by vested capitalist interests, a view which had gained credibility perhaps from the incident of the Zinoviev letter in 1924. Certainly it is true that the bankers had put tremendous pressure on MacDonald to act strongly in order to stem the run on the pound; but this was quite consistent with prevalent economic orthodoxy and also with efforts which the Bank of England had been making since 1918 to restore Britain's prewar status as an international financial centre. In the aftermath of 1931, radicals on the left of the party, men like Cripps and Harold Laski, began to question the efficacy of the parliamentary road to socialism and the assumption that existing administrative institutions were politically neutral. From this came the proposal that any future Labour government should be prepared to pass an emergency powers bill in order to override institutional obstacles to social and economic change. There was generally little support for the idea, however, especially as the immediate impact of 1931 faded. Attlee, who emerged as the new party leader in the middle 1930s, was very scathing of the left wing, even to the extent of pillorying it in verse.

> The peoples' flag is deepest pink
> It is not red blood but only ink.
> It is supported now by Douglas Cole
> Who plays each year a different role . . .[24]

In reality the left's position in the party was very much weaker in the 1930s because of the disaffiliation of the ILP in July 1932. The membership was not unanimous in this decision, however, and the dissenters joined with dissatisfied left-wingers in the Labour party to form the Socialist League. The league's purpose was to provide the party with specifically socialist propaganda and policies, making the test of any Labour party programme whether or not it 'raised the status and conditions of the workers as a class, and correspondingly weaken[ed] the power of the owning class'[25] For a couple of years after 1931, the Labour party — with a weakened parliamentary position, bereft of established leaders, and with morale at a low ebb — was unable to resist quite radical policy resolutions moved largely at Socialist League behest at party conferences. Soon opposition to the league began to crystallise round Bevin. MacDonald's conduct in 1931 had served to deepen his suspicion of intellectuals and strengthen his determination that the unions should exercise much greater control over both party policy and leadership. To this end, he and Henderson had revived the National Joint Council to improve union-party relations. As the party recovered, so Bevin's powerful influence in conference, where he controlled about ten per cent of the two million union votes (it is estimated that the Socialist League commanded about 500,000 votes), enabled him to reverse the tide and reject league policy. The league then began to move away from being merely a propagandist ginger group and challenged for the very soul of the labour movement, organising a series of anti-war conferences in 1935 in conjunction with the ILP and CPGB. The appearance of a joint manifesto from these three bodies, calling for the establishment of a united front against fascism, enabled the NEC to utilise the party rule about non-co-operation with communists to expel those Labour party members who were in the Socialist League. The league was promptly wound up, going the way of so many other left-wing organisations of intellectuals who lacked any root in the unions or for that matter much real experience of working-class life. The ILP also suffered. In 1932, prior to its disaffiliation from the Labour party, membership was some 17,000. By 1935 it had dwindled away to 4,400.

It is against this background that the interpretation of the 1930s as something of a golden age for the left has to be placed. Certainly there was a leftward current among intellectuals who found their economic security undermined and who regarded mass unemployment as a moral outrage. Refugees from Hitler's Germany brought home in a very direct way the horrors of right-wing extremism. The Left Book Club, which began its operations in this decade, reached a membership of 60,000, while the *New Statesman* successfully rallied British socialists of many shades round an anti-fascist platform at the time of the Spanish civil war. Some £2 million was raised to help the republican cause in Spain. Yet far from being some insidious communist front, the Left Book Club merely used communist ideas to serve the British radical tradition, and such ideas were abandoned as soon as they were seen to be inconsistent with that tradition. Communism and Marxism had some appeal to radical intellectuals because of their stress on opposing Hitler and the policies of Baldwin and later Chamberlain which seemed to offer at least moral support to fascism. Yet once Britain actually entered war in 1939 and the CPGB denounced it as a capitalist struggle (until the invasion of the Soviet Union, that is), most intellectuals discovered that they were more interested in defending liberal democracy than the Soviet Union or some vague future notion of a communist Britain. Furthermore, the main bulk of the labour movement and indeed the public at large remained at best indifferent, if not actively hostile to the blandishments of the left. This has been largely obscured, however, for two reasons. The first is that the press made so much of those few places where communist influence in local politics was strong. Thus the *Newcastle Chronicle* drew attention to events in Chopwell, County Durham with the headline 'UNDER THE RED BANNER: CLUTCHING HAND OF COMMUNISM: SPECTRE OF A MINIATURE RUSSIA', while the *Morning Post* described the village as one 'of suspicion, of whispering neighbours and of fear'.[26] Secondly, it is important to remember that most of the writing about the 1930s came initially from the pens of those intellectuals who were politically active at the time. Yet for all the rhetoric and wishful thinking, the left achieved very little, unable to break the unwillingness of labour leaders to support any radical agitation outside the existing institutional channels. In 1934 the TUC issued a black circular advising unions to keep communists out of influential positions. While there were strong pockets of communism among London busmen, Manchester metal workers, and miners in Scotland and Wales – no fewer than 352 officials of the SWMF were party members – total membership remained under ten thousand during the depression. Little impact was made except in a few isolated areas such as Chopwell, Mardy and the Vale of Leven. Even there, it is unclear how far communists owed their influence to their political views and how far to the fact that most of them wore other hats, be they those of trade-union official or local authority councillor. The TUC and official Labour party leadership consistently rejected calls for a united front against General Franco. 'I was against it,' recalled Attlee. 'For I knew that if we made an alliance with the Communists they would stab us in the back. They always have done.'[27] In the same way Kingsley Martin has characterised the attitude of most ordinary people in Britain towards the Spanish civil war as 'lumpish and dull'.[28] Certainly most of the British volunteers for the international brigades were working class, but there were only about two thousand of them altogether. Even in a highly depressed area with a long tradition of militancy such as Wales, the 170 volunteers who went to Spain were negligible besides the six per cent of the total population who migrated in the search for work. Nor were the volunteers' motives always purely idealistic. 'I was an economic burden to my family,' said one, 'and I thought I could be of more use in Spain.'[29] Perhaps more than anyone else, even Orwell, Walter Greenwood caught the flavour of working-class life in his two accounts of the 1930s, *Love on the Dole* and *There Was a Time*. Significantly, there is almost no reference to foreign affairs in either of them. Such interest as there was in foreign affairs took the form of a basic and predictable concern that peace should be preserved. This at least would appear to be the lesson of the East Fulham by-election when a record swing of 26.5 per cent was recorded against the National Government in a campaign dominated by issues of peace, disarmament and the League of Nations. It was confirmed by the results of the Peace Ballot two years later when the majority of the 11.5 million votes cast supported Britain's membership of the League and disarmament.

Equally damaging to the myth of the left's golden age is that in each of Greenwood's books there is only one reference to domestic agitation, a startling consideration in view of the unprecedented scale and duration of unemployment. In the worst year of all, almost three million were officially out of work, nearly a quarter of the insured labour force. With the addition of those not covered by insurance and those who no longer bothered to register, it has been estimated that the true figure was probably nearer 3,750,000.[30] Whole towns lay devastated. The iron town of Stockton, said J.B. Priestley, was 'finished. It is like a theatre that is kept open merely for the sale of drinks in the bars and chocolates in the corridors.'[31] Jarrow was described by Ellen Wilkinson MP as a town that had been murdered.[32] The unemployed themselves hung around street corners, scavenged for coal if it was available, filled up local libraries in order to keep warm, or passed the time at one of the many voluntary centres which were set up to provide facilities for recreation, wood-work, bootmending. A whole generation of workers in the depressed regions grew up not knowing the discipline of regular work; another generation passed into old age, its self-respect and dignity ravaged by years of penny pinching and unemployment. Some 300,000 of those receiving unemployment pay in 1932 had been out of work for more than a year, and they were predominantly older men.

Occasionally, the antagonisms produced by this situation spilled over into violence, as in Belfast and Birkenhead in 1932. On the whole, however, resentment remained private, except at election times when it was channelled through the ballot box. Labour party support held up surprisingly well in the depressed regions, even though the party organised only one official demonstration on behalf of the unemployed. The unemployed never managed anything as spectacular as the protest mounted by naval ratings against pay reductions. Some 12,000 sailors at Invergordon mutinied, though it is worth stressing that they referred to themselves in their petition of grievances at 'loyal subjects of His Majesty the King' and added that they were 'quite agreeable to accept a cut which they consider reasonable'.[33] Such unemployed agitation as did occur was organised in the main by the NUWM whose

activities continued to be carefully monitored by the Home
Office. Its leaders were kept under constant surveillance, and
by the early thirties the organisation had been penetrated at
the very highest level by a police agent.[34] As unemployment
soared in the depths of the 1931 crisis, the NUWM organised
a series of hunger marches so effective that at one time the
National Government was considering legislation to ban
marches, though it ultimately decided to adopt a more subtle
approach, tightening up on the administration of relief in
order to make would-be marchers reluctant to leave home.

The climax of the NUWM campaign really came with the
protests it organised against the National Government's
economy cuts and the introduction of the hated means test.
The cuts came into effect just after Parliament was dissolved
for the general election of 1931. Insurance benefit for an
unemployed man was reduced from 17s. to 15s.3d. and if his
children's allowance remained at 2s. a week, his wife's was
cut from 9s. to 8s. New Anomalies Regulations struck at
134,000 married women who were suddenly deprived of
benefit unless they had paid a certain number of insurance
contributions since marriage. Contributions made while they
were single were simply discounted. Then in October 1931
came the Unemployment Insurance (National Economy)
Order No. 2 which replaced transitional benefit by a new
transitional payments scheme. Although the necessary money
was to be provided by the Treasury, all those who had
exhausted their right to insurance benefit and were entitled
to the new payment had first to submit themselves to a means
test administered by the public assistance committees. The
PACs had been set up to replace the boards of guardians,
abolished in 1929, but many of the old, patronising attitudes
persisted. What was worse, the individual's *family* income was
taken into account, while the rates of payment could in no
case exceed, and were usually less than, the new insurance
benefit scales. Many perfectly respectable, hard working
individuals, to whom the very thought of the poor law had
always been anathema, now found themselves in the doubly
humiliating position of having to submit to a most detailed
scrutiny of their private circumstances administered through
what was to all intents and purposes a revamped poor law.

By January 1932 about 900,000 people were being means tested, and public hostility was not mollified by the fact that many Labour-controlled committees and a few Conservative-controlled ones virtually refused to operate the system and paid relief at the same rate as unemployment insurance. Many young, unmarried men suddenly found themselves with no public income at all if they were living at home. Greenwood's friend, Mickmac, emerged from the local PAC office 'mesmerised with bewilderment and quite unable to grasp the fact that he had been denied the weekly pittance . . . "But I'm out o' work. I told 'em: find me a job," I said. "Find me a job. Anythin'. Aye, anythin'. I don't care what it is, I'll do it." '[35] His more considered response, however, was fairly typical. He moved in to become a lodger with a neighbour, thus entitling himself to benefit as he was no longer living at home.

Greenwood also describes the protests in his home town against the means test, and how the demonstration ended in violence as it did in so many other cities across the country.

> People cowering, tottering, stumbling, the drenched mass breaking into retreat. It was as though the Highways Cleansing Department had been set to work swilling down a rubbish strewn square. The 'mob' dispersed, became individuals with names . . . With the exception of those who were taken into the cells or by ambulance to hospital they retreated in groups, defeated and sodden, making their sullen and embittered way home.[36]

It was a measure of the unpopularity of the means test that membership of the NUWM, which had been some 10,000 in 1929, rose temporarily to 37,000 by the end of 1931. Yet even this was no more than 1.5 per cent of the officially registered unemployed in that year, and it is clear that the movement never succeeded in harnessing popular support. It might perhaps have done more had the TUC or the Labour party offered any formal backing. After all, the one march that remains as part of working-class folklore is the Jarrow march, organised with official sanction by Ellen Wilkinson. At most, therefore, the NUWM campaign provoked a certain amount of public sympathy. At the time of the October 1932 march, for example, service chiefs expressed some reluctance to provide the NUWM with blankets for the marchers. One Conservative commented with some prescience that 'sympathy with the marchers is not confined to our political opponents, if one member died of pneumonia following a refusal to allow blankets it would lead to a public outcry.'[37] For all its rhetoric about destroying the capitalist system, the NUWM did its most valuable work firmly within the framework of the existing system. Some two thousand individual cases were successfully raised by NUWM workers with local Unemployment Assistance Boards, set up in 1934 to deal with those who had never been covered by insurance, together with those whose rights to benefit had been exhausted. Nor did the movement ever succeed in raising any widespread revolutionary fervour among the unemployed. Among documents seized from Hannington when he was arrested on the eve of the October 1932 march were the responses given by various contingents of marchers to the suggestion that they should carry heavy sticks during demonstrations. Only three were in favour.

This general passivity of the unemployed was noted by many of the numerous observers of working-class life in the 1930s, ranging from Hannington and Orwell to the Pilgrim Trust.[38] Many men, wrote Priestley, simply accepted their fate: 'Lots worse off than them. They all say that.'[39] Recent oral history work has confirmed this impression. One inquiry into life in the north-east during the depression produced the conclusion that none of the subjects interviewed 'ever made reference to any form of political activity, or even to any great resentment of the situation'.[40] It is tempting to seek the explanation for this in the better economic conditions which, according, to aggregate statistical measures, prevailed in the 1930s. Depending on the particular index used, economic growth proceeded at between 2.3 and 3.3 per cent a year. Real per capita income rose by about a third, though this had little to do with any government action. Apart from passing the Special Areas Act in 1934, which created relatively few jobs in particularly depressed areas, government was generally content simply to maintain the unemployed and it was left to rearmament and then war to mop them up. That this policy coincided with rising real incomes was the product of a continued trend towards smaller families and a quite fortuitous shift in Britain's terms of trade, making the cost of food-stuffs much cheaper. In 1914 an average working-class family spent sixty per cent of its income on food and sixteen per cent on rent. By 1937 the respective figures were thirty-five and nine per cent. Health standards also improved. Deaths from tuberculosis, the disease most associated with dietary and environmental deficiencies, fell from 1066 per million in 1922 to 687 per million in 1935. All in all, the general impression is that conditions of life got better in the country. John Boyd Orr, a leading dietary expert, argued that while things were still bad, they were 'better than the picture of pre-war days'.[41] In a similar way the Coles had to admit that 'the main body of the working classes is absolutely a good deal better off today in terms of material goods.'[42]

Yet trends in living standards are notoriously difficult to quantify with any precision, because definitions change and individual experiences vary. It might legitimately be asked, for example, what real improvement occurred in the life of an engineer whose real income increased on paper by fifteen per cent if he was unemployed for most of the period 1930–3? Seasonal unemployment continued high in trades such as building and the thriving motor industry, a fluctuation for which many wage statistics do not allow. Kucynski reckoned that in 1938 three million men and 1.8 million women *in employment* earned less than Rowntree's estimate of the minimum necessary to maintain physical efficiency.[43] It seems likely that the vast bulk of the unemployed were also well below his estimate, though it should not be forgotten that many people supplemented their incomes in some small way such as selling firewood or cakes, or hair dressing.[44] Again, there were enormous regional variations behind the aggregates. Most of the increased consumption of fruit, vegetables and meat occurred outside the depressed areas. Testifying before the Committee against Malnutrition in 1936, Mrs Harley, wife of an unemployed Greenock shipbuilder, pointed out that she could not afford to buy any fresh milk and that

on three days a week she bought meat at 2½d a pound and 3½ lbs. of potatoes for 5d. This mixed together was not particularly palatable. On the other four days she bought half a pound of sausages for 2d. She could not afford vegetables every week.[45]

Child mortality in Jarrow was 114 per thousand, 76 in Durham, 63 in Glamorgan and only 42 in the Home Counties. Nor did living standards consist only in what could be measured. The Pilgrim Trust's extensive survey of unemployed life commented on the very high incidence, especially among the long-term unemployed, of medical, psychological and emotional problems. Orwell offers an eloquent comment on the non-material costs of living in a depressed, northern industrial town. Leaving Wigan by train, he noticed a woman kneeling in a backyard, trying to unblock a drain. On her face, he writes, was

> the most desolate, hopeless expression I have ever seen ... She knew well enough what was happening to her – understood as well as I did how dreadful a destiny it was to be kneeling there in the bitter cold, on the slimy stones of a slum backyard, poking a stick up a foul drain-pipe.[46]

Indeed, it was often the women who paid the dearest, most incalculable price. Unemployment was, in a sense, enforced leisure for the main breadwinner; but wives had to continue to run their houses and families, often on reduced incomes. Imagine the pressures on Mrs Holliday from Durham, who followed Mrs Harley in appearing before the Committee against Malnutrition:

> when her children had pneumonia the health visitor informed her that they must have stockings, and wool next to their skin, but she hadn't the money ... She said that the staple meals of the family consisted of mashed potatoes, bread and tea ... They only had one pint of fresh milk on Sundays, and the rest of the week they had condensed. She had to buy pennyworths of bones to boil down for soup. She could manage no more than one blanket on each bed ...[47]

It is impossible to accommodate such non-material factors into any cost of living calculation. Even if it could be done, the significant consideration in the context of working-class attitudes in the 1930s is the individual's perception of his condition, not some objective, statistical assessment of it. Mrs Halliday ended her testimony by saying that 'she knew of people in worse circumstances than herself.'[48] Asked by George Orwell when he first became aware of a local housing shortage, a Lancashire miner replied dourly, 'when we were told about it'.[49] The theory of relative deprivation developed by W.G. Runciman is helpful here, since it argues that resentment is not a function of inequality *per se*, but of a man's assessment of his position relative to others with whom he tends to compare himself.[50] Runciman's survey of 1962 makes it clear that individuals generally compared themselves with those in the same neighbourhood or workplace, and in this context it is worth noting that the unemployed in the 1930s were both geographically isolated from the rest of the country and socially very concentrated in north-eastern pit villages, decaying Lancashire textile towns, and depressed South Wales coal valleys. Indeed, perhaps in a less sophisticated way, Orwell had himself made Runciman's point rather earlier, suggesting that in these conditions there could be little sense of personal failure of the sort which might fuel political disaffection.

Perhaps there is nothing at all peculiar about the quiescence of the unemployed at this time anyway. Writing of the unemployed of Edwardian London, Charles Masterman had remarked that they possessed 'a genial faith in a Deity who is nothing if not amiable and . . . are convinced that tomorrow will see the dawn of the golden age'.[51] Tressell had put it rather more strongly, complaining that the majority of workers were 'like so many cattle', submitting 'quietly to their miserable slavery for the benefit of others'.[52] Yet for most of the period covered by this book the majority of working people had preferred to do just that — and then to get on with their own private lives. Only fundamental discontinuities such as those produced by the French wars and the industrial revolution or, to a lesser extent, the First World War, impinged on their lives so radically as to produce major manifestations of discontent and conflict. By the late nineteenth century, artisan culture in London had become introverted, defensive and conservative, revolving around the pub, the sporting paper, recreation and gambling. Beneath all the tensions and change induced by the First World War, this cultural bedrock remained pretty well intact. Richard Hoggart remarked that working-class life in the thirties put 'a premium on the taking of pleasures now, discouraging planning for some future goal, or in the light of some ideal'.[53] As had always been the case, a small minority concerned itself actively with issues of political power, the distribution of wealth, and the broad nature of society. There were many more in trade unions, which seemed to provide the best guarantee of economic security and protection at the workplace. Most trade-union members and most of the population at large, even in the depths of depression, showed little interest in changing the social system in which they lived, certainly not in any very radical fashion. Orwell reckoned that the average working-class socialist had as his ideal the existing society 'with the worst abuses left out, and with interest centring round the same things as at present – family life, the pub, football, and local politics'.[54] These were the features which in the 1930s remained the central concerns of working-class life, as they had been since the third quarter of the nineteenth century.

A strong sense of community and family pervades most interwar accounts of working-class life. 'We are happy in our own little world,' claimed one unemployed cockney, 'and we know how to . . . get along.'[55] 'People was [sic] knit closely together, there wasn't this apartness like there is now . . . they were hard times, but it did, y'know, it kept people together.'[56] Greenwood caught this spirit in his description of a Christmas celebration in Pendleton, his home town.

She was interrupted by the excited shouts of children and the pounding of running footfalls in the street. Mrs Boarder was at the door immediately. 'The band,' she called to us excitedly. 'It's the band.' We all joined her. Every front door was open, each casting its shaft of light on to the pavement. The Pendleton Silver Prize Band formed a wide circle at the street junction and filled the air with carols and Christmas hymns. There was a drift of neighbours to encircle the band: passers-by joined the attentive crowd

waiting for the grand finale, the ever-favourite tune that brought carousers from the pubs to swell the throng, the song that opened all hearts and sent to the sky the full-throated chorus that, for however brief a time, banished for everybody the worries of the world and its ways:
'Jerusalem, Jerusalem, lift up your heads and sing,
Hosanna, in the highest . . .'[57]

Recreation also remained a central preoccupation, although now it was the cinema rather than the music hall. By 1939, 20 million tickets were being sold each week, and even in a depressed city such as Liverpool forty per cent of the population attended once a week, twenty-five per cent twice. One Lancashire woman confessed to spending eleven pence a week on her weekly visit with three children, 'a big slice in the week's money, but for me it's pictures or going mad. It's the only time I forget my troubles.'[58] Attendances at professional football matches reached unprecedented levels in the interwar years, and some of the best supported teams were in the depressed areas. Even the communists recognised the appeal of sport, organising the British Workers Sports Federation through the medium of the Young Communist League. Primarily, of course, popular interest in sport was connected with gambling. It seems that the proportion of real income spent on betting declined among the working class after 1918, but there is no doubting its appeal.[59] Dog racing and football both became more important in this respect during the period. Once again it is Orwell who captures the implicit introversion of gambling. Local people in Yorkshire, he writes, were totally disinterested when Hitler re-occupied the Rhineland in 1936; but the decision of the Football Association to stop advance publication of their fixtures, thereby undermining the pools, 'flung all Yorkshire into a storm of fury'.[60] By 1938 the pools had ten million clients, but racing remained the central focus of working-class gambling. In Pendleton, Greenwood recalls, librarians cut out or obliterated the racing pages of local papers in order to prevent gambling, but to no effect. 'This was the life! Nothing else to be desired than to stand here smoking, spitting manfully, chatting wisely on racing and forking out three-pence for a communal wager . . .'[61] In Greenwood's novel, salvation in the form of employment comes to the Hardcastle family only when the eldest daughter, Sal, agrees to marry the local bookmaker. Orwell was perhaps going too far when he suggested that 'fish-and-chips, art-silk stockings, tinned salmon, cut-price chocolate, the movies, the radio, strong tea and the Football Pools have between them averted revolution'; but he was drawing attention to the sort of elements in popular culture which had for many years innured working-class people against even quite fundamental deprivations.[62]

9

Postscript: Cradle to Grave?
Labour, 1939-51

For much of the 1930s the shadow of war had hung heavily over Europe. When war finally came in September 1939, the psychological shock was as nothing compared to that of 1914 when, after a century of peace, war had erupted almost overnight out of a seemingly innocuous political assassination in the Balkans. If the psychological shock was not as profound in 1939, the disruptive effects were much more far-reaching. Some five million men and women were enlisted in armed forces which saw service, quite literally, all over the world. To this experience was added a growing political awareness fostered by the educational activities of the Army Bureau of Current Affairs. There were similar upheavals at home. Evacuation brought many middle- and working-class families face to face for the first time. German air raids, while not as devastating as predicted, produced a sense of solidarity in the face of a common hazard, since bombs respected neither poverty nor social status. In addition, there was a great deal of occupational mobility. In one day in May 1940, the government passed its Emergency Powers Act which required all citizens to place 'themselves, their service and their property' at the government's disposal.[1] Through patriotic redeployment and Ernest Bevin's wise use of the enormous powers conferred on him as Minister of Labour, the workforce was reshaped in accordance with the requirements of war. The number employed in the munitions industries, broadly defined, expanded from 3.1 million to 4.3 million. The basic industries increased from 4.6 million to 5.1 million. The armed forces swelled from 438,000 in June 1939 to reach five million by the end of the war. These increases were achieved by absorbing the unemployed, increasing the number of women and young people at work, and contracting less vital sectors. The numbers in food processing, distribution and textiles, for instance, fell to 6.7 million in 1945 as against 10.1 million in 1939.[2]

Combined with the major administrative changes made to improve the efficiency and direction of wartime government and the alliances with the Soviet Union and Roosevelt's New Deal America, the net result of such wartime developments was to hasten the dissolution of old attitudes and to broaden horizons and expectations. Lord Marley's somewhat quaint comment in 1941 expressed the change in terms of social conventions, but it had also more general application. 'It is quite common now,' he is alleged to have said, 'to see Englishmen speaking to each other in public, although they have never been formally introduced.'[3] All in all, there was a distinct radicalisation of opinion, well attested by the government's own inquiries and the surveys of organisations such as Gallup and Mass Observation. Independent radical candidates defeated Conservatives in four by-elections in 1942, for example, and a similar mood was apparent in the electorate's determination in 1945 to have done with the old and to look to the future. In 1918 a grateful nation had handed a massive mandate to the man who won the war. In 1945 a no less grateful nation spurned the hero of the hour and turned instead to the Labour party. An average swing of twelve per cent to Labour, though giving only slightly more than half of the total votes cast, was sufficient to bring with it a comfortable parliamentary majority, Labour taking 393 seats against 213 for the Conservatives and a paltry twelve for the Liberals.

We should be careful not to exaggerate the extent of this radicalisation, however. Only about two-thirds of the three million registered service voters bothered to vote, while turnout at home was about seventy-six per cent of the electorate. In no sense either was the prevailing spirit one of revolution; rather the popular hope centred on those bread-and-butter issues central to working-class life. It had been the same during the war itself. The head of the home intelligence section of the Ministry of Information commented in 1941 that 'material factors mattered more than ideals' in sustaining popular morale.[4] In 1945 one candidate made an almost identical comment. 'Abstract questions such as controls versus freedom . . . seem terribly far away in the streets and factories here. What people want to talk about is "redundancy", housing, pensions and what will happen to ex-Servicemen after the war.'[5] These were precisely the sorts of issues to which Labour had consistently addressed itself even during its participation in the coalition. *Labour War Aims* (1939), *Labour, the War and the Peace* (1940), *Labour's Home Policy* (1940), and *The Old World and the New Society* (1942) all indicated the conscious thought given by Labour to the postwar situation. This was in marked contrast to Churchill's apparent unwillingness to consider the future until the war was finally won. Attlee later recalled that towards the end of the coalition's life he found it 'more and more difficult to get post-war projects before the Cabinet'.[6]

Let Us Face the Future, Labour's manifesto in the 1945 campaign, was hazy on foreign affairs but did lay down a specific programme of reconstruction and welfare which was very attractive, especially when compared with the Conservatives' rather empty appeal to the national interest and the record of Churchill. Its portrayal of a peacetime Britain in which state intervention was to be widely used accorded well with the mood of a nation determined never to return to the laisser-faire wilderness of the thirties. Moreover, massive extensions of government power and control during the war had already broken down many of the psychological barriers to it and had shown just what government could achieve. Not only had the state exercised very close control over manpower allocation, industrial production, and economic priorities; but it had already taken some tentative steps in the direction of universalist (as opposed to selective) social reform. By 1945 many more children were taking milk and dinners at school. Cheap milk was being provided for all children under five, and the Unemployed Assistance Boards had virtually become, in the exigencies of war, all-purpose social welfare agencies. The achievement of the emergency medical service also showed what might be provided by a universal hospital system.

If Labour thus benefited in 1945 from its greater willingness to commit itself to radical solutions to postwar problems, there can be no doubt that the party's image was also much improved by the performance of its leaders in Churchill's government. Under considerable pressure after the debâcle in Norway in the summer of 1940, Chamberlain approached Attlee with a view to his joining the government. After consulting his party, Attlee agreed to join a coalition, but not one led by Chamberlain who was widely distrusted in labour circles. It was a measure of just how little class really mattered in Britain that Labour was quite willing to serve under Winston Churchill. In the ensuing government Herbert Morrison proved effective at the Ministry of Supply and later at the Home Office. Attlee enhanced his own standing considerably by his handling of the war cabinet during Churchill's frequent absences. Arguably it was Ernest Bevin, not even an MP when war began, who made the most significant impact in office.

Quite early on it became apparent that the essence of a successful war effort was going to be manpower planning, since it was the most limited factor of production. As the First World War had shown, the attempt to deploy labour with maximum efficiency was fraught with danger, since government frequently needed to upset trade-union prerogatives and practice. As a trade unionist himself, Bevin was not only trusted by the union leaders but was able to handle sensitive issues with considerable skill and insight. He cut right through much administrative red tape, abandoning the too cumbersome National Joint Advisory Council and replacing it with a seven-a-side Joint Consultative Committee (JCC), which by the end of the war had been elevated virtually to the status of an unofficial government department. Union leaders thus found themselves in a much more influential and less obviously compromised position than they had been under the 1915 Treasury Agreement. It was the JCC which recommended a ban on strikes and lockouts, with outstanding disputes to be referred to a National Arbitration Tribunal for binding decision. This was embodied in Order 1305, and strike activity diminished. Working days lost in 1940 were the lowest since records began; even in the worst war year only 3.7 million days were lost, two-thirds of them in the coal industry. Since all such strikes were illegal, the participants were liable to prosecution; but Bevin used his powers cautiously, seeing the strikes as valuable outlets for fatigue and understandable frustrations. Throughout the war period only 109 prosecutions involving 6,281 individuals were brought. Defence Regulation 1AA, which prohibited incitement to strike and which Bevin forced through against considerable opposition, was never invoked at all. The First World War had shown just how ineffective the law was as a means of dealing with industrial problems. In any case Bevin also appreciated that the natural focus of any discontent, the Communist party, was fully committed to the war effort – at least, once Germany invaded the Soviet Union in 1941. Even before this, however, antiwar conferences organised by trades councils in Cardiff and Glasgow had made no impact. The shop-stewards' movement had re-emerged in the aircraft industry in 1935 but, unlike its First World War counterpart, had relatively few general grievances on which it could batten.

For a start, Bevin stoutly resisted all proposals for wage control, working closely with the unions to encourage voluntary restraint. This was remarkably successful, probably because more regular work, overtime and piece work all combined to raise earnings during the war by eighty-one per cent. Dilution was handled with care and maximum consultation, and the government encouraged the formation of consultative committees to iron out shop-floor production problems. By 1945 there were 4,500 such committees in engineering and 1,100 in the pits. On the other side, Bevin used his powers to ensure that employers recognised unions and improved working conditions. He refused, for example, to schedule any work as being of national importance unless he was sure that the firm concerned had satisfactory welfare arrangements. The replacement of the family means test by a personal needs test in 1941, the freezing of rents in 1939, a points rationing system which combined equitable shares for all with some element of consumer sovereignty, and an excess profits tax of one hundred per cent also reduced the likely causes of labour unrest. Under this benign regime and further strengthened by full employment, unions prospered. Not only were they being widely consulted about many aspects of government policy, but membership increased as well by almost two million. By 1945, there were 7.8 million trade unionists, more than at any time since 1920. Many important white-collar unions were able to take advantage of the government's stance to secure recognition for themselves, and a substantial part of the total increase was accounted for by women.

The concordat which Bevin established with the unions in wartime continued afterwards. The Trades Disputes Act of 1927 was repealed in 1945, and consultation between government and unions continued at every level. By 1948–9 the TUC was represented on no less than sixty government committees as against only twelve in 1939. There was much truth in Arthur Deakin's claim that 'we have an open door in relation to all State Departments.'[7] So fully were the unions integrated into the machinery of government that Keith Middlemas has argued in a powerful book that Britain virtually became a corporate state in which interest groups such as capital and labour had become too powerful to control and were thus admitted to government on an equal footing, to the detriment of parliamentary sovereignty.[8] Corporatist theory had been much explored in the 1930s as a method of consciously reducing social conflict, but – while there is no doubt that the unions did enjoy considerable influence at this time – this was probably due as much to the inherent needs of an industrial society as to any conscious desire to reduce social tensions.[9] Furthermore, the whole basis of the union-government co-operation rested on rather shaky foundations. To some extent it depended on the personnel who had forged it. After the war Bevin moved on to the Foreign Office and was succeeded at the Ministry of Labour by a man of lesser stature, George Isaacs. Similarly, Bevin's successor as leader of the TGWU, Arthur Deakin, was also less able. Walter Citrine left the TUC to join the new Coal Board, and was replaced as general secretary by the less forceful Vincent Tewson. Other prominent union officials also moved onto the boards of various new nationalised industries.

Secondly, the high level of co-operation during the war depended on the continuance of shared aims and priorities between the government and the unions. Yet once the emergency of war was over, divergences began to appear. Labour opted for a Keynesian policy designed to secure full employment. In this perspective unrestricted wage increases threatened price stability, hence demand and therefore employment. Thus Labour, backed by its powerful moderate trade-union allies, called for a continuation of wage restraint; but ultimately this caused considerable rank and file resentment. Government pressure, even if only moral, was seen as an attempt to interfere with the hallowed freedom of collective bargaining, and in any case there was little chance of the policy having much appeal to those many workers who were being paid by results, or where wages were a matter for local bargaining. Mining, for instance, was particularly strike-prone in this period. Much of the trouble sprang from resentments felt by day workers, who were paid a nationally-agreed flat rate, against face workers who negotiated locally and were paid piece rates. In such circumstances strikes flourished, encouraged in some cases by communists who had taken advantage of the suspension of the Black Circular in 1943 to secure complete control of some unions and considerable influence in others. The Fire Brigades Union and the ETU were totally under communist control, while within the National Union of Miners (which replaced the MFGB in 1945) Scottish and Welsh miners were heavily influenced by communist officials. Between 1945 and 1947 prices and wages rose faster than at any time since 1920, an inflationary situation which threatened the stability of the pound and thus the whole basis of the government's strategy for economic recovery. By 1949 Labour had been compelled to devalue sterling and unions found themselves being asked to accept a voluntary wage freeze — knowing full well that prices would rise because of the devaluation. Given that there was no hint of any similar controls on profits and prices, the TUC General Council found it increasingly difficult to hold the line. In 1951 the council's policy on pay restraint was finally rejected by Congress 'until such time as there is a reasonable limitation of profits, a positive planning of our British economy, and prices are subjected to ... control'.[10] At about the same time the TUC demanded, as it was entitled to do, that order 1305 (banning strikes) be rescinded.

Finally, it is doubtful if the concordat would have lasted as long as it did had not the Labour government pursued policies designed to safeguard and improve conditions of work and life. In the space of half a dozen years, Labour brought into public ownership about a fifth of the nation's economic resources, including power and transport. It created a comprehensive welfare state to protect individuals from the cradle to the grave. The new National Health Service dispensed 5.25 million pairs of spectacles and 187 million prescriptions in its first year, ample testimony to the years of neglect it was designed to remedy. At the same time the government was beginning the process of shedding the empire. It was a programme carried out in the face of appalling difficulty — the worst winter in living memory which swept the country in 1947, a war-shattered Europe, the development of the Cold War, and an exhausted domestic industrial base. Constant economic crises blew the government off course. Only twelve million pounds could be provided in 1947 for the purchase of machine tools, though the estimated requirement for industry was thirty million pounds' worth. In housing, financial constraints forced a reduction of the 1947 target figure from 300,000 to 140,000 and such was the general shortage that there was widespread squatting in empty property and particularly in disused military camps. The CPGB was glad to exploit the housing shortage, knowing that it could no longer exploit unemployment as, among its other achievements, the Labour government managed to run the economy at full employment.

Objectively the performance of the Labour government of 1945—50 was impressive, though it hardly represented the fundamental break with the past for which some had hoped and others feared. The much-heralded nationalisation programme, as many workers soon discovered, changed only ownership, not management or practice.[11] What Labour in fact did was to introduce its own variant of a consensus that had emerged during the war about the need for social security, full employment and a closer relationship between the state and industry. Thus family allowances and a new education bill were introduced while the war was still on. Even after the war, Labour's nationalisation programme attracted little real opposition (as opposed to rhetorical flak) except in the cases of road transport and steel, which were profitable and relatively efficient. Generally the emergency of war had swept aside obstacles to reform entrenched in the civil service and the Tory party, showing that government could effectively intervene in a capitalist economy to make it operate more efficiently and humanely.

By 1951, however, the Labour party appeared to have run out of steam, and several of its leading figures were aging or old. As early as 1947 Herbert Morrison had said that 'the half-century-long struggle by the labour movement for social justice was over . . . success had brought a new task.'[12] The trouble was no one was quite sure what that new task was. Notwithstanding the survival of poverty and bad housing, Labour between 1945 and 1950 realised many of the aspirations of the party's founders. It came near to achieving what Orwell had reckoned most working-class socialists really wanted — the present system with the worst abuses left out.[13] For Morrison the way ahead lay in consolidating the gains so far secured. Aneurin Bevan wished to go further down the road to socialism. Embodied in these two were the distinctive strands out of which the party had been forged in 1900 — the bread and butter of Morrison, the visionary dream of Bevan. That the majority of Labour supporters were satisfied with the bread and butter is suggested by the fact that in 1951, even though the Tories won a majority of seats, Labour secured its highest ever popular vote. The party may not have been radical enough for men like Bevan or for middle-class socialists, but then — as Nicholas Davenport once observed of Harold Laski — 'these Marxist intellectuals always got the mood of the people wrong.'[14] In opposition after 1951 Labour bared its soul, publicly airing its schizophrenic personality whether over clause four, nuclear disarmament, or foreign affairs. The reorganised and rejuvenated Conservatives meanwhile proceeded to tap that self-interest which is usually the mainspring of human motivation, with a short-sighted but electorally attractive policy encapsulated in Harold Macmillan's winning slogan in 1959, 'you've never had it so good.' The bills were to come later.

Notes

Bibliographical note: The sources on which this book is based are mainly, though not exclusively, of a secondary nature. The notes give some indication of the most helpful works on specific topics. Otherwise readers are directed to the excellent annual bibliographies published in the spring issues of the *Bulletin of the Society for the Study of Labour History*. All books mentioned in the notes are published in London unless otherwise indicated.

The following abbreviations are used:

Ag.H.R.	Agricultural History Review
Am.H.R.	American Historical Review
B.I.H.R.	Bulletin of the Institute of Historical Research
B.S.S.L.H.	Bulletin of the Society for the Study of Labour History
Ec.H.R.	Economic History Review
Eng.H.R.	English Historical Review
Hist.	History
H.J.	Historical Journal
I.R.S.H.	International Review of Social History
J.B.S.	Journal of British Studies
J.C.H.	Journal of Contemporary History
J.S.H.	Journal of Social History
J.S.L.H.S.	Journal of the Scottish Labour History Society
Llaf.	Llafur
Md.H.	Midland History
M.H.	Maritime History
M.M.	Mariners' Mirror
M.T.	Marxism Today
N.H.	Northern History
P.P.	Past and Present
S.H.	Social History
T.R.H.S.	Transactions of the Royal Historical Society
V.S.	Victorian Studies
W.H.R.	Welsh History Review

INTRODUCTION

1. This thesis is most clearly argued in Tawney's introduction to Thomas Wilson's, *A Discourse upon Usury* (1572), ed. R.H. Tawney, 1923, 17-30. It is also reiterated several times in his *Religion and the Rise of Capitalism*, 1938, 39, 50, 155-6, 207.

2. W.G. Hoskins, *The Age of Plunder: The England of Henry VIII, 1500–1547*, 1976, 105; A. Everitt, 'Farm Labourers' in J. Thirsk (ed.) *The Agrarian History of England and Wales IV, 1500–1650*, Cambridge 1967, 397-9.

3. Phyllis Deane and W.A. Cole, *British Economic Growth, 1688–1959*, Cambridge 1962, 251-2.

4. T.S. Willan, *An Eighteenth Century Shopkeeper: Abraham Dent of Kirkby Stephen*, Manchester 1970, 64.

5. The classic account of the changes occurring within the London guilds is G. Unwin, *Industrial Organization in the Sixteenth and Seventeenth Centuries*, Oxford 1904.

6. E.H. Phelps Brown and S.V. Hopkins, 'Seven Centuries of the Prices of Consumables, Compared with Builders' Wage Rates', *Economica*, n.s. XXIII (1956); reprinted in E.M. Carus-Wilson (ed.) *Essays in Economic History II*, 1962, 179-96.

7. I owe this point to Professor Robert Millward of the University of Salford who allowed me to read his unpublished paper on wage labour in pre-industrial England.

8. J.H. Clapham, *An Economic History of Modern Britain I*, Cambridge 1926, 113.

9. Ann Hughes, *The Diary of a Farmer's Wife, 1796–1797*, ed. Jeanne Preston, 1980, 153. This is a quasi-fictional work; but there is no need to doubt the authenticity of this quotation.

10. J.U. Nef, *The Rise of the British Coal Industry II*, 1932, 140.

11. D.C. Coleman, 'An Innovation and its Diffusion: The "New Draperies" ', *Ec.H.R.* XXII (1969), 417-29; G.D. Ramsey, *The Wiltshire Woollen and Worsted Industry in the Sixteenth and Seventeenth Centuries*, 2nd ed., 1965; W.H.B. Court, *The Rise of the Midland Industries*, 1938; J.D. Chambers, *Nottinghamshire in the Eighteenth Century*, 2nd ed., 1966.

12. *5 Eliz. c. 4*. For a general discussion see E. Lipson, *An Economic History of England, III*, 6th ed., 1956, 252-5.

13. Dorothy George, *London Life in the Eighteenth Century*, 1965, ch. 4. See also Sir John Hicks, *A Theory of Economic History*, 1969, 134-40 for a general discussion of the working of labour markets in pre-industrial conditions.

14. The most recent discussions of migration and vagrancy are Peter Clark, 'The Migrant in Kentish Towns 1580–1640', in P. Clark and P. Slack, *Crisis and Order in English Towns*, 1972, 117-63; P.A. Slack, 'Vagrants and Vagrancy in England 1598–1664', *Ec.H.R.* XXVII (1974), 360-79; Peter Clark, 'Migration in England During the Late Seventeenth and Early Eighteenth Centuries', *P.P.* 83 (1979), 57-90. All these sources emphasise

the extent and frequency of migration rather than its limitation.

15. W.A. Lewis, 'Economic Development with Unlimited Supplies of Labour', in A.N. Agarwala and S.P. Singh (eds.), *The Economics of Underdevelopment*, 1959, 400-49.

16. E.H. Phelps Brown and S.V. Hopkins, 'Seven Centuries of Building Wages', *Economica*, n.s. XXII (1955); reprinted in E.M. Carus-Wilson (ed.) *op. cit.*, 174-6.

17. Adam Smith, *An Inquiry into the Nature and Causes of the Wealth of Nations I* (1776), Everyman edition, 1910, 66.

18. Phelps Brown and Hopkins, *op. cit.*, 174-7.

19. Smith, *op. cit.*, 79-80.

20. *Ibid.*, 89.

21. The fullest discussion of the Statute is W.E. Minchinton (ed.) *Wage Regulations in Pre-Industrial England*, Newton Abbot 1972. For the most recent discussion see D.M. Woodward, 'The Background to the Statute of Artificers: The Genesis of Labour Policy, 1558-63', *Ec.H.R.* XXXIII (1980), 32-44.

22. See C.R. Dobson, *Masters and Journeymen: A Pre-History of Industrial Relations, 1717-1800*, 1980.

23. Corporations of London, Guildhall Library, MS 14, 342.

24. Rowland Vaughan, *His Booke* (1610), ed. E.B. Wood, 1897, dedication.

25. Christopher Hill, 'Pottage for Freeborn Englishmen: Attitudes to Wage Labour', in *Change and Continuity in Seventeenth-Century England*, 1974, 219-38.

26. Thomas Mun, *England's Treasure by Forraign Trade* (1664), Oxford 1925, title page and 3-4.

27. Sir Thomas Smith (1565), quoted in Hill, *op. cit.*, 224.

28. Keith Thomas, 'The Levellers and the Franchise' in G.E. Aylmer (ed.) *The Interregnum: The Quest for Settlement, 1646–1660*, 1972, 57-78; Christopher Hill, *The World Turned Upside Down* 1972, Ch. 3; C. Hill, *op. cit.*, 225-6.

29. Sir William Petty, Political Arithmetic (1690) in *The Economic Writings of Sir William Petty I*, ed. C.H. Hull, 1899, 274.

30. For a generalised discussion see D.C. Coleman, 'Labour in the English Economy of the Seventeenth Century', *Ec.H.R.* VIII (1956), reprinted in Carus-Wilson (ed.), *op. cit.*, 291-308. See also H. Freudenberger and G. Cummins, 'Health and Leisure before the Industrial Revolution', *Exploration in Economic History* 13 (1976), 1-2. For a rare attempt to discuss attitudes to work with reference to specific groups of workers see I. Blanchard, 'Labour Productivity and Work Psychology in the English Mining Industry, 1400-1600', *Ec.H.R.* XXXI (1978), 1-24.

31. John Cary, *An Essay on the State of England* (1695), quoted in Richard Wiles 'The Theory of Wages in Later English Mercantilism', *Ec.H.R.* XXI (1968), 122.

32. Smith, *op. cit.*, 73.

33. England's Great Happiness is quoted by E.A.J. Johnson, *Pre-*

decessors of Adam Smith (1937), reprinted New York 1965, 294. Defoe is quoted by Wiles, *op. cit.*, 121. This article is a discussion of the whole question. See also Charles Wilson, 'The Other Face of Mercantilism', in *Economic History and the Historian: Collected Essays*, 1969, 73-93.

34. Smith, *op. cit.*, 70.
35. E.W. Gilboy, *Wages in Eighteenth Century England*, Cambridge, Mass, 1934, 219-27; Phelps Brown and Hopkins, *op. cit.*, 168-78.
36. Phelps Brown and Hopkins, *op. cit.*, 189.

CHAPTER 1
1. S. and B. Webb, *The History of Trade Unionism*, 1926, 1.
2. Quoted in R.A. Leeson, *Travelling Brothers*, 1979, 257.
3. H. Hikins (ed.), *Building the Union*, Liverpool 1973, 12.
4. W.H. Warburton, *The History of Trade Union Organisation in the North Staffordshire Potteries*, 1931, 28-9.
5. E. Welbourne, *The Miners' Unions of Northumberland and Durham*, Cambridge 1923, 15.
6. S. Jones, 'Community and organisation — early seamen's trade unionism on the north east coast, 1768–1844', *M.H.* 3 (1973), 51.
7. R. Colls, *The Collier's Rant: Song and Culture in the Industrial Village*, 1977, 75.
8. Dobson, *op. cit.*, 154-70.
9. E. Hobsbawm, *Labouring Men*, 1964, 7.
10. E. Hobsbawm, 'The machine breakers', *P.P.* 1 (1952), 59.
11. M. Thomis, *The Town Labourer and the Industrial Revolution*, 1974, 128.
12. F. D'Arcy, 'The trade unions of Dublin and the attempted revival of the guilds', *Journal of the Royal Society of Antiquaries of Ireland* 101 (1971), 113.
13. E. Hopwood, *A History of the Lancashire Cotton Industry and the Amalgamated Weavers' Association*, Manchester 1969, 19.
14. T.K. Derry, 'The repeal of the apprenticeship clauses of the Statute of Apprentices', *Ec.H.R.* III (1931), 78. This statute is more generally and more accurately known as the Statute of ʹArtificers.
15. See E. Hobsbawm, 'The tramping artisan' in his *Labouring Men*, 34-63. For the Scottish chairmakers see I. MacDougall, 'The Edinburgh branch of the Scottish National Union of Cabinet and Chairmakers, 1833-1837', *Book of the Old Edinburgh Club*, 33 (1969), 17-26.
16. Leeson, *op. cit.*, 242.
17. *Ibid.*, 98. For friendly societies see P.H. Gosden, *Self-Help*, 1973; and B. Supple, 'Legislation and virtue: an essay on working class self help and the state in the early nineteenth century', in N. McKendrick (ed.), *Historical Perspectives*, 1974.
18. W.H. Oliver, 'The Consolidated Trades' Union of 1834', *Ec.H.R.* XVI (1964), 77-95. More light is thrown on the question in

M.J. Haynes, 'Class and class conflict in the early nineteenth century: Northampton shoe makers and the Grand National Consolidated Trades' Union', *Literature and History* 5 (1977), 73-94.

19. Webb, *op. cit.*, 121.
20. Membership figures are from MacDougall, *op. cit.*, 21; Warburton, *op. cit.*, 65; W. Kiddier, *The Old Trade Unions*, 1930, 62-3; C.J. Bundock, *The Story of the National Union of Printing, Book-Binding and Paper Workers*, Oxford 1959, 4; H.J. Fyrth and H. Collins, *The Foundry Workers*, Manchester 1959, 32; W.S. Hilton, *Foes to Tyranny: a History of the Amalgamated Union of Building Trade Workers*, 1963, 26.
21. For example, H. Pelling, *History of British Trade Unionism*, 1963, 15; B.C. Roberts, *The Trades Union Congress, 1868-1921*, 1958, 11.
22. N.H. Cuthbert, *The Lacemakers' Society*, 1960, 27 note 4.
23. J.J. Bagley, *Lancashire Diarists*, 1975, 190.
24. A.B. Richmond, *Narrative of the Condition of the Manufacturing Population*, Glasgow 1825, 13.
25. Quoted in D. Vincent (ed.), *Testaments of Radicalism: Memoirs of Working Class Politicians, 1790–1885*, 1977, 132.
26. Leeson, *op. cit.*, 111.
27. J.R. Cuca, 'Industrial change and the progress of labor in the English cotton industry', *I.R.S.H.*, XXII (1977), 250.
28. Pelling, *op. cit.*, 15, argues that it was an obstacle.
29. M. Sanderson, 'Literacy and social mobility in the industrial revolution', *P.P.* 56 (1972), 75-104; T. Laquer, 'Literacy and social mobility in the industrial revolution in England', *P.P.* 64 (1974), 96-107.
30. E.G. West, *Education and the Industrial Revolution*, 1975, 256.
31. T. Laquer, *Religion and Respectability: Sunday Schools and Working Class Culture*, 1977, xi.
32. A. Wilson, *The Chartist Movement in Scotland*, Manchester 1970, 11.
33. H. Weisser, *British Working Class Movements and Europe, 1815–1848*, Manchester 1975, 11.
34. I. Prothero, '*The Beacon*: the first trade union newspaper?', *B.S.S.L.H.* 24 (1972), 33-4.
35. Jones, *op. cit.*, 54.
36. Thomis, *op. cit.*, 128.
37. G. Pattison, 'The coopers' strike at the West India Dock, 1821', *M.M.* 55 (1969), 166.
38. C. Shaw, *When I Was a Child*, 1903, 92.
39. P. Brantlinger, 'The case against trade unions in early Victorian fiction', *V.S.* 13 (1969–70), 37-52. See also P. Keating, *The Working Classes in Victorian Fiction*, 1971.
40. Quoted in D'Arcy, *op. cit.*, 114.
41. S. Pollard, 'Labour in Great Britain', in *The Cambridge Economic*

History of Europe VII, Cambridge 1978, 150-1.

42. Kiddier, *op. cit.*, 36.
43. MacDougall, *op. cit.*, 20.
44. N. McCord and D. Brewster, 'Some labour troubles of the 1790's in north east England', *I.R.S.H.* XII (1968), 36.
45. J. Burnett, *A History of the Cost of Living*, 1969, 250.
46. A.E. Musson, *British Trade Unions, 1800–1875*, 1972, 38-43.
47. For the expansion of the reading public see R.D. Altick, *The English Common Reader*, 1957; and R.K. Webb, *The British Working Class Reader, 1790–1848*, 1955.
48. D.J. Rowe, 'The decline of the Tyneside keelmen in the nineteenth century', *N.H.* IV (1969), 111-31.
49. R.A. Morris, 'Labour relations in the royal dockyards, 1801–1805', *M.M.* 62 (1976), 341.
50. See J. Benson, *British Coalminers in the Nineteenth Century: a Social History*, Dublin 1980, 81 ff.
51. H.A. Turner, *Trade Union Growth, Structure and Policy*, 1962, 86.
52. I. Prothero, *Artisans and Politics in Early Nineteenth Century London*, 1978.
53. Quoted in Pollard, *op. cit.*, 122.

CHAPTER 2
1. E.P. Thompson, *The Making of the English Working Class*, 1972, 12.
2. A. Briggs, 'The language of class in early nineteenth century England', in A. Briggs and J. Saville (eds.), *Essays in Labour History*, 1960, 46.
3. *Political Register*, 27 August 1825.
4. *Penny Papers for the People*, 12 March 1831.
5. J.F.C. Harrison, *The Early Victorians, 1832–1851*, 1971, 21-2.
6. D. Landes, *The Unbound Prometheus*, Cambridge 1969, 9.
7. E.P. Thompson, 'Patrician society, plebeian culture', *J.S.H.* 7 (1974), 396-97.
8. Thompson, *Working Class*, 9-10.
9. G.D.H. Cole and R. Postgate, *The Common People, 1746–1946*, 1946, 142: R. Postgate, *The Builders' History*, 1923, 30.
10. D. Bythell, *The Hand Loom Weavers*, Cambridge 1969, 99.
11. *Ibid.*, 275.
12. Quoted in *ibid.*, 75.
13. *Ibid.*, 76.
14. *Ibid.*, 202.
15. A.R. Wilkes, 'Adjustments in arable farming after the Napoleonic Wars', *Ag.H.R.* 28 (1980), 90-103.
16. Deane and Cole, *op. cit.*, 103.
17. E. Hobsbawm and G. Rude, *Captain Swing*, 1973, 175.
18. *Ibid.*, 189-90.

298   *The English Labour Movement 1700–1951*

19. E. Richards, 'Captain Swing in the west midlands', *I.R.S.H.* XIX (1974), 96.
20. Bythell, *op. cit.*, 203. My italics.
21. F.M. Eden, *The State of the Poor II*, 1797, 497.
22. Diets from J. Burnett, *Plenty and Want*, 1968, 67-8.
23. *Ibid.*, 50-1.
24. E. Howe, *The London Compositor*, 1947, 305-7.
25. D.W. Howell, 'The agricultural labourer in nineteenth century Wales', *W.H.R.* 6 (1972–3), 274.
26. W.H.B. Court, *The Rise of the Midland Industries*, 1938, 211.
27. *Ibid.*
28. *Sheffield Independent*, 28 June 1842.
29. Quoted in I. Pinchbeck, *Women Workers and the Industrial Revolution, 1750–1850*, 1969, 306 note 2.
30. A.J. Taylor (ed.), *The Standard of Living in Britain in the Industrial Revolution*, 1975, xxxi.
31. F. Crouzet (ed.), *Capital Formation in the Industrial Revolution*, 1972, 32.
32. H. Perkin, *The Origins of Modern English Society, 1780–1880*, 1969, 135-6.
33. P. Mathias, *The First Industrial Nation*, 1969, 214.
34. Quoted in S. Pollard, *The Genesis of Modern Management*, 1968, 198.
35. N. McCord, *North East England: an Economic and Social History*, 1979, 40-1.
36. J.D. Chambers, 'Enclosure and labour supply in the industrial revolution', *Ec.H.R.* V (1953), 319-43.
37. J.L. Hammond, 'The industrial revolution and discontent', *Ec.H.R.* II (1929–30), 224-5.
38. F.D. Klingender, *Art and the Industrial Revolution*, 1947, 120.
39. Deane and Cole, *op. cit.*, 119.
40. A. Briggs, *Victorian Cities*, 1968, 140.
41. F. Engels, *The Condition of the Working Class in England*, 1969 (ed.), 69.
42. *Ibid.*, 70.
43. M. Durey, *The Return of the Plague*, Dublin 1979, 44.
44. Quoted in L.A. Clarkson, *Death, Disease and Famine in Preindustrial England*, Dublin 1975, 109.
45. E. Gauldie, *Cruel Habitations: a History of Working Class Housing, 1780–1918*, 1974, 27.
46. Howell, *op. cit.*, 278-9.
47. Quoted in G.E. Fussell and C. Goodman, 'The housing of the rural population in the eighteenth century', *Economic History* II (1930), 64.
48. Durey, *op. cit.*, 201.
49. *Ibid.*
50. Harrison, *op. cit.*, 70-1.
51. On this generally see Burnett, *Plenty and Want*, 99-120.

52. K. Marx and F. Engels, *Manifesto of the Communist Party*, Moscow 1959 ed., 49.

53. *Ibid.*, 69.

54. This phrase is used by K. Wrightson, 'Infanticide in earlier seventeenth century England', *Local Population Studies* 15 (1975), 10.

55. M. Anderson, 'Sociological history and the English working class family: Smelser revisited', *J.S.H.* 3 (1976), 321. See also the same author's *Family Structure in Nineteenth Century Lancashire*, Cambridge 1971, and N. Smelser, *Social Change in the Industrial Revolution*, 1959.

56. See S.D. Chapman, *The Early Factory Masters*, Newton Abbot 1967, and A.E. Musson, *Trade Union and Social History*, 1974, esp. 201-4.

57. I. Pinchbeck and M. Hewitt, *Children in English Society II*, 1969 and 1973, 403.

58. Quoted in E. Hopkins, *A Social History of the English Working Classes, 1815—1945*, 1979, 4.

59. Quoted in T.C. Barker (ed.) *The Long March of Everyman, 1750-1960*, 1978, 83-4.

60. Thompson, *Working Class*, 600.

61. Quoted in D. George, *England in Transition*, 1962, 59.

62. Quoted in Pollard, *The Genesis*, 214.

63. W.R. Lambert, 'Drink and work discipline in industrial south Wales, c1800—1870' *W.H.R.* 7 (1974—5), 304.

64. E.P. Thompson, 'Eighteenth century English society: class struggle without class?' *S.H.* 3 (1978), 133-65.

65. T.L. Jarman, *Socialism in Britain*, 1972, 55.

66. Perkin, *op. cit.*, 188.

67. S. Bauman, *Between Class and Elite*, Manchester 1972, 12.

68. Pelling, *op. cit.*, 13-14. H. Mitchell and P. Stearns, *Workers and Protest: the European Labour Movement, the Working Classes and the Origins of Social Democracy, 1890—1915*, Itasca 1971, 134.

69. A.J. Peacock, 'Bradford Chartism, 1838—1840', *Borthwick Papers* 36 (1969), 1.

70. J. Foster, *Class Struggle and the Industrial Revolution*, 1974, *passim*.

71. Perkin, *op. cit.*, 180.

72. P. Dunkley, 'Paternalism, the magistracy and poor relief in England, 1795—1834', *I.R.S.H.* XXV (1980). On paternalism generally see D. Roberts, *Paternalism in Early Victorian England*, 1979.

73. Freudenberger and Cummins, *op. cit.*, 1.

74. M. Bienefeld, *Working Hours in British Industry: an Economic History*, 1972, 28.

75. This section is based particularly on H. Cunningham, *Leisure in the Industrial Revolution*, 1980, chapter 1.

76. C. Behagg, 'Custom, class and change: the trade societies of Birmingham', *S.H.* 4 (1979), 455-80.
77. Foster, *op. cit.*
78. P. Quenell (ed.), *Mayhew's London*, 1969, 552-3.
79. Quoted in P. H_llis (ed.), *Class and Conflict in Nineteenth Century England, 1815—1850*, 1973, 139.
80. Quoted in A. Tuckett, *The Blacksmiths' History*, 1974, 39.
81. W. Howitt, *The Rural Life of England*, 1844, 201.
82. E.H. Hunt, *Regional Wage Variations in Britain, 1850—1914*, Oxford 1973, *passim*.
83. Howe, *op. cit.*, 305-7.
84. Colls, *op. cit.*, 42.
85. R.W. Malcolmson, *Popular Recreations in English Society, 1700—1850*, Cambridge 1973, 83.
86. T. Coleman, *The Railway Navvies*, 1968, 94.
87. G.D'Eichthal, *A French Sociologist Looks at Britain*, trans. by B.M. Ratcliffe, Manchester 1977, 95.
88. Musson, *Trade Unions*, 15-16.
89. D.J. Rowe, 'Class and political radicalism in London, 1831—2', *H.J.* XIII (1970), 44-5.
90. McCord, *North East*, 16.
91. Foster, *op. cit.*
92. See the debate between Foster and A.E. Musson, 'Class struggle and the labour aristocracy', *S.H.* 13 (1976), 335-66. For a critique of Foster from a rather different perspective see J. Saville, 'Class struggle and the industrial revolution', *Socialist Register* 11 (1974), 226-40.
93. N. Gash, 'After Waterloo: British society and the legacy of the Napoleonic Wars', *T.R.H.S.* 28 (1978), 150-1.
94. M. Elliott, 'The Despard Conspiracy reconsidered', *P.P.* 75 (1977), 46-61.
95. C. Emsley, 'Political disaffection and the British army in 1792', *B.I.H.R.* 48 (1975), 230.
96. Richards, *op. cit.*, 98. It is generally conceded that Nottinghamshire Luddism had no political overtones: see J. Dinwiddy, 'Luddism and politics in the northern counties', *S.H.* 4 (1979), 33-63.
97. A.J. Peacock, 'Village radicalism in East Anglia, 1800—1850', in J.P. Dunbabin (ed.), *Rural Discontent in Nineteenth Century Britain*, 1974, 30.
98. T. Gurr, *Why Men Rebel*, 1970, 341.
99. M. Thomis and P. Holt, *Threats of Revolution in Britain, 1789—1848*, 1977, 43.
100. *Ibid.*, 69.
101. Thompson, *Working Class*, 405.
102. Quoted in Colls, *op. cit.*, 137.
103. S. Davies, *North Country Bred*, 1963, 22.
104. E. Hobsbawm, *Primitive Rebels*, 1959, 126.

105. E. Hobsbawm,'Methodism and the threat of revolution in Britain', in his *Labouring men*, 23-33.
106. B. Semmel, introduction to E. Halévy, *The Birth of English Methodism*, 1979, 29. There are good discussions of the whole subject in B. Semmel, *The Methodist Revolution*, 1974; and R. Davies, A. George and G. Rupp, *A History of the Methodist Church in Great Britain II*, 1978, 252-69.
107. S. Davies, *op. cit.*, 12.
108. B. Hollingworth, *Songs of the People*, Manchester 1977, 22.
109. T. Carlyle, 'Signs of the times', *Edinburgh Review* XLIV (1829), 443.
110. D'Eichthal, *op. cit.*, 78.
111. M. Barkun, *Disaster and the Millennium*, 1974. See more recently, J.F.C. Harrison, *The Second Coming, 1780–1850*, 1979.
112. Harrison, *Early Victorians*, 132.
113. See for example the programme of the Leeds Redemption Society. J.F.C. Harrison, *Social Reform in Victorian Leeds: the Work of James Hole, 1820–1895*, Leeds 1954, 14.
114. Quoted in Hollis, *op. cit.*, 157.
115. J.F.C. Harrison, 'A new view of Mr Owen', in S. Pollard and J. Salt (eds.), *Robert Owen: Prophet of the Poor*, 1971, 1-12.
116. W.H. Fraser, 'Trade unionism', in J.T. Ward (ed.), *Popular Movements, c1830–1850*, 1970, 95-115.
117. Harrison, *Early Victorians*, 165.
118. For example see J.T. Ward, 'The factory movement' in his *Popular Movements*.
119. R.G. Kirby and A.E. Musson, *The Voice of the People: John Doherty, 1798–1854: Trade Unionist, Radical and Factory Reformer*, Manchester 1975, 346.
120. Quoted in *ibid.*, 348.
121. Thompson, *Working Class*, 735.
122. For a rebuttal of the idea that Doherty was really an Owenite see Kirby and Musson, *op. cit.*, 320 ff.

CHAPTER 3
1. Quoted in J.T. Ward, *Chartism*, 1973, 73.
2. *Penny Papers for the People*, 27 May 1831.
3. Quoted in D. Thompson, *The Early Chartists*, 1971, 8.
4. Quoted in Vincent, *op. cit.*, 147.
5. Quoted in Hollis, *op. cit.*, 147.
6. W. Lovett, *The Life and Struggles of William Lovett in his Pursuit of Bread, Knowledge and Freedom*, 1876, 91.
7. Vincent, *op. cit.*, 126.
8. Wilson, *op. cit.*, 37.
9. *Ibid.*
10. C. Godfrey, 'The Chartist prisoners 1838-1841', *I.R.S.H.* XXIV (1979), 205.
11. Ward, *Chartism*, 59.

12. *Ibid.*, 60-1.
13. W. Lovett and J. Collins, *Chartism, a New Organisation of the People* (1840), ed. A. Briggs, Leicester 1969, 12.
14. Ward, *Chartism*, 69.
15. N. Edsall, *The Anti-Poor-Law Movement, 1834—1844*, Manchester 1971, 174.
16. D. Jones, *Chartism and the Chartists*, 1975, 145.
17. A Trowbridge Chartist quoted in A. Briggs (ed.), *Chartist Studies*, 1959, 10.
18. S. Pollard, 'Feargus O'Connor as seen by a contemporary', *B.S.S.L.H.* 24 (1972), 23.
19. J.A. Epstein, 'Feargus O'Connor and the *Northern Star*', *I.R.S.H.* XXI (1976), 51-97.
20. D. Bythell, *The Sweated Trades*, 1978, 217.
21. D.J. Rowe, 'The Chartist Convention and the regions', *Ec.H.R.* XXII (1969), 68-74.
22. See Peacock, 'Bradford Chartism'.
23. Wilson, *op. cit.*, 19.
24. D. Read, 'Chartism in Manchester' in Briggs, *Chartist Studies*, 34.
25. J. Epstein and C. Godfrey, 'H.O. 20/10: interviews of Chartist prisoners, 1840—41', *B.S.S.L.H.* 34 (1977), 30.
26. D.J. Rowe, 'Tyneside Chartists', *North East Group for the Study of Labour History Bulletin* 8 (1974), 30-45.
27. I. Prothero, 'Chartism in London', *P.P.* 44 (1969), 76-105.
28. D. Jones, 'Chartism at Merthyr', *Bulletin of the Board of Celtic Studies* 24 (1971), 236.
29. In no sense, however, were such people *petit bourgeois*. Very often they had been forced from a trade into shopkeeping; their clientele was overwhelmingly working class and none was prosperous. See Godfrey, *op. cit.*, 197.
30. Jones, *Chartism*, 107.
31. Read, *op. cit.*, 141.
32. P. Searby, 'Chartists and freemen in Coventry, 1838—1860', *S.H.* 6 (1977), 761-84.
33. J. Rule, 'Methodism and Chartism among the Cornish miners', *B.S.S.L.H.* 22 (1971), 8-11.
34. Wilson, *op. cit.*, 187, quoting the minister of the Dundee Chartist Church.
35. *Ibid.*, 179.
36. Lovett and Collins, *op. cit.*, 19.
37. Ward, *Chartism*, 109.
38. *Ibid.*, 105.
39. Epstein, *op. cit.*, 92.
40. K. Judge, 'Early Chartist organisation and the Convention of 1839', *I.R.S.H.* XX (1975), 383.
41. T.H. Lloyd, 'Dr Wade and the working class', *Md.H.* II (1973), 78-9.
42. Ward, *Chartism*, 117.

43. *Ibid.*, 118.
44. On the concept of an anti-parliament see T.M. Parssinen, 'Association, convention and anti-parliament in British radical politics', *Eng.H.R.* 88 (1973), 504-33.
45. Jones, *Chartism*, 112.
46. F. Kaijage, 'Manifesto of the Barnsley Chartists', *B.S.S.L.H.* 33 (1976), 23.
47. Read, *op. cit.*, 35-6.
48. Vincent, *op. cit.*, 141.
49. Ward, *Chartism*, 129.
50. Vincent, *op. cit.*, 138.
51. P.A. Smith, 'Chartists in Loughborough', *Leicestershire Historian* 2 (1975), 27.
52. Vincent, *op. cit.*, 136.
53. B. Harrison and P. Hollis (eds.), *Robert Lowery: Radical and Chartist*, 1979, 155.
54. Peacock, *op. cit.*, 20.
55. *Ibid.*, 50.
56. Hollis, *op. cit.*, 261.
57. *Ibid.*, 259-60.
58. C.P. Griffin, 'Chartism and the opposition to the new poor law in Nottinghamshire: The Basford Union workhouse affair of 1844', *Md.H.* 2 (1974), 244-9.
59. Thompson, *Early Chartists*, 27.
60. Hollis, *op. cit.*, 264-65.
61. Useful accounts are in A. Jenkin, 'Chartism and the trade unions' in Munby, *op. cit.*, 75-91; and F.C. Mather, 'The general strike of 1842' in R. Quinault and J. Stevenson (eds.), *Popular Protest and Public Order*, 1974, 115-40.
62. T. and N. Reid, 'The 1842 Plug Plot in Stockport', *I.R.S.H.* XXIV (1979), 71.
63. Ward, *Chartism*, 177.
64. R.Faherty, 'The memoir of Thomas Martin Wheeler, Owenite and Chartist', *B.S.S.L.H.* 30 (1975), 11-13.
65. See, for example, the reaction of Chartists in Kentish London: G. Crossick, *An Artisan Elite in Victorian Society*, 1978, 207.
66. Ward, *Chartism*, 183.
67. *Ibid.*, 205. There was quite a strong Irish involvement in Chartism; despite J.H. Treble, 'O'Connor, O'Connell and the attitudes of Irish immigrants towards Chartism in the north of England, 1838-1848', in J. Butt and I. Clarke (eds.), *Victorian Social Protest: a Symposium*, Newton Abbot 1973, 33-70.
68. J. Saville, *Ernest Jones: Chartist*, 1952, 40.
69. It seems absurd, for instance, to claim that the Chartist leadership of bread riots in Birmingham in the 1850s indicates that they were 'influential enough to assume the leadership of any political or trade union question that roused the working people'. G. Barnsby, 'Chartism' in Munby, *op. cit.*, 101.

70. T.H. Kemnitz, 'Approaches to the Chartist movement: Feargus O'Connor and Chartist strategy', *Albion* 5 (1973), 67-73.
71. Jones, *Chartism*, 56.
72. Harrison and Hollis, *op. cit.*, 7.
73. G. Rudé, 'Protest and punishment in nineteenth century Britain', *Albion* 5 (1973), 1-23.
74. *Red Republican*, 6 July 1850.
75. M. Davis, 'The forerunners of the First International – the Fraternal Democrats', *M.T.* 15 (1971), 51.
76. Weisser, *op. cit.*, 84-98; also *idem*, 'The role of Feargus O'Connor in Chartist internationalism, 1845–1848', *Rocky Mountain Social Science Journal* 6 (1969), 82-90.
77. Harrison and Hollis, *op. cit.*, 9.
78. Hollis, *op. cit.*, 261.
79. Pollard, 'Feargus O'Connor', 22.

CHAPTER 4

1. F.M. Leventhal, *Respectable Radical: George Howell and Victorian Working Class Politics*, 1974, 43.
2. Saville, *op. cit.*, 74.
3. H. Cunningham, *The Volunteer Force*, 1975, 28.
4. D. Philips, *Crime and Authority in Victorian England*, 1977, 284.
5. D. Kynaston, *King Labour: the British Working Class, 1850–1914*, 1976, 39-44.
6. *Ibid.*, 37.
7. S. Shipley, 'Club life and socialism in mid-Victorian London', *History Workshop Pamphlet* 5 (1971).
8. T.H. Marshall, *Social Class and Citizenship*, Cambridge 1950; R. Bendix, *Work and Authority in Industry*, New York 1956.
9. Pelling, *op. cit.*, 62.
10. Leventhal, *op. cit.*, 46.
11. W.H. Maehl, 'The northeastern miners' struggle for the franchise, 1872–74', *I.R.S.H.* XX (1975), 198-219.
12. *Miner and Workmen's Advocate*, 12 November 1864.
13. *Bee-Hive*, 9 February 1867.
14. *Ibid.*, 10 November 1866.
15. C.F. Brand, 'The conversion of the British trade unions to political action', *Am.H.R.* XXX (1925), 257.
16. Royal Commission on Trade Unions (1867–69), *Minutes of Evidence*, q 7484.
17. *Ibid.*, q 818. *Bee-Hive*, 19 January 1867.
18. Anon., 'The despotism of the future', *Quarterly Review* CXXXVI (1867), 200.
19. R. Church, 'Labour supply and innovation 1800–1860: the boot and shoe industry', *Business History* 12 (1970), 25-45; R. Price, 'The other face of respectability: violence in the Manchester brickmaking trade, 1859–1870', *P.P.* 66 (1975), 110-32.
20. I. Ironside, *Trades Unions*, 1867, 17.

21. *Bee-Hive*, 6 April 1867.
22. *The Times*, 21 June 1867.
23. F. Harrison, *Autobiographical Memoirs I*, 1911, 322.
24. Subsequent research suggests that the actuaries may have been correct. C.G. Hanson, 'Craft unions, welfare benefits and the case for trade union law reform, 1867–1875', *Ec.H.R.* XXVIII (1975), 243-59.
25. *The Times*, 8 July 1869.
26. *Bee-Hive*, 26 June 1869.
27. T. Wright, *Our New Masters*, 1873, 5-6.
28. S. Coltham, 'The Bee-Hive newspaper: its origins and early struggles' in Briggs and Saville, *op. cit.*, 175.
29. G.D.H. Cole, 'British trade unions in the third quarter of the nineteenth century', in E.M. Carus-Wilson (ed.), *Essays in Economic History III*, 1962, 213.
30. *Bee-Hive*, 16 March 1967.
31. J. Foster, 'The state and ruling class during the general strike', *M.T.* 20 (1976), 138. Also K. Burgess, *The Challenge of Labour*, 1980, 16.
32. H. Pelling, *Popular Politics and Society in Late-Victorian Britain*, 1968, 37.
33. Bauman, *op. cit.*, 115.
34. Crossick, *op. cit.*, 120.
35. E. Hopkins,' Small town aristocrats of labour and their standard of living, 1840–1914', *Ec.H.R.* XXVIII (1975), 222-42; R.Q. Gray, *The Labour Aristocracy in Victorian Edinburgh*, Oxford 1976.
36. Hunt, *op. cit.*, 358.
37. M.A. Shepherd, 'The origins and incidence of the term "Labour Aristocracy"', *B.S.S.L.H.* 37 (1978), 51-67. See also the recent discussion in *B.S.S.L.H.* 40 (1980), 6-11.
38. Foster, *Class Struggle*, 224 ff.
39. As A.E. Musson tries to do in *Trade Unions*, 20-1.
40. Royal Commission on Trade Unions (1867–69), *Minutes of Evidence*, q 924.
41. R. Church, 'Profit-sharing and labour relations in England in the nineteenth century', *I.R.S.H.* XVI (1971), 2-16; E. Bristow, 'Profit-sharing, socialism and labour unrest', in Kenneth D. Brown (ed.), *Essays in Anti-labour History*, 1974, 262-89.
42. V.L. Allen, 'The origins of industrial conciliation and arbitration', *I.R.S.H.* IX (1964), 237-54
43. R. Harrison, *Before the Socialists: Studies in Labour and Politics, 1861–1881*, 1965, 37-8.
44. F.E. Gillespie, *Labour and Politics in England, 1850–1867*, Durham, N.C. 1927, 177.
45. For one such study see C. Kauffman, 'Lord Elcho, trade unionism and democracy', in Brown, *op. cit.*, 183-207.
46. Allen, *op. cit.*; J.H. Porter, 'David Dale and conciliation in the

northern manufactured iron trade, 1869—1914', *N.H.* V (1970), 157-71; J.H. Porter, 'Wage bargaining under conciliation agreements, 1860—1914', *Ec.H.R.* XXIII (1970), 460—75.

47. C. Fisher and J. Smethurst, 'War on the law of supply and demand', in R. Harrison (ed.), *Independent Collier: the Coal Miner as Archetypal Proletarian Reconsidered,* Brighton 1978, 114-55.
48. K. Burgess, *The Origins of British Industrial Relations,* 1975, 102.
49. R. Price, *Masters, Unions and Men,* Cambridge 1980.
50. B. Harrison, 'Religion and recreation in nineteenth century England', *P.P.* 38 (1967), 102.
51. R. Storch, 'The policeman as domestic missionary. urban discipline and popular culture in northern England, 1850—1880', *J.S.H.* 9 (1976), 481-509.
52. *Ibid.,* 492.
53. D'Eichthal, *op. cit.,* 92.
54. B. Harrison, *Drink and the Victorians,* 1971, 91.
55. L. Shiman, 'The Band of Hope movement: respectable recreation for working-class children', *V.S.* 17 (1973—4), 49.
56. J. Taylor, 'From self-help to glamour: the working man's club, 1860—1972', *History Workshop Pamphlet* 7 (1972), 2.
57. R. Price, 'The working men's club movement and Victorian social reform ideology', *V.S.* 15 (1971), 147.
58. Altick, *op. cit.,* 189.
59. J. Knott, 'Libraries for the working classes in nineteenth century Newcastle', *North East Group for the Study of Labour History Bulletin* 9 (1975), 10.
60. D. Read, reviewing D.S.L. Cardwell (ed.), *Artisan to Graduate: Essays to Commemorate the Foundation in 1824 of the Manchester Mechanics' Institute,* in *N.H.* XIII (1977), 286.
61. E. Royle, 'Mechanics Institutes and the working classes, 1840—1860', *H.J.* XIV (1971), 315.
62. Cunningham, *Volunteer Force,* 21.
63. J. Walvin, *Leisure and Society, 1830—1950,* 1978, 53.
64. J.M. Goldstrom, *The Social Content of Education, 1808—1870,* Shannon 1972, 30.
65. *Ibid.,* 125.
66. T. Tholfson, *Working Class Radicalism in Mid-Victorian England,* 1976, 228.
67. D.G. Paz, 'Working class education and the state, 1839—1849: the sources of government policy', *J.B.S.* XVI (1976), 138.
68. R. Johnson, 'Educational policy and social control in early Victorian England', *P.P.* 49 (1970), 119.
69. R. Colls, 'Oh happy English children! Coal, class and education in the north east', *P.P.* 73 (1976), 93.
70. J. Hart, 'Religion and social control in the mid-nineteenth century', in A.J. Donajgrodzki (ed.), *Social Control in Nineteenth Century Britain,* 1977, 108-37.
71. M. Flinn, 'Social theory and the industrial revolution', in T. Burns

and B. Saul (eds.), *Social Change and Economic Change*, 1967, 14.

72. Thompson, 'Time, work', 38.
73. S. Tamke, 'Hymns for children: cultural imperialism in Victorian England', *Victorian Newsletter* 46 (1976), 21.
74. *Ibid.*
75. Cunningham, *Leisure*, 135-6: P. Bailey, *Leisure and Class in Victorian England*, 1978, 103.
76. Goldstrom, *op. cit.*, 179.
77. B. Harrison, 'Philanthropy and the Victorians', *V.S.* IX (1966), 358.
78. C.M. Turner, 'Political, religious and occupational support in the early mechanics' institutes', *Vocational Aspect* 20 (1968), 70.
79. G. Kitson Clark, *The Making of Victorian England*, 1965, 163.
80. Walvin, *op. cit.*, 55.
81. G. Best, *Mid-Victorian Britain, 1851–1875*, 1971, 218.
82. Harrison, 'Religion and recreation', 115.
83. Laquer, *Sunday Schools*, 239; Harrison, 'Religion and recreation'; J. Lowerson and J. Myerscough, *Time to Spare in Victorian England*, Hassocks 1977, 26.
84. P. Bailey, 'Will the real Bill Banks please stand up? Towards a role analysis of mid Victorian working class respectability', *J.S.H.* 12 (1979), 336-53.
85. J. and J. Rowley, 'The promotion of adult education in Wolverhampton, 1827–1869', *West Midland Studies* 8 (1976), 1-16.
86. Taylor, *op. cit.*, 17 and 20.
87. Laquer, *Sunday Schools, passim.*
88. Tholfson, *op. cit.*, 16.
89. *Ibid.*, 17-19.
90. Harrison, 'Philanthropy', 370.
91. Crossick, *op. cit.*; Gray, *op. cit., passim.*
92. C. Reid, 'Temperance, teetotalism and local culture: the early temperance movement in Sheffield', *N.H.* XIII (1977), 254.
93. See generally P. Joyce, *Work, Society and Politics: the Culture of the Factory in Late Victorian England*, Brighton 1980.
94. *Ibid.*, 170.
95. *Ibid.*, 164.
96. *Ibid.*, 183.
97. *Ibid.*, 233-4.
98. Best, *op. cit.*, 147.
99. Perkin, *op. cit.*, 343 ff.
100. G. Barnsby, 'The standard of living in the Black Country during the nineteenth century', *Ec.H.R.*, XXIV (1971), 220-39; Hopkins, *op. cit.*, 222-42.
101. There is a steady proliferation of literature on the impact of the railways. For a useful recent summary see T.R. Gourvish, *Railways and the British Economy, 1830–1914*, 1980.
102. Vincent, *op. cit.*, 206.
103. D. Fraser, *The Evolution of the British Welfare State*, 1973, 240-1.

104. D.A. Reid, 'The decline of Saint Monday, 1766—1876', *P.P.* 71 (1976), 76-101.
105. Turner, *op. cit.*, 119.
106. E.T. Collins, 'Migrant labour in English agriculture in the nineteenth century', *Ec.H.R.* XXIX (1976), 38-59.
107. E.P. Thompson, 'The moral economy of the English crowd in the eighteenth century', *P.P.* 50 (1971), 76-136.
108. W.H. Armytage, *Heavens Below: Utopian Experiments in England, 1560—1960*, 1961, 269.
109. B. Wilson, *Religion in a Secular Society*, 1966, 48-9.
110. S. Pollard, 'Nineteenth century cooperation: from community building to shop keeping', in Briggs and Saville, *op. cit.*, 77-8.
111. R.D. Storch, 'The plague of the blue locusts: police reform and popular resistance in England, 1840—1857', *I.R.S.H.* XX (1975), 61-90.
112. Philips, *op. cit., passim.*

CHAPTER 5
1. R. Arnold, 'The revolt of the field in Kent, 1872—1879', *P.P.* 64 (1974), 95.
2. Rider Haggard, *Rural England* (1902), quoted in P. Keating (ed.), *Into Unknown England, 1866—1913*, 1976, 208-9.
3. D. Chambers and G.E. Mingay, *The Agricultural Revolution, 1750—1880*, 1966, 193.
4. P. Horn, 'Agricultural trade unionism in Buckinghamshire, 1872—85', *Records of Buckinghamshire* 20 (1975), 76-86.
5. J.P. Dunbabin, 'The incidence and organisation of agricultural trade unionism in the 1870's', *Ag.H.R.* 16 (1968), 114-41.
6. H. Newby, *The Deferential Worker: a Study of Farm Labourers in East Anglia*, 1977; I. Carter, 'Class and culture among farm servants in the north east, 1840—1914', in A. MacLaren (ed.), *Social Class in Scotland: Past and Present*, Edinburgh n.d., 105-27.
7. N. Scotland, 'Methodism and the "revolt of the field" in East Anglia, 1872—1876', *Proceedings of the Wesley Historical Society* XLI (1977), 2-11, 39-42.
8. S. Lewenhak, *Women and the Trade Unions*, 1977, 89.
9. G. Anderson, *Victorian Clerks*, Manchester 1976, 2.
10. Kenneth D. Brown, *John Burns*, 1977, 47.
11. C. Pearce, 'The Manningham Mills strike, Bradford, December 1890—April 1891', *University of Hull Occasional Papers in Economic and Social History* 7 (1975), 58.
12. K. Dawson and P. Wall, *Trade Unions*, Oxford 1968, 37.
13. G. Howell, *Trade Unionism New and Old*, 1892, 162.
14. W. Thorne, *My Life's Battles*, 1925, 129-32.
15. G. Stedman Jones, *Outcast London: a Study of the Relationship between Classes in Victorian Society*, Oxford 1971, 315.
16. H.H. Champion, *The Great Dock Strike in London*, 1890, 6.
17. H. Clegg, A. Fox and A. Thompson, *History of British Trade*

Unions, 1889—1910, Oxford 1964, 95.

18. Hobsbawm, *Labouring Men*, 179-203.

19. S. Hutchins, 'The Communard exiles in Britain', *M.T.* 15 (1971), 90-2, 117-20, 180-6.

20. H. Pelling, *The Origins of the Labour Party, 1880—1900*, Oxford 1965, 17.

21. Brown, *Burns*, 36.

22. G. Aldred, *No Traitor's Gait*, Glasgow 1955, 117.

23. R.M. Fox, *Smoky Crusade*, 1937, 43.

24. Brown, *Burns*, 36.

25. E.P. Thompson, 'Homage to Tom Maguire' in Briggs and Saville, *op. cit.*, 301.

26. P. Stead, 'The Welsh working class', *Llaf.* 1 (1973), 53.

27. J.B. Glasier, *William Morris and the Early Days of the Socialist Movement*, 1921, 144.

28. J. McCrindle and S. Rowbotham, *Dutiful Daughters*, 1977, 65.

29. Pelling, *Origins*, 161.

30. D. Prynn, 'The Clarion Clubs, rambling and the Holiday Associations in Britain since the 1890's', *J.C.H.* 11 (1976), 69.

31. H. Ausubel, *In Hard Times*, 1960, 170.

32. Brown, *Burns*, 72.

33. S. Pierson, *Marxism and the Origins of British Socialism*, 1973, 199.

34. *Ibid.*, 249.

35. *The Times*, 28 January 1903.

36. D. Hopkin, 'The membership of the Independent Labour Party 1904—1910: a spatial and occupational analysis', *I.R.S.H.* XX (1975), 175-97.

37. H. Pelling, *Social Geography of British Elections 1885—1910*, 1967, 11.

38. Figures from G.D.H. Cole, *British Working Class Politics, 1832—1914*, 1941, 272-3.

39. N. Blewett, 'The franchise in the United Kingdom, 1885—1918', *P.P.* 32 (1965), 27-56.

40. Pelling, *Social Geography*, 26-59, 239-87.

41. Kynaston, *op. cit.*, 68.

42. M. Blanch, 'Imperialism, nationalism and organised youth', in J. Clarke, C. Critcher and R. Johnson (eds.), *Working Class Culture*, 1979, 117.

43. R. Tressell, *The Ragged Trousered Philanthropists*, 1971 ed., 454-5.

44. See the conference report, 'The working class and leisure, class expression and/or social control', *B.S.S.L.H.* 32 (1976), 5-18.

45. L. Senelick, 'Politics as entertainment: Victorian music-hall songs', *V.S.* 19 (1975), 150.

46. S. Collini, *Liberalism and Sociology*, Cambridge 1979, 89 note 53.

47. S. Hynes, *The Edwardian Turn of Mind*, 1968, 21.

48. McCord, *North East England*, 191-2.

49. W.J. Baker, 'The making of a working class football culture in Victorian England', *J.S.H.* 13 (1979), 248.

50.   J.O. Baylen, 'The "New Journalism" in late Victorian Britain', *Australian Journal of Politics and History* XVIII (1972), 374.
51.   F. Williams, *Dangerous Estate*, 1959, 116.
52.   J. Springhall, *Youth, Empire and Society*, 1977, 126.
53.   Blanch, *op. cit.*, 107 and 110.
54.   L. Thompson, *The Enthusiasts*, 1971, 23.
55.   Taylor, *op. cit.*, 59.
56.   Kynaston, *op. cit.*, 109.
57.   R. Price, *An Imperial War and the British Working Class*, 1972.
58.   G. Stedman Jones, 'Working class culture and working class politics in London, 1870—1900: notes on the remaking of a working class', *J.S.H.* 7 (1974), 493.
59.   R. Roberts, *The Classic Slum*, 1973, 16.
60.   Jones, 'Working class culture'.
61.   F. Parkin, 'Working-class Conservatives: a theory of political deviance', *British Journal of Sociology* 18 (1967), 278-90.
62.   P. Joyce, 'The factory politics of Lancashire in the later nineteenth century', *H.J.* XVIII (1975), 526.
63.   McCord, *North East England*, 115.
64.   A.E. Dingle, 'Drink and working class living standards in Britain, 1870—1914', *Ec.H.R.* XXV (1972), 608-22. On diet generally at this time see J. Oddy, 'Working class diets in late nineteenth century Britain', *Ec.H.R.* XXIII (1970), 314-23.
65.   A. Mearns, *The Bitter Cry of Outcast London*, 1883.
66.   M. Pember Reeves, *Round About a Pound a Week*, 1979 ed., 39.
67.   Kynaston, *op. cit.*, 120.
68.   Tressell, *op. cit.*, 363.
69.   A.J. Lee, 'Conservatism, traditionalism and the British working class', in D. Martin and D. Rubinstein (eds.), *Ideology and the Labour Movement*, 1979, 84-102.
70.   D. Rubinstein, 'The ILP and the Yorkshire miners: the Barnsley by-election of 1897', *I.R.S.H.* XXIII (1978), 130.
71.   Kynaston, *op. cit.*, 68.
72.   *Ibid.*, 69.
73.   Roberts, *op. cit.*, 148.
74.   J. Brown, 'Attercliffe 1894: how one local Liberal Party failed to meet the challenge of Labour', *J.B.S.* XIV (1975), 75.
75.   P. Clarke, *Liberals and Social Democrats*, Cambridge 1978, 63.
76.   *Labour Elector*, 21 December 1889.
77.   J. Havelock Wilson, *My Stormy Voyage through Life*, 1925, 275.
78.   Figures from B.R. Mitchell, *Abstract of British Historical Statistics*, Cambridge 1971, 72.
79.   G. Alderman, 'The National Free Labour Association: a case study in organised strike breaking in the late nineteenth and early twentieth centuries', *I.R.S.H.* XXI (1976), 309-36.
80.   E. Wigham, *Strikes and the Government, 1893-1974*, 1976, 13.
81.   Pelling, *Origins*, 197.

82. W. Muller, *The Kept Men? The First Century of Trade Union Representation in the British House of Commons, 1874–1975*, Brighton 1977, 3.

CHAPTER 6

1. Labour Representation Committee, *Report of the Conference on Labour Representation*, 1900, 12.
2. Clarke, *op. cit.*, 139.
3. A.W. Purdue, 'Isaac Mitchell and the progressive alliance, 1903–1906', *North East Group for the Study of Labour History Bulletin* 11 (1977), 12.
4. Brown, *Essays*, 234.
5. *Ibid.*, 241.
6. J.R. Clynes, *Memoirs I*, 1937, 124.
7. Quoted in Brown, *Essays*, 235.
8. Tressell, *op. cit.*, 261.
9. H. Pelling, *A Short History of the Labour Party*, 1965, 21.
10. Kenneth D. Brown, 'The Labour Party and the unemployment question, 1906–1910', *H.J.* XIV (1971), 599-616.
11. F. Thompson, *Lark Rise*, 1946, 83.
12. J. London, *The People of the Abyss*, 1963 ed., 86.
13. R. Currie, *Industrial Politics*, Oxford 1979, 256.
14. J. McHugh, 'The Belfast labour dispute and riots of 1907', *I.R.S.H.* XXII (1977), 1-20.
15. D. Egan, 'The Unofficial Reform Committee and "The Miners' Next Step"', *Llaf.* 2 (1978), 33.
16. Wigham, *op. cit.*, 24.
17. Porter, 'Wage bargaining', 460-75.
18. P. Stead, 'Working class leadership in south Wales', *W.H.R.* 6 (1972–3), 337-8.
19. Egan, *op. cit.*, 39.
20. L. Masterman, *C.F.G. Masterman*, 1939, 234.
21. M. Cole (ed.), *Beatrice Webb's Diaries, 1912–1924*, 1952, 15.
22. The Unofficial Reform Committee, *The Miners' Next Step*, 1912, 29.
23. J. White, *The Limits of Trade Union Militancy: the Lancashire Textile Workers, 1910–1914*, Westport Conn. 1978, 91.
24. McCord, *North East England*, 202.
25. V.L. Allen, *The Sociology of Industrial Relations*, 1971, 160.
26. A. Clinton, *The Trade Union Rank and File*, Manchester 1977, 69.
27. *Ibid.*, 72.
28. *Ibid.*, 72-3.
29. *Ibid.*, 79.
30. R. Davidson, 'Wartime labour policy 1914–1916: a re-appraisal', *J.S.L.H.S.* 8 (1974), 3.
31. J. Hinton, 'The Clyde Workers' Committee and the dilution struggle' in A. Briggs and J. Saville (eds.), *Essays in Labour*

History, 1886–1923, 1971, 152-84.
32. Davidson, *op. cit.*, 3-20.
33. C.J. Wrigley (ed.), *The British Labour Movement in the Decade after the First World War*, Loughborough 1979, 1.
34. Clinton, *op. cit.*, 79.
35. *Ibid.*
36. S. White, 'Ideological hegemony and political control: the sociology of anti-Bolshevism in Britain, 1918–1920', *J.S.L.H.S.* 9 (1975), 3.
37. C. Forman, *Industrial Town: Self Portrait of St Helens in the 1920s*, 1979, 30.
38. A.L. Bowley, *Prices and Wages in the United Kingdom, 1914–1920*, 1921, 110-29.
39. R. Charles, *The Development of Industrial Relations in Britain, 1911–1939*, 1973, 231.
40. Barker, *op. cit.*, 205-7.
41. There is a long debate on the failure of social reform after the First World War. It is best approached via P. Abrams, 'The failure of social reform, 1918–1920', *P.P.* 24 (1963), 43-64. See also A. Marwick, *The Deluge*, 1965.
42. B.A. Waites, 'The effect of the First World War on class and status in England, 1910–1920', *J.C.H.* 11 (1976), 43.
43. W. Greenwood, *Love on the Dole*, 1969 ed., 47.
44. F. Thompson, *Lark Rise*, 224.
45. J. McCalman, 'The impact of the Great War on female employment in England', *Labour History* 21 (1971), 36-47.
46. R. Benewick, *The Fascist Movement in Britain*, 1972, 42.
47. White, *op. cit.*, 3.
48. R. Challinor, *The Origins of British Bolshevism*, 1977, 196.
49. S. White, 'Soviets in Britain: the Leeds convention of 1917', *I.R.S.H.* XIX (1974), 165-93.
50. S. White, 'Labour's council of action 1920', *J.C.H.* 9 (1974), 99-122.

CHAPTER 7
1. R. Douglas, 'Labour in decline, 1910–1914', in Brown, *Essays*, 124-5.
2. T. Wilson, *The Downfall of the Liberal Party, 1914–1935*, 1968, 20-21.
3. Pelling, *Popular Politics*, 101-20.
4. Brown, *Essays*, 4.
5. *Ibid.*, 8.
6. G. Hosking and A. King, 'Radicals and Whigs in the British Liberal Party, 1906–1914', in W. Aydelotte (ed.), *The History of Parliamentary Behaviour*, Princeton 1977, 136-58.
7. K. Wald, 'Class and the vote before the First World War', *British Journal of Political Science* 8 (1978), 441-57.
8. C. Cook, 'Labour and the downfall of the Liberal Party, 1906–

1914', in A. Sked and C. Cook (eds.), *Crisis and controversy*, 1976, 38-65.

9. A. Howkins, 'Edwardian liberalism and industrial unrest', *History Workshop* 4 (1977), 147.

10. M.G. Sheppard and J.L. Halstead, 'Labour's municipal election performance in provincial England and Wales 1901–1913', *B.S.S.L.H.* 39 (1979), 39-62.

11. C. Parry, 'Gwynedd politics, 1900–1920: the rise of a Labour Party', *W.H.R.* 6 (1972–3), 313-28.

12. K.O. Morgan, *Wales in British Politics*, Cardiff 1963, 240-55.

13. C. Collard, *Unemployment in Birmingham*, University of Birmingham M. Soc. Sci. thesis 1979, 217.

14. M. Petter, 'The Progressive alliance', *Hist.* 58 (1973), 53.

15. M. Freeden, *The New Liberalism*, Oxford 1978, 149.

16. P. Clarke, 'The electoral position of the Liberal and Labour parties', *Eng.H.R.* XC (1975), 832.

17. P. Clarke, *Lancashire and the New Liberalism*, Cambridge 1971.

18. *Ibid.* See also H.G.C. Matthew *et al.*, 'The franchise factor in the rise of the Labour Party', *Eng.H.R.* LXXXXI (1976), 732-52.

19. M. Bentley, 'The Liberal response to socialism, 1918–1929', in Brown, *Essays*, 42-73.

20. M. Moynihan (ed.), *People at War, 1914–18*, Newton Abbot 1973, 191.

21. J. Winter, *Socialism and the Impact of War*, 1974, 261.

22. *Saturday Review*, 1 December 1923.

23. See the discussion between E.H. Carr, 'The Zinoviev letter' and C. Andrews, 'More on the Zinoviev letter', *H.J.* XXII (1979), 209-14.

24. R. Lyman, *The First Labour Government*, 1957, 259.

25. *Ibid.*, 268.

26. G.M. Young, *Stanley Baldwin*, 1952, 99.

27. P. Wyncoll, 'The general strike in Nottingham', *M.T.* 16 (1972), 173.

28. J. Klugmann, 'Marxism, reformism and the general strike', in J. Skelley (ed.), *The General Strike, 1926*, 1976, 58-107.

29. M. Cole (ed.), *Webb's Diaries*, 94.

30. P. Renshaw, *The General Strike*, 1975, 163.

31. J. Symon, *The General Strike*, 1957, 150.

32. A.R. Williams, 'The general strike in Gloucestershire', *Transactions of the Bristol and Gloucestershire Archaeological Society* XCI (1972), 210.

33. J.H. Porter, 'Devon and the general strike', *I.R.S.H.* XXIII (1978), 333-56.

34. Clinton, *op. cit.*, 127.

35. Symon, *op. cit.*, 49.

36. J. Lovell, 'The TUC Special Industrial Committee, January–April 1926', in A. Briggs and J. Saville (eds.), *Essays in Labour History III*, 1977, 37.

37. T. Davies, *Bolton: May 1926*, Bolton 1976, 1.
38. Barker, *op. cit.*, 207.
39. Gurr, *op. cit.*
40. For example, '1926 remembered', *Llaf.* 2 (1977), 9-30.
41. J. McLean, 'The 1926 general strike in Lanarkshire', *Our History* 65 (1976).
42. E. Trory, *Soviet Trade Unions and the General Strike*, Brighton 1975, 4.
43. McLean, *op. cit.*, 20.
44. G. Short, 'The general strike and class struggles in the north-east, 1925—1928', *M.T.* 14 (1970), 311.
45. Quoted in C. Farman, *The General Strike, May 1926*, 1974, 301.
46. P. Renshaw, 'Anti-Labour politics in Britain, 1918—1927', *J.C.H.* 12 (1977), 702.
47. For company unionism see A.R. and C.P. Griffin, 'The non-political trade union movement' in Briggs and Saville, *Essays III*, 133-62.
48. For example, Pelling, *Trade unionism*, 186-90.

CHAPTER 8
1. K. Middlemas and J. Barnes, *Baldwin: a Biography*, 1969, 507.
2. H. Macmillan, *The Winds of Change, 1914—1939*, 1966, 242.
3. C.L. Mowatt, *Britain between the Wars, 1918—1940*, 1955, 126.
4. N. Branson and M. Heinemann, *Britain in the Nineteen Thirties*, 1971, 50-51.
5. O. Mosley, *My Life*, 1968, 232.
6. R. Skidelsky, *Politicians and the Slump*, 1970, 171.
7. S. Baldwin, *Peace and Goodwill in Industry*, 1925, 35.
8. Skidelsky, *op. cit.*, 67.
9. *Ibid.*, 76.
10. W.S. Churchill, *Great Contemporaries*, 1939, 297.
11. G. Blaxland, *J.H. Thomas: a Life for Unity*, 1964, 221.
12. *Ibid.*, 222.
13. These and all subsequent figures are from B. Gilbert, *British Social Policy, 1914—1939*, 1970, 97 and 162.
14. Branson and Heinemann, *op. cit.*, 9-10.
15. W. Citrine, *Men and Work*, 1964, 240 and 238.
16. Burns of course was never a member of the Labour party, but the general interpretation still holds good.
17. M. Cole, 'The Society for Socialist Inquiry and Propaganda', in Briggs and Saville, *Essays III*, 193.
18. D. Marquand, *Ramsay MacDonald*, 1977, 580.
19. N. Davenport, *Memoirs of a City Radical*, 1974, 63.
20. Blaxland, *op. cit.*, 254.
21. K. Martin, *Harold Laski*, 1953, 81. For a contrary view see R. Miliband, *Parliamentary Socialism*, 1973, 193.
22. D. Howell, *British Social Democracy*, 1976, 65.
23. R. Eatwell and A. Wright, 'Labour and the lessons of 1931',

Hist. 63 (1978), 42.

24. *Clem Attlee: The Granada Historical Records Interview*, 1967, 42.
25. P. Seyd, 'Factionalism within the Labour party: the Socialist League, 1932—1937', in Briggs and Saville, *Essays III*, 212.
26. S. Macintyre, *Little Moscows: Communism and Working Class Militancy in Inter-war Britain*, 1980, 13.
27. Panther Record, *op. cit.*, 17.
28. V. Kiernan, 'Labour and the war in Spain', *J.S.L.H.S.* 11 (1977), 5.
29. H. Francis, 'Welsh miners and the Spanish civil war', *J.C.H.* 5 (1970), 186.
30. Hopkins, *Social History*, 230.
31. Quoted in Mowatt, *op. cit.*, 481.
32. E. Wilkinson, *The Town That Was Murdered*, 1939.
33. Branson and Heinemann, *op. cit.*, 13-14.
34. R. Hayburn, 'The police and the hunger marchers', *I.R.S.H.* XVII (1972), 625-44; R. Harrison, 'New light on the police and the hunger marchers', *B.S.S.L.H.* 37 (1978), 17-49.
35. W. Greenwood, *There Was a Time*, 1969, 181.
36. *Ibid.*, 183.
37. M. Turnbull, 'The attitude of government and administration towards the "Hunger Marchers" of the 1920's and 1930's', *Journal of Social Policy* 2 (1973), 141-2.
38. Pilgrim Trust, *Men without Work*, 1938; W. Hannington, *The Problem of the Distressed Areas*, 1937; G. Orwell, *The Road to Wigan Pier*, 1962.
39. J.B. Priestley, *English Journey*, 1934, 281.
40. E. Bird, 'Jazz bands of north east England: the evolution of a working class cultural activity', *Oral History* 4 (1976), 79.
41. J. Stevenson and C. Cook, *The Slump*, 1977, 21.
42. *Ibid.*, 51.
43. J. Kuczynski, *Hunger and Work* (1938), quoted in Branson and Heinemann, *op. cit.*, 147.
44. For a full study of the black economy in the nineteenth century, see the forthcoming book by J. Benson, *The Penny Capitalists* (Gill & Macmillan).
45. Hannington, *op. cit.*, 63-4.
46. Orwell, *op. cit.*, 16-17.
47. Hannington, *op. cit.*, 64.
48. *Ibid.*
49. Orwell, *op. cit.*, 57.
50. W.G. Runciman, *Relative Deprivation and Social Justice*, 1966.
51. C.G.F. Masterman, *From the Abyss*, 1902, 14.
52. Quoted in Kenneth D. Brown, *Labour and Unemployment, 1900—1914*, Newton Abbot 1971, 167.
53. R. Hoggart, *The Uses of Literacy*, 1965, 132-33.
54. Orwell, *op. cit.*, 155.

55.   Barker, *op. cit.*, 211.
56.   Bird, *op. cit.*, 84.
57.   Greenwood, *There Was*, 165-6. For an identical instance see M. Penn, *Manchester Fourteen Miles*, 1979, 106.
58.   Barker, *op. cit.*, 212.
59.   R. McKibbin, 'Working class gambling in Britain, 1880—1939', *P.P.* 82 (1979), 147-78.
60.   Orwell, *op. cit.*, 80.
61.   Greenwood, *Love*, 56.
62.   Orwell, *op. cit.*, 80-81.

POSTSCRIPT

 1.   M. Gowing, 'The organisation of manpower in Britain during the Second World War', *Journal of Contemporary History* 7 (1972), 151.
 2.   *Ibid.*, 150.
 3.   E. Hopkins, *Social History*, 261.
 4.   K. Middlemas, *Politics in Industrial Society*, 1979, 274.
 5.   Adelman, *op. cit.*, 81.
 6.   Pelling, *Short history*, 92.
 7.   H. Hopkins, *The New Look*, 1963, 114.
 8.   Middlemas, *op. cit.*
 9.   See the review of Middlemas by B. Supple, *Ec.H.R.* XXXIII (1980), 432-7.
10.   K. Hawkins, *British Industrial Relations 1945—1975*, 1976, 28.
11.   See, for example, H. Francis and D. Smith, *The Fed: a History of the South Wales Miners in the Twentieth Century*, 1980, 425 ff.
12.   L. Panitch, *Social Democracy and Industrial Militancy*, Cambridge 1976, 28.
13.   See above p. 280.
14.   Davenport, *op. cit.*, 146. For the emergence of the wartime consensus see P. Addison, *The Road to 1945*, 1975. For a critical assessment of the Attlee administration on the grounds that it followed reformist rather than socialist policies, see. T. Nairn, 'The nature of the Labour party', *New Left Review* 27 (1964), 38-65, and *ibid.* 28 (1964), 33-62.

Index

Aberdeen, 99
Ablett, Noah, 209
Abraham, William, 209—10
Allan, William, 134, 137, 141, 144
Amalgamated Engineering Union, 229
Amalgamated Society of Carpenters and Joiners, 130, 145
Amalgamated Society of Engineers, 37, 140, 172, 209, 217
Amalgamated Society of Railway Servants, 12, 165, 170, 198, 199
Anti-Corn Law League, 109, 116, 122
Anti-Socialist Union, 201, 226, 243
Applegarth, Robert, 130, 137, 141, 145, 146
apprenticeship, 15-6, 30-2, 143-4
arbitration and conciliation, 145-7, 196, 207-9, 222
Arch, Joseph, 166
aristocracy of labour, 142-7, 156-8
Askwith, George, 209, 218
Asquith, H.H., 194, 203
Association of Weavers, 32
Attlee, Clement, 267, 269, 272, 286
Attwood, Thomas, 29, 104, 106

Baldwin, Stanley, 242, 243, 244, 250, 254, 255, 259, 271
Bamford, Samuel, 79
Band of Hope, 149
'bargaining by riot', 30, 42, 83
Barnes, George, 209, 238
Barrow, 256
Bee-Hive, 133, 134, 141
Beesley, E.S., 129
Belfast, 33, 36, 101, 139, 273
Bell, Richard, 199
Bevan, Aneurin, 267, 291
Beveridge, W.H., 204, 218
Bevin, Ernest, 221, 226, 241, 262-3,

269, 270; as minister of labour, 283, 286-8
Birmingham, 47, 63, 71, 81, 132, 162, 187; and Charistism, 107, 109, 110, 112, 113, 114, 116; Political Union, 92, 98, 105
Blatchford, Robert, 181-2, 206
Blincoe, Robert, 66
Board of Trade, 196
Bolton, 36, 40, 52, 77
Bondfield, Margaret, 258, 260
Booth, Charles, 184, 190, 203
Boy Scouts, 186
Boys' Brigade, 186, 187
Bradford, 63, 70, 99, 150, 172, 179, 180, 231; and Chartism, 94, 100, 114
Brandreth, Jeremiath, 80, 82
Brewster, Rev Patrick, 100, 103, 116
Bright, John, 130
Brighton, 249, 250
Bristol, 36, 71, 89
British Empire Union, 226, 243
British Employers Federation, 223
British Socialist Party, 205, 227
Broadhurst, Henry, 179
building workers, 17, 62, 99, 135, 222, 256
Burns, John, 171, 172, 173, 175, 177-9, 180, 182, 184, 194, 198, 202, 234, 264
Burt, Thomas, 132
Bussey, Peter, 94, 100, 104, 106, 113, 123

Canterbury, 54, 55
Carlile, Richard, 38
Carlisle, 36
Carlyle, Thomas, 69, 86, 176
Carpenter, Edward, 177

317

Halifax, 63

Hammond, J.L., 52, 62

Hampden Clubs, 83, 89

Hand-loom weavers, 52-3, 56

Hannington, Wal, 256, 276

Hardie, J.K., 179, 180, 182, 184, 188, 191, 192, 197, 199, 203, 213, 234

Harney, Julian, 103, 105, 117, 120, 123, 124, 125

Harrison, Frederic, 129, 136, 137, 139

Henderson, Arthur, 200, 237, 238, 239, 258, 263, 264, 267

Henson, Gravener, 35

Hepburn, Tommy, 48

Hetherington, Henry, 51, 92, 95, 114

Hobson, J.A., 185, 219

Hornby v Close, 134

Howell, George, 130, 137, 139, 140, 143, 146, 172

Huddersfield, 89

Hughes, Thomas, 136, 137, 146

Hull, 37, 196, 249

Hunt, Henry, 80, 97

Hyndman, H.M., 176, 177, 178, 179, 184, 205, 227

Independent Labour Party, 191, 192, 200, 227, 228, 231, 239, 260, 265; early history, 179-84 *passim;* relations with Labour Party, 198, 203, 205, 258, 260, 269-70

Industrial League, 211

International Working Men's Association, 130

Invergordon mutiny, 273

Irish workers, 12, 63, 65, 77, 143, 217

Iron and steel workers, 13, 47, 143, 194-5

Jarrow, 273, 275, 278

Jones, Ernest, 119, 122, 124, 125, 128, 129

Journeymen Steam Engine and Machine Makers Friendly Society, 43

Junta, 135, 138, 141

Keynes, J.M., 223, 265-6

Kingsley, Charles, 67, 128

Labour church movement, 181, 188

Labour Electoral League, 178

Labour exchanges, 204-5

Labour governments, (1923-4), 239-40, 259; (1929-31), 254-67; (1945-51), 288-91

Labour Party, 200, 201-2, 206, 213, 224, 225, 229, 240, 251, 262, 267, 272, 273, 275, 284; internal divisions, 202-3, 205, 263-5, 270, 291; relations with Liberal Party, 200, 230-38, 264, 268

Labour Representation Committee, 198, 199, 200, 232

Labour Representation League, 132

Lansbury, George, 234, 256, 258, 267

Larkin, Jim, 211

Laski, Harold, 269, 291

Leather workers, 8-9

Leeds, 107, 114, 115, 116, 173, 175, 196; Conference (1917), 227, 240

Left Book Club, 271

Leicester, 34; Sisterhood of Female Handspinners, 34

Leisure, 24, 69, 72, 148-155, 185-8, 280-2

Liberal Party, 192, 197; and Labour Party, 200, 230-8, 268

Liberty and Property Defence League, 194

Liverpool, 28, 32, 36, 47, 63, 165, 173

Lloyd George, David, 200, 213, 219, 223, 233-4, 237, 241, 266; and social reform, 204, 230, 259; and unions, 216, 217, 221

London, 7, 8, 15, 16, 33, 35, 36, 37, 38, 42, 45, 49, 57, 64, 75, 77, 80, 89, 117, 132, 139, 165, 175; Democratic Association, 105; dock strike (1889), 171-2, 173; Working Men's Association, 75, 91, 92, 93, 98, 100, 103-5, 126, 141

Lovett, William, 75, 87, 93, 103-6, 110, 113, 114, 115, 118, 124, 126

Lowery, Robert, 113, 114, 125

Luddites, 53-4, 56, 78-9, 80, 82, 83, 84

Macdonald, Alexander, 132, 146

MacDonald, James Ramsay, 194, 198, 205-6, 213, 232, 234, 237, 239-41, 254, 268, 269, 270; and second Labour government, 258-60, 263-7

Macmillan, Harold, 255, 291

Maguire, Tom, 179, 183